PRAI

BEST FRIENDS FOREVER

"For anyone who has ever had a friend, but especially for those who've ended close relationships, Irene Levine has written a beautiful guide to recovery and healing. It's a book filled with honest reflections and heartfelt advice."

—JEFFREY ZASLOW, *New York Times* bestselling author of *The Girls from Ames* and co-author of *The Last Lecture*

"The end of a friendship is painful and sad, regardless of the circumstances. Dr. Irene Levine explores this difficult subject with insight and heart, plus a look at the latest research. Her guidance is especially interesting and helpful regarding Facebook and other new developments that are changing the meaning of friendship in today's world."

—FLORENCE ISAACS, author of *Toxic Friends/True Friends* and *What Do You Say When...*

"Finally, a book that helps you get through the other type of breakup."

—ANDREA LAVINTHAL and JESSICA ROZLER, authors of *Friend or Frenemy?*

"Dr. Irene Levine's *Best Friends Forever: Surviving a Breakup with Your Best Friend* should be every woman's BFF! Written in a breezy yet thoughtful style and peppered with stories from real-life best friends, this guide shows that female friendships are rich, life-affirming, joyful—but often very complicated too. We women love our friends, but we feel completely alone and confused when those friendships get troubled or even disappear. In her unique self-help guide, Dr Levine gives essential advice and tips for navigating the ups and downs of female friendship."

—JOANNE RENDELL, author of *The Professors' Wives' Club*
and *Crossing Washington Square*

"*Best Friends Forever* explodes the myths about female friendships and is a readable, entertaining survival manual filled with practical advice for girls and women of all ages. The book reminds us that it is the nature of relationships to change over time, and helps us understand and cope with those changes. We don't expect to marry our elementary school sweethearts, and it is equally rare for our best friends from childhood to be there for us forever. This book will help you navigate the choppy waters that complicate friendships, advise you on how to salvage the friendships that can and should be saved, and guide you to move on when necessary."

—DIANA ZUCKERMAN, PhD, Psychologist, President,
National Research Center for Women & Families

"A fractured friendship can be as painful as any other break-up, whether you've been jilted by a friend or been the one to do the jilting. Irene S. Levine understands the complications of friendship—the lulls, the obstacles, and yes, the dissolutions, and offers kind, practical and realistic tools to recover from a break-up and emerge strong, healthy and complete."

—ALLISON WINN SCOTCH, *New York Times* bestselling
author of *Time of My Life*

BEST FRIENDS FOREVER

Surviving a Breakup with Your Best Friend

IRENE S. LEVINE, PH.D.

THE OVERLOOK PRESS
NEW YORK

This edition first published in the United States in 2009 by
The Overlook Press, Peter Mayer Publishers, Inc.
141 Wooster Street
New York, NY 10012
www.overlookpress.com

Copyright © 2009 by Irene S. Levine

LIMIT OF LIABILITY/DISCLAIMER OF WARRANTY:
While the publisher and the author have used their best efforts in preparing this book, they
make no representations or warranties with respect to the accuracy or completeness of the
contents of this book. The advice and strategies contained herein may not be suitable for
your situation. You should consult with a professional where appropriate. Neither the publisher nor the author shall be liable for any loss of profit or any other commercial damages,
including but not limited to special, incidental, consequential, or other damages.

Some of the names and personal details of the women who graciously shared their stories
have been changed to protect their privacy. Any similarity to actual persons is coincidental.

The advice in this book is not intended to contradict or substitute for that of a physician
or mental health professional. This book is intended to provide the type of advice a friend
would offer to another friend. It is strongly recommended that any individual with emotional or mental problems consult with their own doctor.

The author and the publisher expressly disclaim responsibility for any adverse effects
arising from use of the information contained herein.

Cataloging-in-Publication Data is available from the Library of Congress

Book design and type formating by Bernard Schleifer
Printed in the United States of America
FIRST EDITION
1 3 5 7 9 8 6 4 2
ISBN 978-1-59020-040-7

To my old friends, new ones,
and those still waiting to be met

CONTENTS

Contents

Contents

BEST FRIENDS FOREVER

INTRODUCTION

When you lose a close female friend, there isn't a single word in the dictionary to aptly describe the maelstrom of feelings that envelop you: confusion, disappointment, hurt, anger, depression, blame, and even shame, all rolled together. That's because most women are brought up to believe a romanticized myth—*Best Friends Forever*, or *BFF*—that your best friend will always be there for you, and you for her, forever and ever, whatever the circumstances.

In reality, best friends *rarely* are forever. A friendship, like a romantic relationship, is founded on two different personalities, both of whom grow and change, for better or for worse, over the course of time. There is no guarantee that two individuals, however close they once were, will grow in the same direction or remain compatible. Even when a friendship is built on a solid foundation, the odds are overwhelmingly high that it will eventually fracture for one reason or another—leaving one or both women behind in the dust. Except for the outliers (rare exceptions) that we need to learn more about, most friendships, even best or close ones, are fragile rather than permanent.

Yet most of us swallow the myth of Best Friends Forever early on. I was no exception. By the time I was ready to attend kindergarten my mother had lectured me about the golden rule of friendship: *Make new friends, but keep the old; one is silver—and the other gold*. At the impressionable age of six, my Girl Scout troop leader reinforced the theme by teaching us the poem set to music.

In fourth grade, my friendship with my best friend and next-door neighbor, Annie, had become the be-all and end-all in my life. Like Laurel and Hardy, we were sidekicks. She was skinny and I was chubby. We laughed and ate lunch together at school every day, and she endeared herself to me by sharing one of the two Twinkies that her mother put in her lunch box each day to fatten her up. After school, we did homework at her house or mine, sitting on one of our beds or sprawled on the floor of a living room.

One summer, we pricked our pointer fingers with a sewing needle and pressed them together at the spot where they bled so we could become blood sisters. A few months later, we renewed our vows. We closed our eyes and entwined our little fingers—making a pinky-swear promise to remain best friends forever.

Before we graduated from high school, Annie's father accepted a new job and her family moved to Florida. We wrote each other long, mournful letters for several months. Then the letters stopped, and I never heard from Annie again. I felt devastated that my soul sister had unexpectedly disappeared from my life—until I made another best friend to fill the gaping hole that she left.

As I've accreted more friends over the years, I have learned that even best friendships are fleeting. And whenever you lose a friend, whether the choice is yours, hers, or mutual, it is painful. You mull over the reasons and try to take stock of what happened: *Did I do something wrong? Should I have stuck it out? Should we have talked it through? Why aren't I more resilient? Should I have done more to keep the connection? Why can't I just move on and forget?*

Even today, the message consistently reinforced by parents, teachers, friends, and popular media is clear: female friendships are supposed to last forever. For that reason, many of us cling to them long after they are worth keeping, and feel unnecessarily guilty when they end. A friendship lost is viewed as a personal failure, a source of embarrassment to both parties. As such, the social and emotional costs of lost friendships run high. As we morph from girls into women, we are judged by our ability to make and maintain friends.

No one has much sympathy for women who have difficulty finding their friendship niche, even if they are independent, creative, and have a strong sense of self. I remember my first summer job during high school, when I worked as a receptionist at a large marketing firm in Manhattan. Even with my abundant appetite, I would rather starve to death than be caught eating alone in a coffee shop. I assumed that anyone spotted at a table for one would be regarded as a friendless loser! Society looks even more unkindly on women who fail to sustain friendships, labeling their disagreements as "catfights" and friends who drift away as "disloyal."

As strong as the cultural taboos are against ending friendships or having no close friends to begin with, the pain is multiplied exponentially when the decision to end a friendship is one-sided. No one ever likes to feel dumped. We can't help but ask ourselves the same breakup questions we would when dismissed without recourse by a love interest: *Wasn't I good enough for her? How could she do that? Who does she think she is? Does she ever think about me? Is there something I could have done to prevent this?*

In the case of being dumped, there are strong parallels between a friendship and a romantic relationship. Being tossed aside by a best friend is just as painful as being jilted by a boyfriend, husband, or lover. The ambiguity of not knowing why adds to the sense of abandonment and betrayal. Making matters worse, there are few supports to draw upon when you lose a close friend. If you split up with a romantic partner, divorce your husband, or lose your spouse, a circle of caring people embraces you. Losing a female friend, on the other hand, provides the bricks and mortar for a wall of silence. After all, how do you explain to another female friend that you have parted ways with someone you thought of as your best friend? Won't she think of you as a loser, or a fickle friend? Or will she be jealous that this other friendship was so important to you?

As a result, women are reluctant to speak openly or acknowledge these painful endings, despite the fact that each of us has at least one breakup (and more likely, many of them) in our history. So great is the shame that only a handful of those I interviewed for this book were willing to use their real names or provide those of their friends. When women have conversations about fractured friendships, they are held behind closed doors with therapists or confided to close friends, generally prefaced with the phrase, "Please don't tell anyone . . ." Whether consciously or unconsciously, each of us carries skeletons in our closets—secrets about the friendships we lost, the friendships we killed, and the ones that simply disappeared. If only we were able to share our stories!

As we experience various milestones in life—graduations, marriages, divorces, physical moves, new careers, childbirth, and retirement, to name a few—we learn the bitter lesson that even the strongest friendships are vulnerable to change. Like most women, I have a rap sheet of former best friends—women I left behind, those who left me, and those who simply drifted away. During our friendships, I had been certain they would be part of my life today. I still think about those lost friendships and wonder whether they can be rekindled.

I do have a remarkably indestructible bond with an elementary school teacher who has remained my mentor and friend for nearly fifty years. Somehow, our friendship has that special ingredient that makes it stick while so many others have dissolved. I know I am lucky to have her, and her continued presence in my life is proof that some friendships *are* forever. So what is it about our friendship that makes it invulnerable to the strange and unpredictable factors that have broken up other relationships?

Most women have more questions than answers when they begin to dissect their friendships, past and present. For example:

- Why does the nature of a friendship change over its lifespan?
- Is it wrong to rely solely on one or two best friends?

- Is it wrong to end friendships that feel toxic? How can I do so without being vicious?
- Once hurt, will I ever be able to open up to another friend again in the same way?
- Do all women suffer the same pain when a close friendship falls apart?
- Is it sacrilegious to sacrifice time from work and family to make more time for friends?
- Since it's so hard to talk about a lost friendship with other girl-friends, what approaches can I use to heal from such a loss?

Trained as a clinical psychologist, I am a keen observer of human behavior. In addition, I've immersed myself in studying and collecting data about female friendships, but even I can't claim to have all the correct answers to these difficult questions. Human emotions are fascinating and complicated, and every single friendship has unique hallmarks, like fingerprints, that set that particular relationship apart from any other in the world. Although there is infinite variation and no universal rules, I've come to realize that there are some guidelines that can help us understand damaged relationships and begin the healing process.

To learn about these issues, I developed a dialogue with real experts: other women. When I posted a survey on the Internet asking women to share stories of their close friendships, I was overwhelmed by the number who responded, by their need to express themselves, and by their candor. As long as I promised anonymity, women were willing to tell their stories and disclose their secrets uncensored. Within months, more than 1,500 women—ranging from those in their teens to those in their seventies—completed the Fractured Friendships survey, expressing the mix of intense feelings enmeshed in these relationships. Thus, this book has been informed by the rich outpouring of anecdotes from women of different ages, racial and ethnic backgrounds, and ways of life.

Donna was one such woman who shared her story with me. She and her friend Gayle, now both 45, were "bosom buddies" until their mid-twenties. From the time they first met in a college English class, they felt completely comfortable with each other and were almost inseparable. Not only did they become best pals, they were also roomies. They shared each other's clothes and commingled their dirty underwear in the same laundry basket. "We viewed life the same way and laughed at the same stuff," says Donna. "We saw each other through some truly interesting life experiences (not all good, of course), bad bosses, near-poverty, boyfriends, family issues, etc.," she says. They even worked together for several years at two different companies. Donna could never imagine the relationship coming to an end because, for as long as they knew each other, they never even had a squabble.

By their sophomore year, Gayle had gotten involved with a wealthy guy who was a few years older than they were. Donna was with her when she met him at an off-campus bar. He and Gayle began dating regularly and he offered Donna a part-time job at his company (twenty hours a week), a job she was grateful to land to help pay her tuition and living expenses. Although her new boss seemed pleasant enough from afar, while working in his native habitat she got to know him better and concluded that he was "quite a jerk." In the workplace, he was a completely self-centered and chauvinistic boss. Gayle, his girlfriend, saw him in a much different light; she had found her true love. Donna didn't want to burst her friend's bubble or come off sounding jealous, so she kept her concerns to herself.

"He wined her and dined her and jetted her off to Europe while I stayed home alone in our dumpy old apartment," Donna recalls. Gayle began sleeping at his apartment most nights and announced that she would be officially moving in with her boyfriend by the end of the semester. The two girlfriends began spending less and less time together. Donna felt hurt that Gayle never thought about including her as part of a threesome to hang out, go for dinner, or see a movie. "When certain yearly events came up that we always attended together, Gayle informed me that she'd now be going with her boyfriend and his friends," Donna says. "I felt truly left out. I was dumped."

The winter break that year was a sad and lonely time for Donna, who felt like she had outlived her usefulness as a friend and had been tossed aside. For the first few months, she dreaded the thought of coming home to an empty apartment. Then Donna realized that she needed to pull herself together and complete her college education. Like the stereotype of a lonely, single woman, she even adopted a Himalayan cat.

During the spring semester, she met a guy whom she began to see regularly, changed jobs, and made new living arrangements because she didn't make enough money to support the apartment she and Gayle had lived in together.

Years went by without any contact between the former friends. "I never heard from her, but I'd heard through the grapevine that she and the 'true love' that she had dumped me for had broken up," says Donna. A lesser friend might have gotten some perverse pleasure in hearing about the split, but not Donna: "I was glad because he wasn't a good egg, and I had wondered about how she was doing. I missed her still, but so much time had passed that I figured she was gone from my life forever."

That was indeed the case until one Sunday afternoon, almost ten years later, when the phone rang and it was Gayle. "She had tracked me down where I was living across the country in Oregon," says Donna. Her friend apologized for what had happened and admitted that she hadn't been a good friend. Gayle told Donna how bad she had felt. She said she even had disturbing dreams about that time in her life.

"She had missed me as much as I missed her," says Donna. "The funny thing was that I was thrilled to hear her voice and I forgave her immediately. We basically picked up where we'd left off, except now I was living thousands of miles away with my fiancé and Gayle was married to a different guy and had three kids." The reconnection was almost instantaneous. The two friends remain in touch, sending each other birthday and Christmas gifts and emails, and catching up on the phone whenever they can. "I flew out to Michigan and had the chance to spend some time with her and her family," says Donna. "It's great to have Gayle back in my life. It was like a hole had been filled up again, and I think we'll be friends forever."

Only in retrospect could Donna begin to understand and put her fractured friendship in perspective. Like most best friends, Donna had hoped that her friendship with Gayle would be a constant in her life. After all, they clicked immediately and had an intimate, reciprocal friendship while it lasted. While she was disappointed and hurt when she was abandoned for a guy who turned out to be a dud, Donna chose to let her friend make her own decisions about romance. If she had told Gayle that her "true love" was a jerk, her friend never would have accepted it; she had to discover it herself. Donna gave her time, space, and acceptance. There were no harsh words or recriminations. That's why they were able to reconnect after so many years.

Not every failed friendship comes full circle and ties together so neatly at the end. But when you look analytically at friendships, yours and those of other women, you are able to see some of the myths that pervade the culture of friendship and make breakups painful. "You grow from these experiences, learning to be more accepting and not to do those [same] things again," says one woman.

Much of what women learn about female friendships from their mothers, teachers, and girlfriends are clichés that bear little resemblance to real life and their own experiences. Women tenaciously cling to the belief that a lost friendship is a fluke—a once-in-a-lifetime heartache, an anomaly, an exceptional circumstance—that will never happen to them again. (If only this were true!) Still others succumb to the natural tendency to dig deep: to figure out exactly why the friendship failed. They spill their guts to coworkers, therapists, spouses, boyfriends, other friends, or whoever else will listen, to make sense of their experience. Many others are too embarrassed or even ashamed to talk about their losses. They swear off best friends entirely, saying *never again*.

Introduction

They resolve to protect themselves by keeping a safe distance from other women, sometimes deciding that they can only trust men.

As I heard the stories of hundreds of women, I realized that although the specifics were different, there were many common themes. It became abundantly clear that female friendships are shrouded in myths that need to be reexamined:

Common Friendship Myths

Myth   **Best friends are forever.**

Reality   Most friendships don't last forever, even the best of them. Rather, the large majority of friendships tend to be fragile and impermanent relationships over a season of our lives. It's not unusual for best friends, who once played leading roles in the story of our lives, to fade away completely or only to return to make a cameo appearance. The quality of a relationship rather than its duration is a more realistic measure of the meaningfulness of a friendship.

Myth   **The meanings of the terms *friend* and *friendship* are universal.**

Reality   While the need for friends and friendship is universal, the terms are subjective and vary in meaning depending on who is using them and how they are being used. Every woman has different needs and expectations of friendship, needs that are shaped by genetics and environment.

Myth   **You can only have one best friend.**

Reality   Most women relish being the chosen one, the *best friend*. However, friendships characterized by exclusivity and jealousy are more likely to be pathological ones. It is more realistic to think about having simultaneous or sequential best friendships, each one special and meaningful in its own way. For example, there may be a friend from your past who knows your history; a mom-friend, so you can have playdates for your kids; a shopping friend who knows all the best bargain haunts; a kindred spirit to understand your emotions;

---

philosopher friend who challenges your intellect; and an outgoing friend who can introduce you to other people. Each of these friendships is distinctly important in your life, and choosing only one or designating which woman you are closest to may be unnecessary.

Myth   **You only need one best friend.**

Reality   Unless she is superwoman, no one friend can be it all or do it all. Different friends enrich our lives in different ways. If you depend on one person for everything, she may start to feel like you are sucking her dry. Women need to liberate themselves from that one-or-none thinking. It is often more viable to patch together a few different satisfying friendships to substitute for the perfect best friend.

Myth   **A friendly person will always have close friends.**

Reality   There are times when it is more or less difficult for even very sociable women to sustain their close friendships (e.g., it may be more challenging when there are other competing demands, such as family or career), and women tend to have greater needs for friendships when they are single, widowed, divorced, or retired. When it comes to friendships, it can be feast or famine, with periods of addition and attrition.

Myth   **A best friend is always supportive.**

Reality   Hopefully not. A best friend may need to tell you things that sound negative, or that you don't want to hear. For example, if you are engaging in self-destructive or unhealthy behaviors, she may confront you because your well-being is more important than the risk of alienating you.

Myth   **All friendships are inherently good.**

Reality   Not all friendships are good for you. Some may well be toxic, and even good ones aren't necessarily good all the time.

Myth   **Technology is a friendship-killer.**

Reality   Many women worry that the time we spend on cell phones, PDAs, and computers takes away from face time, and is potentially destructive to friendships. Not so: new modes of communication have made it possible to enhance our female friendships. Asynchronous communication (such as e-mail, which doesn't require two people to be available at precisely the same time) facilitates staying connected across miles and different time zones.

Myth   **Having a best friend is like looking in a mirror; she is a reflection of you, your values, and your attitudes.**

Reality   Some best friends seem like our twins but are really attractive to us because they have qualities or characteristics of the person we aspire to become. Differences—in cultures, hobbies, or outlooks, for example—can add zest to a relationship, and enable us to grow and learn new ways of being.

Myth   **Best friends never argue and their relationship is conflict-free.**

Reality   To keep a friendship going, friends need to communicate and work out the conflicts that inevitably occur. If a close relationship is totally conflict-free, at least one of you is probably swallowing hard and seething inside.

Myth   **You should be able to say whatever you want to a true friend.**

Reality: You can say what you want, but some words hurt so much and are felt so deeply that they will never be forgotten and can result in the demise of a friendship.

Myth   **It always pays to be honest when you are ending a friendship.**

Reality: Perhaps you can't stand being with your friend because she is stuck in an affair with a married man that you know will come to an unhappy end. After many long conversations, you realize that she's unable to hear your concerns, let alone act on them. You can lash out at her in frustration and tell her you think she's a fool, or you can tell her you want to spend your time with friends who can spend more time with you. It may be more prudent, as well as more humane, to tell the white lie and preserve the feelings of your once-close friend. The latter approach leaves the door open for reconciliation.

Myth **When a friendship fractures, you'll soon get over it.**

Reality: Yes, you will get over it, but getting over such a loss may be slow and painful. With time, you will be able to accept what has happened and you'll grow to appreciate the good parts of the friendship as well as the lessons you learned. Really!

This guide is intended to empower women of all ages to better understand their friendships; to recognize and accept the inevitable fragility of these relationships; to identify the red flags that signal problems (sooner rather than later); to reexamine some pervasive myths; to understand what makes a friendship worth saving; to help women break out of the emotionally confining shackles of toxic friendships that stifle personal growth and happiness; and to recognize the self-defeating patterns of behavior that may be impeding, impairing, or destroying their friendships. Most of all, I hope it will allow them to recover and to trust again after a loss.

A few caveats: this book expresses the collective wisdom of the many women who contributed their experiences—through the survey, personal interviews, posts, and e-mails directed to my blog (*www.TheFriendshipBlog.com*), and stories I have been told by friends and strangers. To protect their anonymity and privacy, I have changed their names and altered other identifying information as necessary. I've also truncated some of the stories and quotes, although I did my best to preserve their integrity.

Any advice contained in this book is intended to be practical rather than clinical, the type I might give or get from my own female friends, although I hope that my training as a clinical psychologist has enhanced my ability to be a good listener, and to analyze and interpret responses. Female Friendship 101 isn't a course found among the offerings of most schools of higher education.

Also, although there are two sides to every friendship story, I surveyed individuals rather than pairs, so the anecdotes reflect one subjective side of the equation. But that's precisely what I was interested in: women's feelings and perceptions about their own friendships. While many of the questions I asked tapped into the negative aspects of female friendships, this was done to illuminate the common pitfalls of these complex relationships. The women I surveyed were generous in describing the unanticipated heartbreak of their failed friendships.

Many of the women who completed the survey told me that just thinking about their own friendships, past and present, was a useful exercise that changed their attitudes and behaviors. I can certainly say the same for me. Spending many months placing my own female friendships under the microscope has left me eager to carve out more time to strengthen these wonderful relationships. I have already tried to selectively breathe life into some that have fizzled, and to find ways to cultivate new ones to sustain me over the years that lie ahead. I realize that such a commitment will entail a reordering of my priorities, but I am convinced that female friendships are worth it. They are crucial to every woman's well-being, including my own.

If you are reading this book, I hope it will inspire you to take a close look at your own friendships and their endings, and to find comfort in knowing you are not alone. Remarkably, whether we are 5, 55, or 75 years old, whether our friendships end slowly (almost imperceptibly) or abruptly, these endings play havoc with our emotions—leaving many unresolved, painful feelings in their wake. But most women agree, as painful as breakups can be, they make us wiser and make our future friendships stronger and more resilient.

CHAPTER 1

UNDERSTANDING FEMALE FRIENDSHIPS

"Each friend represents a world in us, a world possibly not born until
they arrive, and it is only by this meeting that a new world is born."

—ANAÏS NIN

Why do women enjoy watching endless reruns of TV classics like *I Love Lucy*, *Friends*, and *Sex in the City*? Like our mothers and grandmothers before us, we are fascinated by the joys, the angst, and the intensity of female friendships. Women are still riveted by the antics of two best friends, Lucy Ricardo and Ethel Mertz, on a sitcom that initially aired more than fifty years ago. We crave relationships like that of Rachel (Jennifer Aniston) and Monica (Courtney Cox), who are close friends both on and off the show. We mull over the lessons Carrie Bradshaw offers in each episode of *Sex and the City*, a show that was really as much about nuances in adult female friendships as it was about sex or the city. One thing is for sure: we never tire of observing, thinking, and talking about women's friendships on screen and off.

The term *friend* seems relatively straightforward, but it is mired in imprecision and ambiguity, and means different things to different people. This is because every person views the world (and his or her friendships) through different sets of lenses, which vary based on the person's background, temperament, and experiences. Since every friendship is a product of two people, if we simply multiply this variability times two, we can conclude that, like snowflakes, no two friendships are ever the same.

Some experts have tried to characterize friendships and describe them based on their complexity, depth, and intimacy. For example, simple friendships have one main basis for connection; more complex ones tend to be multidimensional. Say you have a close friendship with a colleague who has children (about the same age as yours) and whom you see at and outside of work. That friendship has more bonds than your friendship with a neighbor whom you only see once in a while. In the case of two friends you like equally, you probably feel closer to the one with whom you have greater shared history, values, experiences, and trust.

People you call friends can range from a distant acquaintance you recognize by sight to a confidante and soul mate (a best friend), and friendships of all different shades of gray in between. Friendships also vary in terms of their frequency of contact and sense of permanence.

While there is no commonly agreed upon lexicon, one simple way to categorize the broad distinctions between different types of friendships can be illustrated in a Friendship Pyramid, an equilateral triangle divided horizontally into three slices.

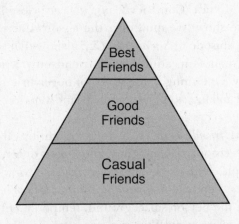

The Friendship Pyramid

Casual friends make up the base of the triangle, the largest slice, since they tend to be the greatest in number. These might include people whom you know from your neighborhood or from your office or school. They are people in your personal universe to whom you feel connected, but only casually; people you know but don't really know well. These relationships are superficial, loosely tied, and linked to situational circumstances—for example, the happenstance or serendipity that you live near each other, or that you have the same lunch hour or belong to the same soroity, house of worship, or civic organization—but you still consider these people friends. Such relationships are highly vulnerable to fading away if the situation or circumstances that brought you together change (e.g., one or both of you move or change jobs).

Good friends occupy the middle slice of the pyramid. These are friends with whom you feel close, and with whom you choose to hang out and spend more time. A good friend may be one you meet for lunch or coffee regularly; someone you do homework with; a parent of your child's friend with whom you discuss child-rearing problems or meet at the park so the kids can play; or someone you know from high school or college whom you still talk to and/or e-mail fairly often. It may be a single or divorced friend whom you enjoy spending time with on long weekends or vacations. Although closer than a casual friendship, a good friend relationship lacks the sense of intimacy and closeness that typifies a best friendship.

Best friends are at the apex of the pyramid. While fewer in number, these relationships are solid in terms of intimacy and trust, and tend to be characterized by more frequent contact than typically occurs between either good friends or casual ones. These relationships feel like they will be long-term, even if they ultimately wind up not being permanent, and cause the most pain when lost or fractured.

Characteristics of
Strong Friendships

Complexity
Depth
Intimacy
Closeness
Trust
Shared history, values, and experiences
Frequency of contact
Feeling of permanence

FRIENDSHIP COUNTS

One question that invariably arises when people talk about friendships is *How many are enough?* Most of what is known is anecdotal. While there are census counts of households and individuals, there are no official friendship counts. Surveys use different definitions and look at different groups (in terms of their sex, age, nationality, and socioeconomic status), making them hard to compare, so quantifying how many friends a woman typically has or needs is an inexact science. Nonetheless, every woman is interested in getting a general sense of how her friendships compare to others.

One of the most ambitious studies of modern friendships looked at 10,000 Brits, both males and females, in 2003. According to the study the average number of friends a person had in the United Kingdom was thirty-three, the "magic number." Two years later, that number increased to fifty-four friends (the increase attributed to the way technology has enhanced communications). But only one-sixth of them, about nine people on average, are considered close friends who make it to the "inner sanctum" as opposed to social (casual) ones. Although those surveyed ranked their friendships as the most important thing in their life—above money, career, and even family—people generally only stay in contact with one out of twelve of the average number of 396 friends they make in a lifetime.

Ironically, both women and men tend to see social (or casual) friends more often than the people they think of as their closest friends. On average, women see their social friends every 3.5 days while men see their social friends every 5 days; both sexes see their close friends once every eight weeks, only six times a year.

There are some noteworthy gender differences. Men typically have 20% more friends than women and their friendships are marginally longer-lasting (32% of men compared to 27% of women have known their close friends for more than twenty years), but men tend to have fewer close friends. Also, women are twice as likely as men (10% vs. 5%) to only have friends of the same sex.

Nearly three-quarters of the 1,500 women who responded to the Fractured Friendship survey have between two and five very close or best friends. One in ten say they have only one best friend, and another one in ten say they have six to ten very close or best friends. Women who admit to having no best friends say that it isn't out of choice, and they still hope to find one or more.

Aristotle, the Greek philosopher, pointed out that when it comes to "friendships of good" (philosopher talk for our concept of best friends) there are limits to the number of relationships that can be juggled simultaneously. Aristotle was writing about friendship more than two thousand years ago, but the same is obviously true today. No doubt, the exact number of manageable relationships varies from person to person. Recently, a daily poll of Facebook users asked both sexes the question: *How many best friends do you have?* Women are more likely than men to have just one best friend; they are almost half as likely to have ten or more best friends than men; and are about half as likely as men to have no best friends. These quick and dirty findings suggest that women favor a smaller, more intimate circle of friends than men.

A study in the 1990s at Liverpool University found that most people have about five close friends and an extended network of

150 people they consider more distant acquaintances, which is somewhat consistent with other surveys. Around the same time, British anthropologist Robin Dunbar studied social groups of non-human primates to estimate the number of social connections that a human being could handle at one time. Dubbed "Dunbar's Number" (which was popularized in Malcolm Gladwell's book, *The Tipping Point*), 150 is the maximum number of friends, casual and close, that Dunbar concluded humans are functionally hardwired to handle at the same time, the number limited by the volume of the neocortex of the brain.

Friendship Numerology: More Art than Science

Some of the soft conclusions that can be drawn from friendship research include:

- People have only a small circle of best friends relative to good (close) ones and casual ones (as illustrated in the pyramid).

- While there is wide variability among different women, most women have between two and five very close or best friends.

- Women tend to favor a smaller, more intimate circle of friends than men.

- The friends women see most frequently are often not the people they think of as their closest friends.

- Most people think they have fewer friends than their friends have.

Compared to male friendships, female friendships tend to be far more intense and intimate. While there are individual differences, as a group, women are more likely to provide each other with emotional support, while men tend to share companionship and activities: a run in the park, seats at a football game, a set of tennis, or several hours at the lake sitting silently beside one another as they fish for bass. Often the shared activities of male friends are competitive and create distance between them. (Many female friendships are also fiercely competitive but the competition is less overt.)

Women tend to have and need a greater number of best friends with whom they share their lives than do men. One social scientist described female friendships as "face-to-face" and their male counterparts as "side-to-side." There is growing evidence that the different ways in which women and men experience friendship is ingrained and may have a genetic basis. Some say these differences are evolutionary, harking back to the days when men went off to hunt and women stayed behind to support one another during times of extreme stress, such as war or famine. UCLA psychologist Shelly E. Taylor speaks about how women are more likely to "tend and befriend, as opposed to men, who instinctively 'fight or flee' under stressful conditions."

A study of infants found that baby girls pay more attention to facial expressions than do baby boys, suggesting that even soon after birth females are more in tune with other people's feelings and emotions. As youngsters, girls prefer the exclusivity of best friend relationships while boys tend to play in groups.

These gender differences remain as boys and girls get older. As females mature, their friendships become even more tightly interwoven. Many women are inseparable from their best friends: attached at the hip, talking to each other multiple times during the day—sharing confidences about their bodily secretions or fears of exposing their bodies in a bathing suit—things they would hesitate to share with their lovers.

As we learn more about the human brain and genetics, we may discover the extent to which our friendship choices and the number we need and can juggle simultaneously are predetermined by biology as opposed to environmentally influenced by choice and opportunity. It is likely that both factors affect the type of friendships we make, those we retain, and those that flounder—and that there are innate and learned differences between the sexes.

THE ESSENCE OF FEMALE FRIENDSHIP: SHARED INTIMACY AND RECIPROCITY

"Friendships are discovered rather than made."
—HARRIET BEECHER STOWE

The willingness of two women to become increasingly open with each other, to reveal their true selves—with all their frailties and foibles—is the essential ingredient that turns acquaintances into good friends, and good friends into best friends. Both of them need to be willing to step out of their comfort zones and risk exposure. It means taking off a public face, or the social façade they present to the rest of the world, and allowing a friend to get to know the real person underneath.

But intimacy isn't entirely a matter of choice or volition. Some women let down their guard more easily than others; to them, self-disclosure to a close friend feels instinctive and natural. Other women are inherently more guarded because of their innate temperament and personality style. Still others are cautious about self-revealing due to a range of experiences that have shaped them, which can run the gamut from traumatic childhoods to the personalities of their parental role models to the disappointments they've had with past friendships.

For example, if a woman's mother was narcissistic and aloof, or if she is just recovering from a best friendship gone sour, she may hesitate to open up and be vulnerable to that hurt again. Or if she lacks confidence and self-esteem, and is embarrassed about an aspect of her life situation (personal demons such as alcoholism or drug abuse, a relative with a stigmatizing disability, a recent divorce, underemployment, etc.), she may feel threatened to expose herself, particularly to someone who appears "to have it all." This doesn't mean that she is incapable of being close, but she may need to work on overcoming her natural tendency.

Intimacy usually doesn't happen overnight. Some relationships are easy from the beginning while others aren't. Yet, the degree to which two women are able to be emotionally honest and intimate with each other is the most important measure by which women ultimately judge the quality of a friendship. When a woman feels safe and secure in a relationship, it frees her to be authentic and real. She can be her true self: willing to share and talk openly about everything and anything without the fear of being judged, ridiculed, or rejected. In such a close friendship, trust begets trust so the openness is reciprocated, strengthening the foundation of the relationship.

For a friendship between two women to take hold (or stay together), there also needs to be some sense of common ground: a sense of reciprocity, a mutual feeling that each one is getting her fair share from the relationship. This doesn't mean that the relationship is balanced all the time, but the giving and receiving equals out over time.

Although two friends may be of different backgrounds, ages, or socioeconomic classes, they can share certain qualities or attributes that bond them together. A woman going through infertility, premature childbirth, breast cancer, or divorce may connect with another who is empathetic because she has been through a similar experience. Even differences can be the basis of a strong attraction between two people. For example, one woman may like to "mother" her friends, and another may have a strong need to be "mothered" by someone who is older, wiser, or more experienced.

There may be times when one friend feels needy and looks for support, and other times when she is in a position to be supportive and extend herself. One friend may be reeling from a recent series of life events, but doesn't feel burdensome to the friend providing support because the second friend's life is on an even keel at the moment. She realizes that there were times when she felt more like an underdog and now the roles have reversed. The relationship isn't always equal across every domain, but there is enough balance so that it doesn't feel like one person is always a giver and the other is always a taker.

When relationships begin to weaken, one or both of the women find some reason to withdraw and move on. In fact, unlike the legal or blood ties we have with spouses, partners, or relatives, friendship is a totally voluntary relationship between two people

Favorite Friendship Flicks

Movies can provide a glimpse into the lives and friendships of other women, and thus alert us to what to expect of our own. If you haven't seen these classic flicks, rent one with a girlfriend or two, sit back with some popcorn, and use it as a springboard for talking and thinking about your friendships.

Beaches (1988)
Mystic Pizza (1988)
Steel Magnolias (1989)
Bagdad Cafe (1990)
Thelma and Louise (1991)
Fried Green Tomatoes (1991)
A League of Their Own (1992)
First Wives Club (1996)
Divine Secrets of the Ya-Ya Sisterhood (2002)
The Sisterhood of the Traveling Pants (2005)
Sex and the City (2008)

SOURCE: Suggested by Jane Boursaw, *ReelLifeWithJane*

who *choose* to befriend each other, and the relationship can be ended summarily by either party. "Friendship is a non-event—a relationship that becomes, that grows, develops, waxes, wanes, and too often, perhaps, ends, all without ceremony or ritual to mark its existence," says sociologist Dr. Lillian Rubin.

Yet almost uniformly, women are caught surprised when a friendship that was once close—and that appeared to be life-long—turns casual or comes to an unanticipated and jolting end. Friendships are fluid, characterized by permeable boundaries that change over time. In many cases, it is difficult to pinpoint precisely when a friendship begins and when it ends. The same person who was once a colleague, acquaintance, or schoolmate can evolve into a best friend, confidante, sidekick, or soul mate; conversely, someone who was a best friend can turn into an old acquaintance, or even someone from whom you are completely estranged. It is usually disappointing when someone occupies a more peripheral role in your life than they did before.

THE ENDURING NEED FOR BEST FRIENDS

Despite the fragility of these relationships, the need for close female friendships begins early and never seems to abate. As young girls and adolescents, our best friends enable us to take our first steps out of the proverbial nest, the protective unit of the nuclear family. Best friends allow us to try on new roles, craft an image of who we would like to become by opening up a wide new universe of other girls and women apart from our mothers and sisters.

It's natural to want to affiliate with other girls and women. No one wants to sit alone in the lunchroom or to be the last one picked in a softball game. That's why some of our most painful life experiences as young women occurred when we were excluded, bullied, victimized, or dumped during the middle and high school years. Often, one girl is dumped not only by her best friend but also by a whole clique, part of the "mean girls" phenomenon.

Friends are vital to development because they help us see ourselves in a virtual mirror: if we do something silly, they laugh. If we do something nice, they smile. If we do something dumb, they let us know. Childhood friendships are the training ground for adult ones. Over the years, girlfriends continue to help us define our sense of style, values, and career paths, and hold our hands as we struggle with the challenge of aging. If we are lucky and wise as older women, we can still count on our very best girlfriends for pleasure, comfort, and practical support. Since these are among the most meaningful and important relationships in a woman's life, it's important to understand their pitfalls and potentials.

CHAPTER 2

BEST FRIENDS: WE JUST CLICKED

"A bosom friend—an intimate friend, you know—a really
kindred spirit to whom I can confide my inmost soul. I've
dreamed of meeting her all my life."

—LUCY MAUD MONTGOMERY, *Anne of Green Gables*

Since it was first published in 1903, *Anne of Green Gables* has
been a perennial favorite among girls and women around the
world. After all, who among us can't relate vicariously to the
joy of a once lonely young girl making her first best friend?

Anne Shirley, an eleven-year-old orphan who moved from
place to place, never had a girlfriend until she arrived at Green
Gables. Yet she had a vivid imagination and always dreamed of
one day finding a "bosom friend." When she met Diana Barry,
a neighbor's daughter who lived at Orchard Slope, she instantly
knew that she had found her kindred spirit and convinced
Diana to take an oath that the two would remain devoted
friends forever.

In many ways, the two girls made an odd couple. Anne was
homely but bright and spirited. With raven hair, Diana was pretty
but only had an average imagination—in fact, she may have been
a little boring. Despite their differences, the two quickly forged a
close friendship until Anne accidentally served her friend an alco-
holic drink, which resulted in Diana's mother forbidding them
from seeing each other again.

In a highly emotional parting, Anne laments: "Why, Diana, I didn't think anybody could love me. Nobody ever has loved me since I can remember. Oh, this is wonderful! It's a ray of light which will forever shine on the darkness of a path severed from thee, Diana."

After Anne saves Diana's little sister's life, Mrs. Barry finally recants and allows them to resume their friendship. Somewhat predictably, as Anne's world and her experience expand, the idealized friendship recedes into the background of her now richer life.

Friendship Through Rose-Colored Glasses

Like Anne, nearly all young girls—and many grown ones—have fantasies of finding a very special female friend—a *best friend* who will be a soul mate who makes her feel accepted and understood, and whom she accepts and understands. Anne's need for a best friend was so great that she overlooked her friend's foibles.

How does someone know when she's found a best friend? French women—yes, the kind who don't get fat—would say it is a certain *Je ne sais quoi* (English translation: something indescribable). In responding to the survey that helped set the stage for this book, over and over women used phrases like *we clicked* or *we connected* to express the feeling of being at one with a female friend. More often than not, finding a best friend is based on emotion rather than on rational thinking.

Like romantic relationships between men and women, the synergy that makes for close female friendships is complex and even hard to understand if you try to dissect it. A best friendship is characterized by honesty, openness, generosity, and loyalty. But most of all, it feels comfortable: women say it just feels right when best friends are together—as comfortable as slipping into a favorite pair of blue jeans that have been washed with hot water and fabric softener at least a hundred times. Even before she got to know her, this was the sense that Anne Shirley had about Diana. She immediately knew they were meant for each other, or so it seemed.

With a best friend, you don't have to censor your thoughts, measure your words, or think before speaking; nor do you need to spell-check your e-mail. Conversation flows naturally and easily. You are able to laugh about the same things and understand one another's humor. If you're an avid fan of a particular TV show or movie genre, it's hard to imagine being close with a friend who "doesn't get it."

Attempting to describe the indescribable, one woman compared the warmth of being with her best friend to "hugs and cups of tea." Others remarked that while they can easily finish their friend's sentences (as is often said of romantic relationships), it also feels totally okay to spend time together in silence. Best friends rarely tire of one another. Being with a best friend makes shopping, seeing a movie, or going to the gym more fun, but best friends are also comfortable and relaxed doing nothing.

Some women call this type of closeness a feeling of sisterhood. In fact, a woman without a sister feels like she's found the sister she never had. A woman with one or more sisters may consider her friend another sibling. "If she needed anything from me, I would be there for her, just like my other sisters," says one woman. In some cases, women feel closer to a best friend than to a blood relative.

Two best friends often share a history of common interests or similar life situations. They may share a deep sense of spirituality or have the same political beliefs. They may have gone to the same high school or college, lived in the same town, or raised their children at the same time. They may have both been the sibling who had to be responsible for the rest of the family, the youngest sibling, or an only child. Sometimes the friendship expands beyond the two individuals and embraces their respective families—husbands, children, parents, or siblings—making everyone feel part of something larger than themselves.

Although less common, some women *click* because they are polar opposites who complement one another in terms of their interests, attitudes, politics, or personalities. Even though two friends come from different backgrounds and walks of life, they speak the same language (figuratively), generally share similar values, and can put themselves in each other's shoes. One woman called her best friend, who was a few years older than she, a quasi-fortune-teller because she could help her predict the next chapters in her life.

Friends recognize strengths that we don't see in ourselves and help us evolve into the person we want to become. Together, two best friends form a spiritual bond that overcomes each one's sense of isolation and that buffers them from the anonymity and indifference of their larger social circle and even the world around them. One woman remarked, "Meaningful friendships have gotten me through the divorce of my parents, my own divorce, and the premature births of my children. The power of female friendships continues to amaze me each and every day."

In short, when you're with someone who is best-friend-worthy, there's a special chemistry between you. Each woman can express herself in an authentic way without compromise and feel understood. A woman can trust her best friend with her secrets, share her insecurities openly, and count on her loyalty. Friendships provide women with a safe harbor that allows them to gripe and commiserate about roommates, romantic crushes, unrequited loves, and their husbands, sisters, bosses, mothers, and children. Being able to talk through and mentally rehearse problems with a third person helps immeasurably in working them through and transcending them.

These relationships, at their best, aren't possessive. Instead, they help strengthen dating and marital relationships by providing a woman with a sounding board to work out feelings and resolve problems, with both other women and men. Thus, they can help improve parenting and friendship skills.

One woman uses the term "soul friend," which comes from

the Gaelic tradition of the *Anam Cara*, to describe this relationship. She writes: "It means a lot of things to me, including that someone may not make you happy but makes you grow into the highest and best you are meant to me. And at its most, it's joyful. This soul friend is there sharing the journey with you until the end, your outer triumphs and sorrows, and your inner joys and demons— and loving you, making you laugh, loyal, listening, and support- ive—yet in your face when she needs to be. She is simply part of your life in some form every day."

In the book *Eat, Pray, Love*, author Elizabeth Gilbert trans- lates the Italian phrase "un'amica stretta," which means a close friend. She goes on to explain, "*stretta* literally means tight, as in clothing, like a tight skirt. So a close friend, in Italian, is one that you can wear tightly, snug against your skin."

A best friend is the exclusive friend we all want to have and the one we all strive to be: someone who is chosen from the pack to share the greatest degree of intimacy and closeness. Because these relationships are so exalting to the spirit, we feel like we've gotten the wind knocked out of our sails when they sour.

REAL VS. IDEAL

Unfortunately, the sentimental notion that all close friend- ships do or even *should* last forever—at a consistent level of intima- cy—is more the hyperbole scrawled on T-shirts, greeting cards, and posters than it is reality. Sociologist Dr. Rubin points out that, like the shows we watch on the boob tube, most definitions of friendship are "idealized" and incorporate only positive attributes such as *trust, honesty, respect, commitment, safety, support, generosity, loy- alty, mutuality, constancy, understanding, and acceptance*. Real friend- ships, however, are far more nuanced and multidimensional.

One woman admitted that her definition of a best friend sounded so mythical, even to her, that she wasn't sure she had one. She describes a best friend as someone "who would be there for you at any time, who would drop other things for you, who would think about the things going on in your life (e.g., when you had your next appointment for a mammography), and a person whom you would feel completely comfortable with and her with you." As wonderful as they may be, even our best friendships have their warts. And while we expect every close friendship to be enduring and last forever, this usually isn't the case.

Too often, women romanticize the notion of a best friend (or even a very close friend) as someone who is a near-clone of her, the other half that makes them whole, the kindred spirit who will remain the same and be there for them forever, unconditionally. Because this can never be the case, relationships based on this ideal often end in bitter disappointment.

Instead, a friendship involves not one but two different people on two separate—not identical— trajectories, which intertwine in a unique way, defining and redefining their relationship over time. When a relationship is working, women are making seamless accommodations to each other by focusing on their common ground and appreciating their differences. One woman may be a stay-at-home mother and the other a working mom, but they bond on the soccer field as they chat and watch their kids' weekend games. Before long, they come to count on one another both in practical ways, such as carpooling and information sharing, and for support and consolation when either one has a day that's overwhelming.

When a side of a friend emerges that you never saw before, you suddenly realize that she is more imperfect than you had thought. One woman felt that way when she found out that her best friend who was married had been using her as a cover for her sexual indiscretions. Or you may discover that the fun-loving girlfriend who was your best friend in elementary school isn't the same person as the self-centered woman who won't let you get a word in edgewise.

One 25-year-old woman named Hannah told me how sad she felt when she first realized that even close childhood friendships could end unexpectedly. Hannah and her best friend Jade, whom she met when she was only 9 years old, had spent ten seasons together in summer camp and maintained the relationship over the remainder of the year, even though they lived far apart.

When they both were accepted at the same college, they were together constantly. They had a relationship that was so close and long that there never seemed to be any reason for secrets between them. During the second half of their freshman year, the two women became good friends with David, a guy in their dorm, and the twosome soon turned into a comfortable threesome who felt like siblings. They had meals and studied together, and knew everything about each other's lives. When they had dating problems, David could provide a male perspective.

Through another girlfriend, Hannah learned that Jade's relationship with David had become intimate over the summer. She would have better handled the shock had she heard it from her best friend first rather than from a casual acquaintance who lived in their dorm. She was both hurt and embarrassed, and confronted Jade. She accused her of living a lie by keeping the relationship hidden from her.

Jade was contrite, explaining that she just couldn't find the right words to explain what had happened. She had wanted to tell Hannah but the timing was never right. She said she cherished her friendship with Hannah and wouldn't do anything to jeopardize it. Hannah accepted her apology, but the friendship was never the same. Hannah never thought that anything could upset such a solid friendship but it did. "I'm starting to realize that this is normal—friends come and go, especially when you're friends with someone during the transformative years of your life," says Hannah. "You are both bound to change."

Because people change, their friendships are dynamic. Friendships intensify, become frayed, remain somewhat the same, or end. At some phases there is a pull that brings two women together, and at others there is a tug that tears them apart. Some changes are temporary; others are permanent. Sometimes changes are so subtle that they take place with little or no awareness; other times, friends consciously decide to alter their relationship.

A CASE OF FRIENDSHIP LOST

The story of two ex-friends, Jess and Merry, is noteworthy. While the circumstances surrounding their split are hard to fathom, it illustrates how a friendship can go awry, seemingly without any rational explanation. This one came as a huge disappointment for Jess, who could never have imagined it would end in this way.

Jess, now 33, grew up in Los Angeles, where she played competitive squash with her friend Merry from the time they were 12 years old. They attended the same schools, shared the same girlfriends, and experienced the same highs and lows of winning and losing games. They were co-captains of their team and took pride in wearing the same uniform. "I just knew we would be best friends forever," says Jess.

She describes the relationship as one of "fire and passion." Jess admired her best friend, a charming and charismatic person who was fun to be with and who attracted friends like bees to honey. "My connection to such an outgoing, fun-loving friend drew me into her social limelight, too," she says. Sometimes, she thought Merry's antics and practical jokes were over-the-top, but never once were they directed at her or were they done at her expense.

She spent a lot of time at Merry's home and grew close to her friend's family as well. "Her dad was a great guy; he reminded me of my father," says Jess. "He was a professional athlete—very loving to her, although I think he spoiled her. She always thought of herself as Daddy's little girl."

Years later, when the two women both ended up applying to Stanford University, their friendship slowly started to unravel. Merry was accepted under early admission but suddenly changed her mind about going after she learned that Jess was later accepted to the same university. Jess found it hard to believe that Merry didn't want to be at the same school as her best friend and didn't know what to make of it. Merry opted to attend an Ivy League college on the East Coast, and despite the separation, the two remained long-distance friends, calling and visiting each other.

Jess didn't think twice about asking Merry to be a bridesmaid at her wedding, and was glad Merry was there on her special day. Several months afterwards, Merry left for London, where she began dating a lawyer. About a half-year later, Merry and her new boyfriend returned to the States to live in Los Angeles. The boyfriend wound up moving in with Jess and her husband in the Sherman Oaks neighborhood for a short time, and Merry moved into a tiny apartment with a female roommate.

"The threesome living arrangement, with her boyfriend living at our apartment, didn't last long," says Jess. "We found out he was surfing porn on our computer each day while we were out at work. He even brought a gorgeous French woman to our apartment, ostensibly to see our dogs. That's when we confronted him and asked him to leave."

Merry ended up getting engaged to the guy anyway, and the two moved in together. She invited Jess and her husband to their destination wedding, which was taking place in Italy, because Merry's mother was born there. Through the wedding planner, Jess made arrangements for a babysitter to stay with her then-infant daughter. "Not long after we purchased plane tickets, I received a long e-mail from Merry's father suggesting that we not attend," says Jess. She was stunned.

"I was in tears, unsure of what was happening," she says. "Was I actually being disinvited?" When she called to find out what was happening, Merry's dad said that the perils of traveling with a newborn in Europe would be too much for them as a young couple and for the baby. The excuse was so far-fetched that Jess didn't know what to make of it.

"I was completely shocked and wrote an e-mail back saying

that I had never been so hurt and disappointed in my life," says Jess. When she confronted Merry, her friend wasn't explicit about whether the "disinvite" had been her idea or her dad's. The long and short of it: Jess could only conclude that her best friend, who had been her bridesmaid, didn't even want her to take part in her wedding.

Neither Jess nor her husband could ever understand what had happened. With indignant anger and consternation, Jess blurted out the story to everyone in their circle of friends, but it still felt like a terrible loss that no one else could explain or understand. "She is someone that I have fond memories of from my college years, and it's sad that we aren't best friends any more," says Jess. Years later, Jess still thinks about what happened from time to time.

One possible explanation: More than once Merry seemed to cut off her relationship with Jess at the point of her making a significant life transition. At those junctures, it seemed like Merry wanted a clean slate and a new identity, leaving her old self behind. She chose discontinuity over continuity in her relationships. The best explanation of behavior is often found in patterns from the past.

Like an unrequited love, the terms of a friendship like Jess and Merry's aren't always equal. One friend may be more committed to the relationship than another and one may unilaterally decide to break off the friendship for a host of reasons. If you consider someone your best friend and she doesn't rank you among hers, it usually destroys the relationship. One woman I interviewed told me that when she overheard her best friend tell a member of her monthly book club that someone else was her best friend, she felt as if she were impaled because the remark seemed to invalidate her friendship.

All friendships, even those between best friends, have their highs and lows, and can present friends with unexpected twists and turns. Yet the fantasy of Best Friends Forever remains pervasive. Jess learned how perfect a friendship can be at the beginning and how imperfect it can turn out at the end. Adding to the pain was her inability to ever figure out what happened.

Clearly, best friendships are richer and more complicated than as portrayed on TV or as implied by the BFF acronym that has been used so flippantly over the last two decades as a kind of shorthand for female relationships. Pop culture has deemed that best friends *are* forever—reinforcing the very best friends myth at the heart of our collective consciousness. Tragically, generations of women grow up with that idea and either stay in toxic relationships or feel confused, pained, and taken off guard when a relationship ends.

CHAPTER 3

WHY FRIENDSHIPS FALL APART

"One who looks for a friend without faults will have none."

—HASIDIC SAYING

With the high hopes and expectations we place on female friendships, the loss of a friend is nothing short of an emotional jolt. When two women who were once intimates, a comfortable twosome, suddenly feel separate and very ill at ease, it's normal for each woman to be left questioning whether she really knew the other at all.

When friendships end, regardless of how or why, there's a profound sense of disappointment over the loss of a relationship that once felt like it was meant to last forever. We tread so carefully at the beginning of romantic relationships, getting to know someone before gradually trusting them to get emotionally close to us, and resisting pinning hopes on that person until we have passed through a series of relationship hurdles. But with a female friend, we tend to barrel into a relationship assuming that it never has to end. Although breakup-like scenarios between best friends are fairly common, we are not, for good or ill, culturally encouraged to tread carefully or fear fallout. Instead, we're taught to assume the very best. After all, if either woman in a friendship had ever anticipated an eventual demise or dissolution of that friendship, the two never would have been become so close.

The emotional scars are deep and long-lasting, as described to me by a woman named Rachel. Living in the same freshman dorm and taking several classes together, Rachel and Julie became fast friends—and before long, best friends. In the middle of their sophomore year, Julie started dating Rob, a good-looking guy who lived in a frat house not far from the school. Rachel could tell her friend was smitten, although Julie didn't admit it to anyone, not even to Rachel. Julie and Rob dated other people, but Rachel sensed it wasn't by choice as far as Julie was concerned. Sadly, Julie was much more into Rob than Rob was into Julie.

As if her friend needed one more reason to pursue this elusive and hard-to-pin-down guy, Julie's mom always had strong opinions about her daughter's boyfriends and this time was no different. She kept pushing Julie into this relationship because Rob was pre-med, on his way to becoming a doctor. Rachel never thought much of Rob because he was so awkward socially and she saw that he never treated Julie with respect. However, Rachel made the decision to keep her misgivings to herself.

When Julie studied abroad for a semester in her junior year, Rachel found out that Rob had moved on to another relationship, probably before her friend had time to unpack her bags. "I wanted to tell Julie but felt I couldn't e-mail something like that to her while she was in another country," says Rachel. So she kept the secret to herself, knowing she would have a heart-to-heart with her friend the moment she returned.

By the time Julie returned, she had already found out on her own that the relationship was over and she was devastated. "She was a mess like I had never seen her before. So I made the decision, perhaps stupidly, not to tell her what I knew," says Rachel, who was thinking, "Why throw salt on her wound?" Not totally unexpectedly, as sometimes happens in volatile relationships, it wasn't long before Julie and Rob got back together. He apologized for messing up a good thing with her and she quickly forgave him.

"She knew I still hated him so much and asked me why," says Rachel. Not quite knowing how to handle it, Rachel dodged the bullet. Before long, Julie also saw qualities she didn't like in Rob and had second thoughts about him, so she enlisted Rachel's help in composing an e-mail to Rob explaining why the relationship wouldn't work. The two women wrote the note, clicked "Send," and went to sleep at Rachel's apartment, where Julie was spending the weekend. They had a relaxed brunch on Sunday morning, and Julie left for home.

A couple of days later, Rachel called Julie at her office to find out how things were going and her friend said she was too busy to speak. "I e-mailed her, called her, wrote her a letter. She never spoke to me again, or to any of our other common friends," says Rachel.

Rachel had been dumped by her best friend. Perhaps Julie had second thoughts about shooting off the e-mail and couldn't face the humiliation of telling Rachel, who she presumed would never understand why she wanted to get back with Rob. Julie's reaction was nothing short of perplexing, says Rachel. "We were so inseparable that it took me a long time even to tell my family. When I finally did, I was hysterical."

Julie experienced what psychologists call cognitive dissonance. After she made the decision to keep Rob in her life, most likely based on his persuasiveness, Julie knew that Rachel would not agree with the wisdom of this decision based on their previous conversations. When such a mismatch (cognitive dissonance) occurs, people tend to find a way to minimize the psychological conflict; in this case, Julie got rid of Rachel.

Now, almost six years later, both women are 29 years old and happen to live in the same neighborhood in New York City. They run into each other from time to time, Rachel always wondering if she should nod and say hello or pretend she doesn't see Julie. "She always looks away, pretending she doesn't see me," says Rachel. Through a mutual friend she learned that Julie had gotten back together with Rob for a few years. Then, when he pulled the same thing again, she finally ended it for good. Through another friend, she heard that Julie got married to someone else about a year ago.

"I never stop wondering if she ever thinks of me," says Rachel. "She shaped my life so much, and there was no closure or mutually agreed upon ending. No fight. Just my own theory on what she was thinking. And, as good of a person as I always believed she was, I learned that she had her shortcomings too." Rachel never had the grit to confront Julie directly. She thought she would have gotten over this disappointment by now, especially since so many years have elapsed since college. But almost all of her college memories involve Julie in some way, and all of those memories feel tarnished.

However it occurs, losing a once-close friend, someone you hoped would be your friend forever, is like getting punched in the stomach. Commonly, women are stunned when this happens, and the abandonment feels nothing short of catastrophic. One woman described it as "losing a part of her self." Another called her breakup with her friend a "divorce."

Rachel had a premonition that Julie's relationship with Rob wouldn't last, but she never suspected that their friendship would become history too. Julie had been her closest college chum and she genuinely cared about her as much as she cared for her family members. She hesitated blurting out the honest truth about Rob because the last thing she wanted to do was to hurt Julie. In fact, Rachel went out of her way to protect her, supporting her decisions while worrying privately about her friend's well-being. Rachel felt like she never had done anything so heinous that warranted Julie shutting her out of her life. Given the chance, she would have been able to understand Julie's ambivalence given the strong feelings she had for Rob.

Even so, why hadn't Julie called after she split with Rob? Rachel suspects that Julie couldn't handle the humiliation of her friend, or anyone else, knowing that she had thrown herself at Rob, only to be rejected over and over. Or maybe Julie was harboring a grudge against Rachel for not being more assertive in warning her about Rob's infidelity. Perhaps somewhere in her heart, Julie felt that Rachel betrayed her by not taking a different stance. Of course, Rachel will never know, since Julie totally cut her off without communication.

Rachel's worst fear about her ex-friendship, which she still worries about six years later, is that Julie never gives a moment's thought to Rachel or the close relationship they once had. Unlike romantic breakups, there's no standard protocol for a hemorrhaging friendship that obliges the dumper to be chivalrous or kind—to offer the courtesy of polite parting words, an explanation, or an apology to the friend she is leaving. As a result, the dumpee almost never has closure about a failed relationship. Most likely, Rachel will never know why she was dumped or what Julie was thinking; she'll just have to get over it on her own.

When friendships fracture abruptly, the hurt is palpable—especially if you can't pinpoint exactly when, how, or why how it occurred. If you are in the midst of such a breakup now, you may be feeling vulnerable, angry, guilty, or depressed. Given the significance that intimate friendships play in the lives of women, the intensity and duration of the feelings are easy to understand—at least, by other women.

Rachel was depressed for months, clinging to the thought that Julie would one day call her, tell her what happened, and apologize for the silence. When that never happened, the void she felt was even more painful than when she had broken up with boyfriends in the past. Julie was her confidante; she knew everything about her. They were used to spending so much time together that they could almost read each other's thoughts.

Although the psychic wounds remain, Rachel now accepts that the friendship is truly over and she has to move on. She still feels hurt when she catches a glimpse of her ex-friend in the neighborhood, and goes out of her way to avoid places where she might run into Julie. The experience has made her question her own worthiness as a friend. It also has raised other questions in her mind: *Is she capable of being a good friend? Is she worthy of close friendships? Will other friendships similarly fade away? Can she trust again?* Clearly, she hasn't been ableto move past the loss.

WHY FRIENDSHIPS FADE AND FRACTURE

When friendships fall apart, they end for different reasons and in a variety of ways. Sometimes the ending is one-sided, as happened to Rachel and Julie. Other times, two friends mutually decide that the friendship is over, perhaps because of a blowup, disappointment, or because they have simply grown apart.

Frequently, a friendship dump hinges on something the dumpee said, something she did, or something she didn't do or say—a small matter that might have been patched up at other times, but which, for reasons of her own, the dumper cannot make herself face at the moment it ruptures. A one-sided ending is particularly painful, especially when the split is unrelated to the friendship, per se, but may have more to do with other things going on in the jilter's life.

Other endings are mutual, with the friendship falling apart because of a misunderstanding, betrayal, or blowup. When this occurs, both women can generally pinpoint the time or event that transformed the friendship. The large majority of friendships have ambiguous endings, with two women drifting apart and never really able to understand what happened or to determine precisely what led to the demise of a once-close friendship. Just as no two friendships begin the same way, the factors leading to their demise are never the same, although patterns begin to emerge.

DISAPPOINTMENTS

There is an implicit contract between friends: they will be there for each other. Thus, minor disappointments can assume gargantuan proportions between close friends because of the intensity of the feelings between them. There are a range of ways two women can disappoint each other, but some common disappointments are associated with important milestones in a woman's life—childbirth, deaths, birthdays, and weddings. These are times when women tend to be emotionally vulnerable, when small infractions or insults become magnified or exaggerated. That's what happened to Karen.

NOT BEING THERE

Woody Allen once said, "Eighty percent of success in life is just showing up." When it comes to friendships, not being there can also make an important statement. Karen and Megan had been best friends since college. They saw the world the same way and even shared an offbeat sense of humor that was often elusive to other friends. They were both vegans and political liberals on a largely conservative college campus. After graduation, although they saw less of each other, they still got together for girls' nights out and considered each other best friends.

When they were 24 years old, Megan's father died. Karen had no car and lived more than four hours away from where the funeral was being held. Clearly, there was no easy way for her to get to the funeral. She reconciled herself to the idea of not attending the service by planning to spend "alone time" with Megan afterwards, which she thought would be even more meaningful. She reasoned, or perhaps rationalized, that mutual friends would surround Megan in the days immediately after the death and she would be there with her when things settled down.

Karen was stunned when Megan refused to see her after the funeral and then never spoke to her again. "Having never lost a parent of my own, I didn't realize how great her need would be to have me beside her," says Karen, who is now in her late forties. "If I'd known how devastated she would be, I would have done whatever it took to get there," she says.

Worse than the loss of that one special friendship, it turned out that none of their mutual friends spoke to Karen again, either. They had been a close-knit group who had been together from the first weeks of college through graduation and beyond. For Karen, this sudden severance was an extraordinarily painful time in her life, which she still remembers more than twenty years later. She knows that she screwed up and regrets it, and has never made that same mistake again.

As far as Megan was concerned, Karen "blew it" (the relationship) by not showing up at the funeral. There is no way she could forgive Karen, even though she came to realize that the hurt wasn't intentional. From Karen's perspective, she thought the relationship was strong and forgiving enough to make allowances. But there are certain life situations—most frequently, the milestones listed earlier—where all bets are off, and where sometimes the close emotional allegiances and history we bank on to get us through are unable to prevent feelings from being hurt. When anyone's feelings are wounded, emotions can trump rational thinking. Perhaps if Karen had discussed her decision with Megan, she would have realized the importance of showing up that day, and could have found to get there.

OVERLOOKING MILESTONES

Birthdays are milestones which, when forgotten or overlooked, can cause an unexpected schism in a long-term friendship. Depending on how a woman has been raised to feel about birthdays, what else is or isn't going on in her life at the time, or the significance of the particular birthday, what happens or doesn't happen between friends on that single day can assume mammoth proportions.

Some families make a big fuss over the birthday girl, no matter her age—showering her with cakes, celebrations, and gifts. These women often grow up expecting their own family members and friends to carry on the same tradition. If one friend was raised to view birthdays as "just another day," it can create an awkward mismatch between her and a friend who lives for birthdays.

Aside from expectations not matching up, birthdays aren't always happy occasions for everyone. Often a birthday girl feels riddled with fears, doubts, and disappointments about herself on

Tenets of Friendship at Times of Loss

- Above all, be there. Reach out even if you find out about what happened from a third party. Don't pretend you didn't know or hear what happened, even if you are uncomfortable or unsure of the distance between you two at that moment. "Sometimes you put out your hand and it isn't taken," says Anne Roiphe, author of *Epilogue*. That doesn't mean the effort won't be appreciated.

- It's normal to feel awkward and not know exactly what to say to someone who has experienced a recent tragedy or loss. Remember that the words you use aren't as important as your being there to listen to what she has to say.

- Don't tell your friend that you know what she's going through, even if you or your aunt in Detroit went through something similar. Every experience of loss and grief is unique.

- Focus on what you can do, whether it's providing a meal or an afternoon's diversion, rather than on what you can't do or change.

- Keep your curiosity in check. Don't pry with questions. Let the other person take the lead in deciding how much detail she wants to provide.

- Most people appreciate a warm hug and a simple expression of thoughtfulness, like a special tea or coffee.

- If you don't know what to say, the most simple and heartfelt message is: "I care and I'm here for you if you need me."

- Don't relay your expressions of sympathy through someone else

- If you are the one grieving or who has had a loss, realize that your friend may feel awkward and uncomfortable, and cut them some slack.

Celebrating Birthdays in Style

- Send a card or note on pretty stationery telling her why you treasure your friendship.

- If today is her birthday and you've forgotten until this very minute, it's still not too late to call her. Sometimes a quick phone call is the most personal and touching birthday gift.

- Whether it's a meal or a walk in the park, suggest a way to spend time with her on her special day. If you live far apart or have to work the actual day of her birthday, make sure she knows you have concrete plans for a rain check for celebrating with her.

- Leave fresh flowers on her doorstep.

- Surprise her. Make something, buy something, or do something she wouldn't ordinarily do for herself. Make a special dessert, send her flowers or cupcakes at work (unless she's the type to get embarrassed), offer to babysit so she can go out with her husband, or find some other way to indulge her. A little surprise goes a long way.

the milestone day, making the occasion particularly emotionally charged. Certain birthdays are more significant milestones, such as a woman's 18th, 21st, or 35th birthday or the round-number birthdays that mark the passage of another decade, and women like to share them with a circle of friends. However, if a woman is at a low point in her life, when things don't seem to be going in the right direction—perhaps because she just broke up with a partner, hasn't met Mr. Right, has lost her job or feels stuck in an unsatisfying career, has health or financial problems, isn't able to conceive, has lost a parent, is mildly depressed, has lost a good friend, or has too few female friends—she may have unrealistic expectations of how her friends should treat her on that day.

April, now 42, severed a friendship over hurt feelings that were brought into sharp focus around a milestone birthday. April, who is single with no children, was friends with Diana, who was married with two kids in elementary school. April acknowledged every milestone and event tied to Diana and her kids—birthdays, communions, graduations, anniversaries, and gymnastic tournaments. Since Diana had no sisters, April felt like an aunt to her friend's daughters. "I was there for her through her husband's affair, the birth of her children, and all those momentous occasions," says April.

For three years in a row, Diana never recognized April's birthday—not even her 40th, which was a significant one for April. She had always hoped she would have been married by then, so the passage of that year was tinged with sadness as she heard her biological clock ticking away. On the evening of her birthday, which fell on a Saturday, she had a pleasant dinner with her parents and younger sister at a favorite restaurant in the city. She was sure she would return home to a message from Diana, but when she checked her voice mail, no one had called.

About a month later, after hearing about the dinner, Diana finally "tossed a card in my direction," says April. In a moment of frustration, April made it known how disappointed she was and complained to a mutual acquaintance that only one person remembered her birthday, apart from her family. This third person passed the information on to Diana.

"She called me and said that I hadn't given her time to wish me a 'Happy Birthday' and called me a 'bitch,'" says April, still angry and upset over the incident. "As a single woman, I refuse to feel bad for wanting to be recognized for my birthday at least one day out of the freakin' year," she says.

It's been months and the two women haven't spoken. It's easy to see how April could feel overlooked by a friend who appeared to "have it all" but who had no compassion for someone else who wasn't feeling at the top of her game. Though she never kept a scorecard, even in terms of the money she shelled out for gifts, April began to feel cheated. Soon after the 40th birthday explosion, their once-close friendship started to drift apart.

Perhaps April had grown too needy and was jealous of her friend. Or perhaps Diana was a mother and wife who was at a point in her own life when she no longer had time or patience to focus on a needy single friend. Maybe Diana grew up in a home where birthdays weren't important and attached less meaning to them than her friend. If that was the case, Diana might even have thought that April's reaction was childish or uncalled for, while in fact Diana's behavior hurt April deeply. Whatever the reasons, there was a shift in the dynamics of their relationship so it was no longer reciprocal.

Psychologically speaking, empathy is required to take on the perspective of the other person in a friendship. Clearly, Diana was not as empathic to her friend's needs as was April to hers. But negotiating our relative empathy levels is an important part of creating a working dynamic in a relationship. If you notice that your friend's feelings tend to bruise more easily than yours, or that your friend seems to be more in tune with and worried about your joys and concerns than you are with hers—or vice versa—you need to be alert to your respective differences. Once you understand and accept how the two of you might differ, you can take steps to help your friendship stay balanced, even through rocky moments.

Often, with a little forethought, you can avoid disappointments that lead friendships to unravel:

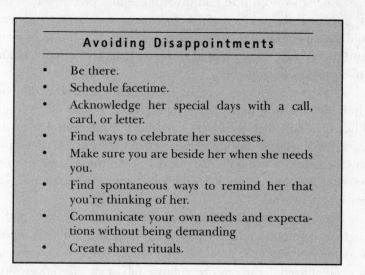

Avoiding Disappointments

- Be there.
- Schedule facetime.
- Acknowledge her special days with a call, card, or letter.
- Find ways to celebrate her successes.
- Make sure you are beside her when she needs you.
- Find spontaneous ways to remind her that you're thinking of her.
- Communicate your own needs and expectations without being demanding
- Create shared rituals.

FAMILY FEUDS

Another common friendship fallout arises when a friend says or does something hurtful to someone in our family, sometimes to a husband or to our kids. As blood boils, it suddenly becomes thicker than water.

Desiree described a friendship that came to such an abrupt end. Her girlfriend, Vanessa, had a child of the same age. The two women had given birth only weeks apart; each of their children referred to their mom's friend as "Auntie." Once a month, the couples shared a babysitter and went to dinner without the kids. Then one day, Vanessa's young son began acting aggressively to Desiree's daughter, pulling her hair without provocation. Had the situation been reversed, Desiree would have reprimanded her daughter right away, but Vanessa not only didn't reprimand her son, she admonished Desiree's daughter for being a cry-baby and fighting back.

Desiree couldn't believe what she was hearing. How dare Vanessa discipline someone else's daughter when she couldn't take care of her own son, who had thrown the first punch? From that day forward, the relationship between the two moms and their children was never the same. Desiree accused her friend of being blind to her own son's antics at Desiree's daughter's expense, and said that was unacceptable.

After that incident, Desiree called her friend and told her calmly that she was being too lenient with her son, and it would ultimately cause her problems. Despite the attempted heart-to-heart, there was no rapprochement after what had occurred that day. Soon there were no more playdates and the women stopped speaking. Neither friend was willing to give in to repair the relationship. The end.

How did it come about that two women who ostensibly had so much in common suddenly broke up over one isolated, minor incident? Although the breaking point was a single event, the disagreement itself became representative of larger differences. Both women seem to have realized that their parenting philosophies were irreconcilable—Vanessa's was more hands-off, while Desiree's was more authoritarian. Perhaps since the well-being of their children was in question, the small incident became indicative of deeper differences. Those irreconcilable philosophies were important enough to each woman that neither could think well of her former friend for not admitting she was wrong about her approach.

The fact is, family is often prioritized over friendship. While children and how they are raised are probably among the most common reasons mother friends fall out, there are other reasons a woman might feel her once-best friend has come between her and her family. Susie and Pam were neighbors as well as friends who had one such misunderstanding after years of friendship between their families. They all vacationed together at least three times a year and kept a small boat they shared at the lake. When Susie's husband lost his job, the family had to cut back on their discretionary spending. Susie and Pam still chatted each day but Pam seemed to have little sympathy for what Susie and Mark were going through as a couple.

Mark was so depressed that he had a hard time mobilizing himself to look for work. His unemployment insurance didn't go very far and Mark sure didn't seem to enjoy being home and feeling useless. More than once, Pam called Mark a "couch potato" in front of his kids. Pam thought she was being funny; perhaps she could cheer him up a bit. He had been looking so dour, she thought. The third time she did it, Susie snapped. Was Pam purposely trying to demean her husband when he was already down? How could she be so insensitive when she knew what was going on?

The next day, Susie called Pam and said she thought it wasn't "healthy" for the two families to be as close as they once were. Pam apologized and said that perhaps she was tactless. But after that conversation, things were never the same.

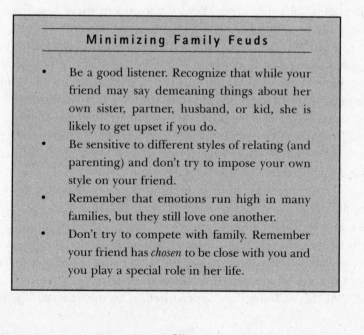

Minimizing Family Feuds

- Be a good listener. Recognize that while your friend may say demeaning things about her own sister, partner, husband, or kid, she is likely to get upset if you do.
- Be sensitive to different styles of relating (and parenting) and don't try to impose your own style on your friend.
- Remember that emotions run high in many families, but they still love one another.
- Don't try to compete with family. Remember your friend has *chosen* to be close with you and you play a special role in her life.

GROWING APART

Another deal breaker: as time passes, people change and they get to know each other on different levels. Two friends may realize that their values clash or that they see things so differently it creates an insurmountable gulf between them. Such was the case for Holly, who lost not one but two best friends because of emerging differences in values.

Holly, Ann, and Bev had known each other since elementary school. They lived in the same neighborhood, went to the same schools, attended the same church, and ran in the same circles. After high school, however, the three friends went their separate ways—Ann went to college, Bev partied and worked various odd jobs, and Holly went on to complete graduate studies. By the time Holly was done with grad school, they happened to all live in the same city again, and they started to hang out together and had a great time. It was as though there had never been a break in their friendship, and they were the same group of three best friends they had been since childhood.

"I got engaged with my boyfriend of eight years, and it just seemed fitting that they would be my bridesmaids," Holly recalls. Trouble started brewing during the year leading up to Holly's wedding. "We all spent tons of time together and I started feeling self-conscious, saddened, and emotionally drained after spending time with them. I couldn't figure out why I had these negative feelings." Holly would come home to her fiancé and complain about her friends, which was totally out of character.

Then there were a series of disagreements about the bridesmaids' dresses and other wedding arrangements. Holly felt as if Ann and Bev had opinions about everything and were ganging up against her. She wanted a somewhat modest affair. They accused her of being cheap and told her she would always regret the decisions she was making about her special day.

"As the wedding date approached, it hit me!" says Holly. She realized that she hardly had anything in common with either woman anymore. "They were superficial, and obsessed with appearances—weight, dieting, plastic surgery, and gossip—whereas I was more down-to-earth and laidback," she says. Over the four years they were apart, the friends had been shaped by different experiences and veered in different directions.

A CLASH OF VALUES

Friendships often come to an end when one friend disapproves of another's behavior or finds fault with her character, morals, or values. There are two discrete schools of thought about whether or not you should let someone know when she disappoints you. Some women feel that good friends should never judge one another—that the basis of any true friendship is unconditional support. "Friends may need to step back to let us make mistakes and learn from them," says one woman. "To cut off someone because of a poor choice, even though she realizes she made a mistake and apologizes, isn't being a good friend. Sometimes, these lapses are due to immaturity and we all learn as we grow."

Others feel that close friendships are predicated on honesty and therefore you should tell a friend when you disapprove of something she says or does. Problems arise when the two members of a friendship have different beliefs about how honest or supportive a good friend should be. Sometimes the answer isn't black or white, but more a matter of degree.

Cherise, age 50, was dumbfounded when her close friend ended their long relationship because of a presumed clash of values. Cherise had lived with her fiancé, Warren, for six years before they married in 1990. Her childhood buddy and best friend, Betsy, made it clear from the time the couple were first engaged that she thought Cherise was settling for less than she deserved. Warren was an easygoing, laid-back guy, who showed little ambition. He wasn't sure what he wanted to do after college, although he had the option of working in his father's business (a busy retail drugstore). For the immediate future, the couple planned to live on Cherise's salary as a teacher while Warren scoped out the job market.

Of course, her best friend's negative opinions about Warren gave Cherise some cause for concern, but she was certain she knew him a heck of a lot better than Betsy did. He was extremely capable and bright, and she was sure he would eventually find a satisfying career path. She loved his easygoing nature, his generosity, and that he was always doting on her. She was so in love that she was nearly blind to any of his imperfections. When Betsy repeatedly reminded her of these shortcomings, Cherise dismissed them as a product of her friend's envy.

Despite Betsy's admonitions, Cherise married Warren. He turned out to be a diligent worker who went on to law school at night to become a trial attorney. Betsy, who was unwilling to settle for a man who wasn't perfect, never married. Cherise and Warren had a child, and for the next five years, Warren was frantically busy, either working part-time in the drugstore or glued to his law books.

With lots of time on her hands, Cherise began what turned out to be a long-term extramarital affair. Betsy began to pull away. "She didn't approve of my affair," says Cherise. "I was involved with my high school sweetheart, a boy she hated intensely in high school, whom she didn't trust then and didn't trust now. She might have been jealous that I seemingly had it all, a great husband, great life, didn't have to work, nice kid, beautiful house . . . and a man on the side."

Cherise received a three-page, single-spaced typewritten letter in the mail from Betsy telling her that she could no longer be her friend. "This was after twenty-nine years of friendship!" exclaims Cherise. "I reread the letter to make sure of what I was reading, immediately shredded it, and we have not had contact with each other since. I was disappointed that she had put moral boundaries on our friendship, whereas I never did."

Cherise was more angered than hurt. She was brought up to believe that a best friend never judges: "A best friend knows how to keep a secret, and you keep hers." Betsy had a distinctly different opinion about the role of best friends: She thought that she was doing right by Cherise by showing her "tough love," trying to send her a wake-up call because Cherise was behaving in ways that seemed self-destructive and potentially hurtful to her family. She believed that a good friend has a responsibility to call her friend on the things she can't see or doesn't want to hear.

Like Cherise and Betsy, women fall on both sides of the fence, and a clash of values about the roles and responsibilities of friends can be divisive. Differences in religious views, attitudes towards money, parenting styles, and even discrepant political views can divide friends. During the polarizing presidential election campaign in 2008, the politics and values of the two candidates were so discrepant that many people had to face the issue of whether or not they could remain friends with those who backed the other candidate.

Speaking Out: When Candor Is Called For

- Your friend is self-destructive or being abusive to someone else.
- She is being abused.
- Her health, emotional well-being, or safety is at risk.
- She is breaking the law and putting herself in legal jeopardy.
- She is compromising your integrity or reputation (by asking you to do something dishonest or illegal).
- You just can't take it anymore.

BETRAYALS

A betrayal sets the stage for a particularly painful ending because it is a moral lapse directed at you. Being betrayed by a friend whom you once considered an intimate is as jolting as being rear-ended at a stoplight. Such was the case for Linda, now 45, who was betrayed by her best friend Susan.

BREAKING A CONFIDENCE

When they both turned 30, Linda and Susan were following parallel paths. The guys that they each were dating, and later married, happened to be close friends. Soon after marriage, each woman gave birth. Two years later, both women gave birth again. Each couple had a boy and a girl, with the same-sex children being roughly the same age. To further cement their already close friendship, the young families moved within a couple of blocks of one another and the women spent most days together with their children in tow at the playground or in each other's homes.

Linda and her husband divorced about five years later and she and her children went through a rough patch. The children felt like their lives had been turned upside down. By that time, Susan's first husband had died of leukemia and she had remarried. Her children, like Linda's, were having difficulty dealing with their changed lives.

"My daughter was especially rebellious, blowing off her schoolwork," says Linda. "She was deeply depressed as a result of having to deal with the dissolution of our family as she knew it." As a single mother, Linda was never sure whether her teenager's erratic moods were a result of the divorce or something more.

When Susan offered to help—to talk to Linda's daughter—Linda breathed a sigh of relief. Susan recounted her success as a youth minister, in addition to her long relationship with Linda's kids, and assured her that her intervention could help Linda reconnect with her daughter in a positive way. Nothing could have prepared Linda for what was to come.

"Her way of helping: she told my daughter that my son was conceived out of wedlock, something we had hidden from them and intended to tell them one day in our own time," says Linda. "She also told her that her Dad and I never loved each other (not true) but that we married because we 'had to' (again, not true). It threw my daughter into an emotional tailspin and made her despise me even more. It added to her depression instead of helping it."

After her daughter recounted the details of the "counseling session," those transgressions were the only things Linda remembered about her former friendship with Susan. She considered her friend's actions a betrayal of the worst kind and never spoke to her again. "She harmed my daughter emotionally by divulging what I had told her in confidence, telling her something she had no business telling her. When it happened seven years ago, it made for a very rough patch in my relationship with my daughter," says Linda. "Fortunately, my daughter and I weathered it and are extremely close now."

"I never could decide if she was being spiteful or just stupid," she says. "I tend to believe she was being spiteful, although she explained it away as plain stupidity. She hurt my daughter, and I erased her from my life. It wasn't that hard."

Susan may have been harboring unexpressed anger at Linda that led her to "act out" by saying these terrible things to her daughter. Had she been able to express her feelings to Linda more directly, this fallout might never have happened. Whatever Susan's motives might have been in sharing what she did with Linda's daughter, it created a fatal breach in Linda and Susan's friendship. Linda couldn't find any way to condone or explain the way Susan had hurt her child. As far as she was concerned, any semblance of trust between the two friends was gone and could never be rectified. In this friendship, as in many, there may have been a host of unexpressed grievances.

Other betrayals are relatively minor when looked at it retrospect, but while they are happening, or soon after, they make a

What Not to Talk About:

If a friend consistently says the wrong things (e.g., criticizing your appearance or taking every opportunity to make an undercutting jab) or talks too much about certain subjects, it may place a friendship at risk. Here are some topics that call for discretion:

- **Money:** It's generally uncomfortable for people to talk about the nitty-gritty of how much they make, how much they owe, or how much they spend—so if you choose to, make sure your friend is as comfortable doing so as you are. Sizeable disparities in income between women (or their families) are likely to increase the odds of an uncomfortable discussion. Yes, you can mention getting a salary increase or losing money on your stock portfolio, but it's best not to dwell on dollar amounts unless you are business partners.

- **Other people:** Gossip can be an immediate friendship killer. Be extremely cautious about talking about your friend behind her back, particularly if it is unfavorably. A good general rule: don't repeat or say anything that you would not want to get back to your friend. Don't put down her friends or relatives; you can criticize their behaviors without tearing them apart as individuals.

- **An excess of success:** Friends like to share in each other's successes (as well in the successes of their significant others) but when it reaches the threshold that might be considered bragging, be cautious. Use judgment in talking about your son's grades if your friend's son is struggling. Don't talk about your designer handbag if she does all her shopping in thrift shops.

- **Dating problems:** Adolescent girls love to share stories about guys. In doing so, they provide each other with advice, support, and confidence—and are able to resolve problems and worries. But there can be too much of a good thing. Psychologist Amanda Rose of the University of Missouri-Columbia has done research on the problem of co-rumination: the problem of talking too much about anything. Specifically, she found that when girls rehash their problems excessively, it leads to depression, anxiety, and a sense of hopelessness.

woman feel like her friend has turned a blind eye to her feelings. I remember how hurt I felt when my best friend Lenore had chosen the same June wedding day as mine. With the limited availability of caterers and the brief window between graduation and summer, she said she had no choice. But I had wanted her to be my maid of honor! Didn't she know that? How could she betray my feelings? Many years and a couple of marriages later, we laugh about it, but at the age of twenty it felt like a major slap in my face. Our expectations of our friends aren't always realistic, and when they're not met, it feels like betrayal.

NOT KEEPING A PROMISE

Another woman, Missy, age 20, told me the story of her friendship with Georgia. During their senior year in high school, Georgia met a man online who lived in Pennsylvania. They began e-mailing and texting regularly. Missy was sure that once the two girlfriends moved into their dorm at Syracuse University, Georgia would meet guys on campus and this virtual relationship would be over.

That didn't happen. In November, over the Thanksgiving holiday, Georgia flew to Pennsylvania without even telling Missy. "She married the Internet boyfriend within two weeks of meeting him and never returned to finish school," says Missy. It was impossible for her to understand how an intelligent woman could abandon her plans and goals for the future for a relationship with a man she hardly knew. "I felt like it was a betrayal to me as well as to her," says Missy. After several months, the friendship between the women was history.

Although it may have never been discussed explicitly, Missy assumed she and Georgia had made a pact. They would be roommates throughout their four years of college—or at least through the first semester. When Georgia doused their plans, Missy felt as if she was abandoned for a boyfriend Georgia barely knew. It made her wonder if she really knew Georgia at all.

Promises can be explicit or implicit (like the one between Georgia and Missy). Although a promise between two friends is usually an honest expression of affection and closeness when it is made, it may lose currency over time. For example, two friends may promise to stay single, but then one meets her mate. Or two women may promise to have children at the same time, but one suddenly finds herself pregnant. Because life yields so many unpredictable twists and turns, a promise two friends make to take care of each other in old age isn't as likely to be kept (or considered unforgivable, if broken) as a more practical, short-term promise such as to accompany a friend to an appointment with a surgeon next month, to drive her home from the bar if she has too much to drink, or to tell her immediately if she hurts your feelings.

BEING BLINDSIDED

When Tracy, 21, and Alexis were first introduced, they just seemed to click. The conversation flowed fast and easy. They initially met at a party where Tracy also met a guy named Brad, who was friendly and flirty. "He was flirting with both of us but a bit more towards her," Tracy recalls. Since Alexis was already involved with someone, Tracy didn't think anything of his play for her friend.

About eight months later, Tracy ran into the same guy at a club, and this time they really hit it off. They started seeing each other regularly and the relationship got serious. "Alexis was supportive during all of this and I never suspected that she wanted him too, especially since she was on her third boyfriend since that party," says Tracy. Tracy and Brad dated for several months and he became her first lover, which made the bond feel that much stronger and significant.

"I never saw it coming," says Tracy. "One day I stopped by Alexis's house for a surprise visit on my way home from campus. She was rushing out of the shower and looked really flushed, but I presumed it was just from the shower." When Alexis asked her to come back later without inviting her in, it struck Tracy as odd.

As she started to leave, she saw Brad's shoes on the doormat. "I felt so betrayed," says Tracy. "I mean, I could expect it from a guy—but she and I were so close!"

Even though Alexis subsequently apologized, Tracy still feels hurt. "I ended up losing two best friends that day," she says. Tracy was betrayed by two people whom she cared for deeply—but she says that having a female friend act in such an uncaring and duplicitous way hurt her even more deeply than her first lover's infidelity. And because she had lost the friend with whom she used to commiserate, there was no one she could go to for comfort.

UNFAITHFUL

The dissolution of the friendship between Rebecca, now 31, and her friend Hayley was long overdue—and the infraction so egregious that it's hard to understand how it lasted as long as it did. Yet some friendships are so strong that they tolerate the unimaginable: "What led to our friendship ending was that she had an affair with my husband while I was pregnant with our fourth child," says Rebecca. "At first, I readily forgave her because I saw her as vulnerable and weak, a victim of a very abusive marriage. She and my husband had been seeing each other for a little over a month when I first found out—and it was supposed to be over. However, the two of them continued to sneak around behind my back."

As odd as it sounds, Rebecca continued to have sympathy for her friend who was sleeping with her husband. "I was still trying to help her get out of her marriage," she says. One day Hayley called Rebecca from the cell phone in her car, crying hysterically. Hayley was so upset that she wanted to drive off the road. Rebecca talked her out of it.

The last straw came during Rebecca's eighth month of pregnancy, when she found a strange cell phone bill in her mailbox. It was for a private line that her husband had set up for himself and Hayley. For the first time, she realized that her friend wasn't really a friend. "I called her cell phone (the secret one) and left a scathing message, and that was the last time I talked to her, although my husband talked to her off and on for another two years. It was awful," Rebecca recalls.

"It affects me to this day," she says. "I'm still so angry with her. I will never understand why I wasn't important enough to her to stop trying to wreck my family and steal my husband, especially when she knew from firsthand experience how awful it is to be cheated on."

Instead of being furious about being betrayed by her husband and her best friend, Rebecca felt sorry for Hayley. She identified with her friend so closely that, even though she knew she was sleeping with her husband, she saw Hayley as the victim. Somehow Rebecca never even recognized that her husband was complicit in the affair. Perhaps her expectations of friendship were greater than her expectations of marriage—or else her self-esteem was so low that she wasn't able to defend herself until she got clobbered over the head. (Still married, Rebecca says she remains there for the sake of her children.)

Avoiding Betrayals Between Friends

- Err on the side of honesty.
- Keep lines of communication open.
- Ask rather than assume.
- Keep your promises.
- Apologize sooner rather than later.
- Don't take advantage of a friend.

BLOWUPS

Friendships sometimes blow up when one or both women reach a point when they are no longer able to tolerate the other. One volatile incident (an explosive argument, for example, or an unforgivable betrayal) or the culmination of a string of disappointments results in the undoing of a close relationship in an instant. If you've had a blowup, you can generally pinpoint the precise moment when your friendship went awry.

Sometimes women are unable to express their feelings until they are ready to explode. They hold them in, hoping they'll resolve themselves, but that usually doesn't happen. Jen, age 22, had an argument that escalated into a major blowup. Jen and her friend Sara truly understood each other, but some stylistic differences between them seemed to get in the way of their friendship. Jen was far more spontaneous and willing to make last-minute plans than Sara, who liked to plan and schedule everything way in advance.

Jen would call Sara and ask her to take a walk to take advantage of the beautiful weather or to catch a new movie together, but her invites were always turned down unless she was already on her friend's calendar. Sara would have one excuse or another about why she was too busy to get together. Jen felt like they only saw each other when she was "booked" at Sara's convenience. "I began to see her as arrogant and selfish," says Jen.

After being rejected many times, Jen reached her boiling point. "I confronted her about this and it escalated into a huge yelling match, filled with accusations and insults," says Jen. The argument wasn't merely about Sara's unwillingness to go to the beach on a hot summer day; it was about her need to control, and her rigid and unyielding manner with Jen. "Friends simply don't treat friends that way," says Jen. That blowup marked the end of their friendship because there was no way to undo all the harsh words they had hurled at each other.

Blowups aren't always in-your-face disagreements. They can take place by snail mail or e-mail as well. Unfortunately, such letters and electronic messages (that don't allow for real-time dialogue, facial expressions, or body language) increase the risk of completely blowing a relationship out of the water. Unintentionally, the delivery of the message can turn out more hurtful than was ever intended. Caroline, age 58, shared such a story with me.

Caroline and Judy were once very close but they no longer lived in the same city. Judy e-mailed Caroline asking why they were seeing less and less of each other. Feeling that Judy had given her an opening to be honest about why she had refused so many invitations to visit, Caroline, who was divorced, wrote back and said that as much as she enjoyed spending time with Judy's family, she felt like her friend's husband, a psychologist, was analyzing every word she was saying.

She waited several weeks for Judy's response, which seemed long overdue. "After that, I never heard from Judy again. But a mutual friend told me how hurt she was by the letter," says Caroline. "I had no idea I had come across so strong. I didn't mean to end our friendship."

Had the discussion taken place in person, the two women may have been able to find a way to resolve their problem without either one feeling slighted. The distance, the passage of time, and the fact that the offending words were in black and white, made the insult harder to ignore or work out.

PERSONAL JEALOUSIES

Some friendships end because a new person enters the picture and changes the dynamics of a preexisting friendship. The third person may be male or female; the new relationship may be romantic or platonic. It can even be an infant that consumes a new mother's time. Whatever form it takes, the change is significant enough to upset the precarious balance of a friendship and makes it less viable.

RELEGATED TO "JUST A FRIEND"

The promise of romance, love, and desire is often so strong that women disappoint and drop close or long-term female friends in favor of what often turns out to be a transitory relationship with a guy. This is particularly painful when two women are attracted

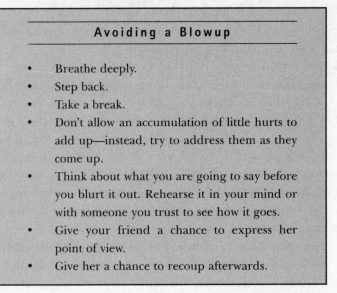

Avoiding a Blowup

- Breathe deeply.
- Step back.
- Take a break.
- Don't allow an accumulation of little hurts to add up—instead, try to address them as they come up.
- Think about what you are going to say before you blurt it out. Rehearse it in your mind or with someone you trust to see how it goes.
- Give your friend a chance to express her point of view.
- Give her a chance to recoup afterwards.

to the same person—possibly a lover, partner, or spouse—and one comes out on top. It can destabilize and split the relationship between the two females.

Often it's surprising and hurtful when a very good friend suddenly prioritizes a potential lover over us, but the situation is hardly uncommon, even among the closest friends. Sometimes it's a matter of not knowing exactly where our friend stands on the importance of romance versus the importance of friendship; sometimes it is simply giddiness about the prospect of romance that blinds us to how we are hurting our friend in the process of pursuing it. Sue recently broke up with a guy she was dating because the relationship didn't seem to be going anywhere. During the time the two had been seeing each other, she had introduced her boyfriend to quite a few of her female friends. One girlfriend, in particular, was having a difficult time, so Sue tried to include her in things she did with her boyfriend. "She became friendly with my ex, but they only knew each other through me," says Sue.

Soon after the split and before the proverbial body was cold, the girlfriend called Sue to see if it was okay for her to go skiing with Sue's ex, who had now invited her on the trip they had planned as a threesome. "I told her she could do whatever she wanted, but I found the whole thing inappropriate," says Sue.

After thinking about the call for several days, Sue couldn't believe that her friend had been insensitive enough to ask her. She expected more from her girlfriend than she did of her ex. Even though she had broken up with her boyfriend, she still felt disappointment that the relationship didn't work out the way she had hoped it would. With this transgression, Sue no longer trusted either of them and decided to make her girlfriend an "ex" too.

Another instance of how a romance can kill a friendship is that of Nicole and Lacey. The two women met soon after they both moved to the same town. They hit it off immediately. "We were both adrenaline junkies, partners in crime who enjoyed outdoor activities. Sometimes we thought of each other as twin sisters or maybe more like teenage brothers," says Lacey, who is a lesbian.

Nicole was bisexual and the two women dated briefly. "Nicole wasn't that interested and I decided to end it when she started avoiding me, although I would have preferred otherwise," says Lacey. The two remained friends, but Lacey began to see a cruel side to her friend's personality after they stopped dating. "She started to make condescending and dismissive remarks if I wanted to talk about what was bothering me about us." If she met a new friend, Nicole would ask Lacey to sit in the back of her car so her new friend could sit in the passenger seat. Lacey felt as if she was being relegated to the rear of the bus.

Yet Nicole felt comfortable enough to call Lacey crying about her boyfriend who dumped her or to pick up girls in front of her while at clubs. She even started getting "frisky" with one of them in front of Lacey. Lacey was feeling increasingly sore and sensitive. She confronted Nicole about her behavior, but Nicole made no apologies. She told Lacey that they were friends, not exes, since they were never in a long-term relationship. "She seems to have conveniently ignored that I still had romantic feelings for her," says Lacey.

The anger kept escalating and Lacey admits to becoming passive-aggressive at times. Nicole requested a break. Several months passed and the two women tried to be "just friends" again, but it never worked. Lacey learned how exceedingly difficult if is to downgrade a romance to a platonic friendship after someone has been dumped. In her case, there was too much residual hurt and anger.

THREE'S A CROWD

Threesomes can easily become friendship killers when two women have an extremely close relationship and a third person, male or female, suddenly enters the picture.

In the case of Carey and Jillian, a possessive boyfriend killed the friendship. Carey, now 24, and Jillian had been best friends during elementary and middle school as well as their first two years of high school. People teased them because they were always at each other's side. Carey became part of Jillian's family and Jillian became part of hers. They did homework together, joined the same clubs at school, and had many friends in common. They spoke about taking trips to Europe and living together after high school.

Their relationship changed when Carey's family moved away, but Carey and Jillian still spoke on the phone and saw each other twice a year. Through their senior year in high school, Carey would spend Easter week with Jillian's family and Jillian would return the visit towards the end of summer vacation.

Carey was commuting about forty miles to work in a hotel in downtown Chicago, where she was a front desk clerk. It wasn't an easy time for her. When she got home each evening, she seemed to argue constantly with her parents. Her parents didn't like her coming home late and disliked her new boyfriend, Marc, her supervisor and the manager at the hotel. Marc was in his early 40s, considerably older than she was, and divorced with two children. With alimony and child support payments, there wasn't much money left from his salary to spend on himself or anyone else. He lived frugally in a small studio apartment not far from work, where they often met after hours.

Carey impulsively decided to move in with Marc after a couple of months, hoping to minimize the hassles with her parents and to reduce the length of her commute. She was able to walk to and from work and she liked him "enough" even though he didn't seem like "marriage material." The space was small, but they made do. When she told Jillian the news, her friend was angry beyond belief. "She felt that I had ruined our plans to live together after high school," says Carey.

Carey and Jillian did live together eventually—just not as they had originally planned. When Carey and Marc realized they could afford a larger two-bedroom if they found a third roommate, Carey thought that inviting Jillian to move in with them might be a fix for more than one problem. With their recommendations, Jillian was able to get a job in the same hotel and achieve some independence from her family. Carey loved the idea of having her best friend nearby, and with Jillian contributing a third of the rent, she and Marc could have more space—or so she thought.

They may have acquired more square feet of apartment, but the diminished psychological space began to feel oppressive. Jillian had moved in with the expectation that she and Carey would pick up where they left off, certainly thinking they would spend more time together as housemates. But whenever she asked Carey to go out with her, Carey wouldn't go because Marc would make her feel bad about leaving him.

One night, the three roommates went out drinking together. When they returned home, Jillian was plastered and told Marc that Carey had cheated on him. He reacted violently. "He beat me up and threw me out the door," says Carey. "She just stood there and watched, so I took a knife to her car and scratched it because I felt so betrayed. She blamed the whole thing on me, and from that night forward, we weren't friends." Carey couldn't understand why Jillian would make up such a lie. It was unforgivable. She moved into a rented room and never heard from Marc or Jillian again.

Time and again, I have heard stories about how a third person destabilized the precarious balance of a close or best friendship. There is, sadly, no antidote to prevent its occurrence because friendships are dynamic, changing with the circumstances of our lives. But looking back at the friendship and talking about it helps us heal and learn.

MEAN GIRLS

Some of the cruelest betrayals occur when a clique of three or more female friends suddenly turn on one in their midst. This is extremely common during the middle and high school years, but it can inflict long-lasting scars that remain when these girls become women. Grown women also lament their exclusion from PTA committees and mom groups.

In middle and high school, the cafeteria is the most common backdrop for exclusion by the clique. Emily, now 20 years old, has vivid memories of the tears she shed when she became a lunchroom exile. Emily and her friend Marissa were on their way to lunch after math class during their sophomore year. While Emily was paying for lunch, she noticed that Marissa headed toward a table with a group of friends she was going to eat with. "They were my friends too," says Emily.

Looking for a place to sit, Emily joined Marissa and the rest of the group but soon noticed there were no more chairs. "They had all decided to *not* save me a seat," says Emily. She was stunned. "And I'm talking like these were people I knew since grade school, and all of a sudden I had no one to sit with."

When Emily saw Marissa after school, she asked her what had gone down at lunch. Marissa lashed out and accused Emily of being too negative all the time and said that she had decided to surround herself with people who were more positive. Emily felt dizzy and sick to her stomach. "I spent every day in the library after that, and the friendship just went out the window," says Emily. "I was depressed for months. It was like a part of me had died. I saw her with other people, having such a good time, and I always felt like I had let her down. It affected the rest of my high school career."

Whether Emily really let Marissa down or not, Marissa was unnecessarily cruel in the very public way she handled the split (although common in the culture of middle school). She instigated their mutual friends to participate in the group dump of Emily, not realizing or caring how it would shatter her former friend.

At some point in their lives, many women suffer an indignity like this one that often goes on to affect their trust in future relationships. Another woman told me how her friend excluded her from a group in seventh grade. The two reconciled the next year and became good friends and remained very close into adulthood. "But I'll be honest—to this day [some fifteen years later], when I'm mad at her about something else, I think back resentfully to how she shut me out at the lunch table," she says.

Age is no barrier when it comes to one person being cast as the odd woman out. In a memorable episode of the HBO series *The Sopranos*, mobster Paulie Walnuts returns from prison and is shocked to find out that his mother has been excluded from the "girls" at Green Grove Nursing Home. When Paulie complains to the director of the facility, he responds, "Nursing homes are like high schools with wheel chairs." Whatever your age, being dumped by one friend is awful, but being dumped by a group in public is humiliating. You not only wonder what your friend was thinking but what she told everyone else, and how you can face other people.

Meaningful friendships depend on a foundation of trust. When friends betray us or disappoint us, it can easily undermine that sense of security. The more egregious the lapse in judgment and/or the more often it happens, the less trusting of that person we become and things begin to fall apart, either slowly or suddenly.

In addition to the dangers that lurk within, friendships are also subject to insults that occur from outside. A new lover, partner, best friend—or even a change in circumstances, such at income, career, lifestyle, or neighborhood—can rattle a very close friendship to the core. The loss of a friendship, however it occurs, whatever the reason, is almost uniformly unpleasant. Yet the one common upside to these breakups is that they provide an opportunity for reflection that may lead us to better friendships, better choices, and better endings in the future.

CHAPTER 4

GETTING OVER
GETTING DUMPED

"Men kick friendship around like a football and it doesn't
seem to crack. Women treat it like glass and it falls to pieces."

—ANNE MORROW LINDBERGH

She's gone. Your once-close friend hasn't called, returned your
calls, responded to your e-mails, or otherwise acknowledged
your existence in hours, days, weeks, or months—depending
on the frequency of contact you have come to expect. She was a
close friend, perhaps even a best friend, and now you've suddenly been defriended. It's almost as if she clicked a big "DELETE"
button that eliminated you from her IM list, cell phone contacts,
and e-mail address book. She may have done all that, too.

Being dumped by a best friend doesn't hurt just once. On
many levels, emotional, social, and physical, you are reminded con-
tinually of your former companion by her absence. You're reminded
of her when you have a fight with your mother—you would usually
call your ex-friend immediately, and now there's no one who quite
knows the situation or characters well enough for you to share your
frustration. Or you had been hoping to catch that new movie and
she was the one most likely to go with you. Now what do you do?
She was such an integral part of your life that the hole feels gaping.
To top it off, each gape is a reminder that something you were
taught was sacred—your best friendship—went terribly wrong.
The wash of strong feelings is almost exactly what a woman experiences when dumped by a lover: embarrassment that she wasn't

good enough; anger at the dumper for her callousness; sadness for thwarted dreams of a future together. When it comes to friendships, the more significant they were, the harder you fall. The pain, fury, and shame at having been dumped lessen only gradually.

There's no way around it. Getting dumped really hurts. Like Randi, you may not have even seen it coming. Randi, who is 32, recently phoned her girlfriend Nicole, just to see how she was doing. "She hit me with a bombshell," says Randi. "She told me politely, but in no uncertain terms, that there was no point in continuing our friendship." Since the last time they had spoken, Nicole had decided to make some "positive changes" in her life. Ending her friendship with Randi was part of that plan.

Randi was dumbfounded at Nicole's pronouncement. The two women only had one prior disagreement over the six years they had known each other. In a moment of anger, harsh words were exchanged between them, a disagreement that was, at least on Randi's part, insignificant and long forgotten—until now, as she struggled to understand what was happening.

"We were both Americans living abroad, and we found creature comfort in talking to a fellow countrywoman," says Randi. They shared joys and tears and supported each other through difficulties. Because they were busy moms who lived in different towns, most of their interactions had taken the form of long phone calls when the kids were napping or asleep for the night. Randi had three sons under the age of five and her husband usually worked long hours, while Nicole was a single mom with an only child. Randi often babysat for Nicole's daughter, Chelsea, whenever she was asked, and included her in all her children's birthday parties. With families that close-knit, what could have been the breaking point?

"I had to respect her decision, but was confused about why she felt the need to cut our friendship off entirely," says Randi. Nicole said she was looking for a best friend who was more available and accessible, someone with whom she could go out and have drinks—something Randi never had time to do, with her three small children and her husband's long work hours. Nicole said she didn't feel like putting any more energy into a "phone friend." "Could she only have one friend at a time?" asks Randi, who felt humiliated and rejected.

These were two women whose lives had taken different paths and whose friendship needs had diverged. For Randi, this "friendship-lite" added an important dimension to her harried life as a busy mom living abroad. For Nicole, it simply wasn't enough. "I understand her need to cut loose, but I thought she understood my situation, too," says Randi. "I am sad. I miss our girl chats. I miss being her Dr. Freud." Although Randi knows many people where she's living, her relationship with Nicole felt like her special lifeline to the United States. She never had to explain herself to Nicole because her friend always knew. "I really feel alone now," she says.

Randi is not the only woman to have been unilaterally dumped by a friend. This is an experience many women have—the "it's just not working for me" phone call so akin to a romantic breakup, or, in some cases, a face-to-face meeting in which one woman redresses her friend for her friendship failings. But not all friendship "dumps" are so clear, or so acknowledged. Because best friendships are not exclusive and categorical, like most romantic relationships, best friend breakups are generally confusing and messy.

For example, Stephanie and Anna, both in their twenties, met while they were graduate students. Because they shared several classes as well as an advisor, they recognized each other by sight. When they found themselves in the library at the same table one evening, they immediately began chatting and realized how much more they had in common. The conversation flowed easily and they soon became soul mates, talking multiple times a day (and night) and sharing their lives with each other.

When they graduated the next year, Stephanie helped Anna get a job in the same firm where she had been working part-time. The two friends became inseparable. "We did everything together, from going to dinner or the movies to jogging in the park," says Stephanie. "We spent a lot of time texting and instant-messaging at work, too."

Then Anna met a "new best friend," a woman named Lisa

who lived on the same floor of her apartment building. Little by little, Anna was spending more time with Lisa and less time with Stephanie, who felt like she had been replaced. Anna made no secret that she and Lisa were going bar-hopping, swimming, and to yoga classes, things Stephanie had never wanted to do with her.

One day, after Stephanie dropped Anna off at home for lunch, Stephanie texted her friend saying that maybe they should give their friendship a break because they seemed to be getting into so many little arguments over the past couple of months. Stephanie was probably worried that she would be dumped, and made a defensive, preemptive strike to avoid any more psychic pain. She was still shocked when Anna texted back: "Fine and take care."

Stephanie swallowed hard and felt bad about what she had done. The next day she texted Anna again, apologizing for her impulsive message borne out of frustration. She said she hoped that her friend would forgive her. Anna texted back what seemed like a prefunctory message: "There is no need for you to be sorry."

The two women had it out when they saw each other at work. Stephanie asked what was going on. Anna exploded and told Stephanie that she was simply too needy. Anna was sick of listening and keeping her company all the time. She admitted that she felt bad saying it but she couldn't be that kind of friend for her. With those words, Anna essentially ended the relationship, but said that the two would still be work acquaintances. How could that play itself out? Stephanie couldn't help but find the message insulting and unsettling.

The two once-best friends haven't spoken since. They avoid each other at the office whenever possible, because they both feel so awkward. Stephanie tried texting Anna several times, asking to get together again to talk. "I told her that I will always continue to value her friendship and would like to work things out with her," she says. Anna texted back: "Our relationship just doesn't work for me anymore and you need to move on with your life. I have nothing to say to you."

Stephanie is desperately seeking what she terms as "closure."

She asks: "Should I try to reach out to her one last time or just let go? Seeing her every day at work and not speaking to each other is very painful. I still want to reconnect and be her friend."

As difficult as it is to be dumped, having to see your once-best friend on a daily basis (at work, at school, on the block) makes it that much more painful. It reopens a wound that never had a chance to really heal. Although texting isn't a good way to handle sensitive discussions, it isn't likely that Stephanie's friendship broke up because of that one provocative text message. There had been many red flags along the way: Stephanie and Anna were beginning to argue more often. Anna made a new best friend without making any effort to draw Stephanie into their circle or offering any explanation. The text message may have simply given Anna the excuse she was looking for to opt out of the friendship.

While it is natural for a friend who has been dumped to hope for some "feel-good" or palliative closure (e.g., an apology or face-saving explanation), Anna made it clear that she wasn't willing or ready to rehash her friendship with Stephanie. This left Stephanie with no choice but to back off and do some soul-searching to figure out what really happened and why. Stephanie would have to achieve closure on her own.

Warning Signs of a Waning Friendship

- Having less time for each other
- Feeling out of touch and/or out of sync
- Having less to share
- Having to work harder to make conversation
- Feeling you have less in common than you once did
- Increasingly preferring to be with other people (friends or family)
- Increasingly frequent miscommunications and misunderstandings

A third—and very common—kind of friend-dumping is the de facto kind, when one friend ceases to be present in the relationship but never addresses her friend or whatever the problem may be. Instead, the breakup initiator simply distances herself or disappears completely, forcing the dumpee to come to her own conclusions about what might have gone wrong.

To this day, Gwen, 35, reels from the loss of her friendship with her college best friend, Sara, whenever she thinks about it. When Gwen met Sara in the dorm on their first day of college during their freshman year, they bonded instantly. They spent most of their time together for three years, in and out of school. They studied together; had long talks about life, love, and heartaches; and shared their innermost secrets.

While still in college, the two were involved in a terrible car accident that almost took Gwen's life. Sara had been driving the car. "I know she felt responsible and even guilty about what happened," says Gwen. Perhaps as a function of her own guilt, or perhaps unsure whether Gwen wanted to see her, Sara pulled away. "She visited me only a couple of times while I remained in the hospital for nearly a month," Gwen remembers.

When Gwen returned to school, Sara came around even less. Although Gwen was quick to forgive and forget, other friends pointed out Sara's absences, drawing attention to what they felt was bad behavior on Sara's part, which caused Gwen to pull away as well. "Sadly, neither of us tried very hard to get things back on track," Gwen says. "Our friendship ended."

Gwen was devastated. On top of having to deal with the physical and emotional trauma of her accident, she was left wondering why her once-best friend no longer wanted any contact with her. The dissolution of their relationship haunted Gwen for several years. Yet despite her feelings of loss and confusion, Gwen still thinks warmly of Sara. "I often wonder how Sara is, and what she's doing," she says.

With time, Gwen was probably better able to accept the separation because it was precipitated by an identifiable trauma, the car accident. It gave her an alibi to explain the lost friendship to herself and others. She believed that the trauma of the accident made it extraordinarily difficult for Sara to maintain or revisit the friendship. But even this semi-ambiguous ending left Gwen with unanswered questions about what happened to her friend and whether their friendship had been real at its core.

Of course, not every breakup story has such a clear-cut cause as Gwen and Sara's. One such breakup story is that of Amy and Alexa. Amy, now 32 years old, had been a close friend of Alexa's since her early twenties. The women met when Amy became Alexa's boss in a small company where they both worked. "I interviewed and hired her, but as time went on we grew friendly outside the office," says Amy. They stayed overnight at each other's homes after evenings out and shared intimate details of their personal lives (especially about men and the traumas of dating).

Amy was a few years older than Alexa and became somewhat of a mentor to her friend. "Alexa was delightful, a highly intelligent person who made me laugh so much," Amy says. She encouraged her protégé to take risks, to advance her career, and tried to protect her from any landmines along the way. Alexa had a vulnerable side that appealed to Amy because it reminded her of herself during her younger years.

"We had a lot of fun, danced, sang, and cried (if crying can be fun), and went through a lot together, at that kind of key twenty-something time when you're falling in and out of love—the classic heartbreak and party years," says Amy. "When she was sad and sick, I gave her massages."

When the two women were assigned to work in different locations, they had less time to spend with one another. While their careers were on separate tracks, Amy still considered Alexa a good friend, always acknowledging her birthday and congratulating her on her successes. They got together several times a year, and each time it felt as if they had never been apart.

Then Amy made yet another career move, to the UK from the States. She heard later through common friends that Alexa had moved overseas as well, but to a different part of the UK. Both women had married Americans, and Amy was excited about the prospect of reconnecting to share their common bonds and experiences.

Amy contacted Alexa by e-mail. "Her first response was courteous but lukewarm," says Amy. "I visited her region for several months as part of my work, and tried to see her while I was there. She brushed me off repeatedly. I knew she was due to have a baby, and was also holding down a very pressured job, so I didn't take it too personally, although warning bells sounded," she says. Since Amy and Alexa were now close geographically, both expats and old friends, Amy thought it odd that her friend seemed to put off their getting together.

When she returned to the States, Amy sent e-mail messages and birthday greetings, but Alexa didn't respond. "In a way, that was better than the lukewarm messages she sent me earlier, which were painful. After two or three years of still sending messages (even after they were met with stone silence), I finally realized I had to give up," says Amy.

Amy has no idea why her friend disappeared from her life. "I know she had some big mother issues that she may have projected onto me, but don't we all?" Amy taxed her memory to figure out what had gone wrong. She thought that something had soured the friendship for Alexa, perhaps a remark that had made Alexa angry more than a decade ago and which, from Amy's perspective, was part of the past. "I immediately apologized to her at the time for a comment that was well-intended," says Amy. But since Amy still remembers the comment more than ten years later and wonders if it was a factor in the breakup, it is likely that Alexa remembers the comment as well.

At the time, Amy told Alexa that she wouldn't intentionally do anything to hurt her. "I realized that I cared for her so much that her feelings were more important than arguing the point that I hadn't done anything so wrong," says Amy. "Anyway, I thought we'd cleared that up. Part of me wonders if she held on to it, or some other resentment. This is the only conflict I remember."

It may well be that geography, marriage, and Alexa's coming

into her own personally and professionally changed the nature of their friendship, irrespective of that remark. For a while after Alexa cut off contact, Amy even wondered if something had been wrong with Alexa's baby or with her marriage, or whether her once-best friend was at some other difficult place in her life. Amy realizes that when someone is suffering, it's sometimes painful to talk to people, even good friends. "That's why I persevered in contacting her, on the off-chance that she might reply one day. Finally, I took the hint and gave up."

The friendship had started to fall apart roughly around the time the two women both married. Although they had connected in the workplace and maintained a relationship as singles, they weren't able to sustain their friendship afterwards. Breakups often take place for idiosyncratic reasons that can be unfathomable to outsiders, and often remain beyond the conscious awareness of the two former friends themselves—especially the one who is dumped. Perhaps Alexa married someone who she worried wouldn't bless her relationship with her old friend, or perhaps she feared that her old friend wouldn't bless her new husband.

All Amy could figure out was that something toppled the relationship between the two women—a relationship Amy hadn't realized was at risk—and the breakup left her dumbfounded. Unfortunately, "three's a crowd" thinking is common when a woman feels that a friendship is threatening to her allegiance with her life partner. In this case, as often happens, Alexa resolved the conflict by dropping the less significant relationship, her friendship with Amy.

Being dumped like Randi, Stephanie, or Amy is far more common than you may think. Yet it always comes as a shock. Whether it's by the friend of the moment or the friend you walked to school with on the first day of kindergarten, it is always painful and embarrassing to be unceremoniously dumped—because dumping is one-sided, unexpected, and generally comes without a clear explanation.

FROM SHOCK TO ACCEPTANCE

When they realize they have been dumped by a friend, women typically experience a range of reactions that include shock and denial, loss, self-blame, embarrassment and anger before they reach a state of acceptance and relief. Not every woman goes through every stage, nor do all women go through these stages in the same order, but eventually most will move from utter shock to reluctant acceptance.

STAGE 1: SHOCK AND DENIAL

When the ending of a friendship is one-sided, it often comes out of the blue for the friend who has been dumped. The jilter may have been trying to find a way to extricate herself from the relationship for weeks or even months, but when she drops the news on you, you're caught totally off guard and unprepared. Or there may have been problems festering for some time that both friends conveniently buried beneath the surface.

Because of the element of surprise (this occurred on your friend's timeline and not yours), you're likely to be baffled. The last few times you've asked your friend to get together, she responded that she was too busy with this or with that. You cling to the fantasy that she really is and that it has nothing to do with your relationship. Face it: you are in denial.

When you finally realize you've been dumped, it's natural to try to figure out what led to the breakup. You replay your last conversations over and over, searching for clues as to why the friendship veered off course, hoping to find a way of patching things up. Even if you already know the basis for her decision—either because she told you or because you saw signs that the friendship was unraveling—it's hard to deal with the feeling of being rejected by someone you care about.

The reasons for some cutoffs are readily apparent and, for

others, more elusive. You may realize that the two of you really weren't a good fit to begin with or that your lifestyles or values had become too discrepant.

The jilter may simply be tired of her relationship with you—and may have found someone else or be looking for someone else with whom she prefers spending time. Time is finite, and she's decided that you are no longer first on her speed dial. She may not be able to tolerate her jealousy towards you anymore; she feels that she can't hold a candle to you in terms of your ability to attract partners or other female friends, succeed at work, handle your kids, or juggle it all. Or she may have decided that she is giving more than she is getting and that the relationship is no longer reciprocal; you are always asking for more than you are able to give. While you can speculate about a bunch of maybes, you may never be able to pinpoint precisely what's happened.

STAGE 2: LOSS

It's natural to feel a sense of grief, loss, and pain when someone who was important in your life suddenly disappears. You are going to need time to heal, but be assured, you will, despite the challenges. In Randi's case, Nicole was unnecessarily blunt and showed little consideration for her friend's feelings in her kiss-off. In Stephanie's situation, she had to face her once-best friend every time she went to work. Amy felt like she had invested so much of herself in mentoring Alexa, and was overlooked and unappreciated.

In situations such as these, the hurt runs very deep. Many women use the same language they use to describe the feelings of being jilted by a female friend as when they are jilted by a lover or abandoned by a husband. You may also experience physical symptoms: headaches, lost sleep, eating too much, eating too little, or trouble focusing. These symptoms can last for weeks, months, or even years.

Making the loss more stinging, disagreements or misunderstandings you may have had in the past fade into the background and you tend to selectively recall, idealize, and miss the positive aspects of your relationship: sharing feelings and confidences, having someone to bounce ideas off of, talking about your love lives or problems at the office, sharing clothes or recipes, IM-ing one another, getting her cell phone calls in surprising places (even in the ladies' room), shopping and hunting down bargains at T.J. Maxx, just being together or not even being together physically, but knowing you are there for each other. Having a close friend makes a woman feel connected and less alone.

Memories of time spent together are marked by obsessive thoughts of what you could have possibly done to alienate her. The loss is so one-sided that it seems inexplicable, ripping at your self-confidence and playing havoc with your emotions. A cloud of confusion, guilt, and shame hangs over you. Aren't friendships supposed to last forever? Was the friendship even real to begin with?

STAGE 3: SELF-BLAME

Shock, denial, and loss are soon followed by self-blame and feelings of shame. You ask: *What role did I play in bringing this friendship to an end?* and *What will others think of me when they hear that I've been dumped?*

Although there is the tendency to blame yourself after the loss of a meaningful friendship, being dumped doesn't necessarily mean you, or even your friend, did something wrong. Remember: Friendships are organic relationships that change when people change as a result of their various life experiences. Just like there are no-fault divorces and auto collisions, it isn't necessary or helpful to assign blame or fault for the demise of a friendship. You may have changed, she may have changed, or you both may have changed.

When Randi began to think about why she was dumped, seemingly out of the blue, she realized that her friendship with Nicole was imperfect to start with. While the two women were both expats, they had fundamentally different lifestyles (a single mom of an only child versus a married mom with three little ones), and lived in different towns with few opportunities to see one another face-to-face. While none of these differences are necessarily *relationship killers*, there weren't enough shared interests or solid emotional ties to bind them to each other (at least from Nicole's perspective).

The inconvenience of their friendship was a major factor that contributed to a mismatch, putting the relationship on shaky grounds almost from the start. Randi mentioned that she liked being her friend's "Dr. Freud," which suggests that she was on the giving end of the relationship and implies there was not enough give-and-take. When relationships are tipped too much in one direction, they are often prone to fracture.

Randi's life had become increasingly constricted. Her husband had long working hours; she was still adjusting to living in a foreign country away from old friends and extended family, and she had limited childcare options. Her desperate need for the lost friendship was greater than Nicole's, who had more time and opportunity to pick and choose the people with whom she wanted to socialize. Nicole wanted to barhop and look for male companionship and preferred being with women who shared the same pursuits. Randi took the loss especially hard because she knew this was a tough time for her to make new friends and carve out time to be with them. For her, having a "phone friend" was convenient.

Of course, feelings of guilt and sorrow are exacerbated when you recognize that something you did, perhaps inadvertently, played a role in ending the friendship. You might remember the story of Karen, who missed her friend's father's funeral. After her friend dumped her, Karen realized that she should have been there when her friend really needed her. Letdowns such as this one take many different forms, but all of them can lead to guilt and feelings of responsibility. It may be an offhand remark you made that you can't take back, a lapse in judgment that can't be undone, an insensitive joke that hurt her feelings, or an irreparable breach of trust.

We all hope that our friendships will be strong enough to allow forgiveness, but that isn't always the case. For example, Kat, 22, accidentally revealed a secret to a group of mutual friends that her best friend, Luisa, had been hiding for year. When Luisa was younger, she had been obese, and became the butt of painful jokes from all the kids in her middle school. It was an exceptionally painful time in her life. She attended a new high school and slimmed down considerably, so no one knew anything about Luisa's past. In casual conversation, in Luisa's presence, Kat mentioned her friend's metamorphosis to a group in the lunchroom, not knowing that it would embarrass her friend or that it had been told to her in confidence. Luisa turned beet red and tears welled up in her eyes. She refused to speak to Kat until months later, and despite her acceptance of her friend's apologies, the damage was irrevocable, and their relationship became that of somewhat distant acquaintances rather than close friends.

Kat wished she could have taken back her remark when she saw her friend's face, but there was no undoing it. She had no one to blame but herself.

STAGE 4: EMBARRASSMENT AND SHAME

When you are the one who has been dumped, it's also a natural tendency to worry about what others will think of you and the role you played in bringing the friendship to an end. It's common to evoke negative reactions because of the ubiquitous myths associated with female friendship. Couldn't you keep a friend? What did you do to make her run in the other direction?

Outsiders (very often, boyfriends, fathers, brothers, and husbands) who have a hard time relating to the strength and intensity of female friendships might ask, "I thought you girls were best friends. What happened?" They may casually attribute the breakup to catfighting, behavior stereotypically attributed to women. Even your mother might ask, "What did *you* do wrong?" For Randi, a serious concern was how she would explain the breakup to her kids and to her husband. Stephanie worried about what the people at work would make of her fallout with Anna.

Women have every reason to be anxious about what other women will think of them because of the stigma associated with lost friendships. It might be an innocuous remark like, "I usually see you with your friend Judy. Don't the two of you see each other anymore?" And there is the additional concern of how the woman who initiated the breakup (your former friend) will portray the breakup to those around her.

The people around you may not understand that you had a falling-out that's painful for you to explain and/or talk about, or they may not believe that you don't quite know what happened yourself. Even the people "in your camp" may not fully believe your side of the story.

STAGE 5: ANGER

Unless you are the one person who was totally responsible for the breakup (which isn't often the case), before long, you're bound to feel intensely angry and disappointed at what your girlfriend has done to you. You may say to yourself: *I put up with her drama for so long and was always there when she needed me* or *How could she do this after all I've done for her?* or *The friendship wasn't perfect but I hung in there. Isn't that what friendship is about?*

You trusted someone who ended up treating you like a doormat when she gave you no opportunity to weigh in on the decision to end the friendship. You are likely to be furious and wonder whether you can ever trust another woman enough to have a best friend again.

Even when they aren't at fault, this is the stuff that drives women into psychotherapy to determine why they are so angry and what role they played in bringing this on or allowing it to happen. Some swallow pills to ease the unbearable anxiety, others run marathons, some drink a few too many cocktails, and some over-dose on chocolate or whole pints of Ben & Jerry's ice cream.

One way to deal with the anger is to stay active. Even if you aren't a gym person, this is the time to work out or take long walks. It will relieve the stress and distract you from your loss. If you can't do that, organize or de-clutter your home. Again, you'll feel a sense of accomplishment and feel better about yourself. Meditate and practice forgiveness. You don't necessarily have to condone your friend's actions or leave her blameless, but you need to let go of your anger so it doesn't gnaw at you.

The pain over being jilted and having had no say in the matter can last a very long time. It may interfere with future friendships or cause anger to seep out inappropriately, either in the workplace or at home. But with time, awareness, and under-standing, the anger and sadness usually diminishes or dissipates completely.

STAGE 6: ACCEPTANCE

It takes time to come to grips with a broken friendship and to let go of the anger—but it will happen. The more meaningful the friendship, the harder it will be and the longer it will take. Having had no say in the matter also makes it hard to accept the finality of your friend's decision. Acceptance is a process.

Even after time has passed, you may wrestle with the notion of contacting the friend one last time to apologize or to find out what happened, even if you are sure you didn't do anything wrong. If you are aware of something you did that led to the breakup or if your friend overtly blamed you for the fractured friendship, you may feel that the transgression wasn't so egregious that it should have severed all ties between you, and feel a need to restate your case.

You may cling to the hope that you can rectify the problem and that she'll realize that she's blowing things out of proportion. You may hope that being brutally honest about your weaknesses, mistakes, or insecurities will allow her to accept you as a real rather than idealized friend, warts and all. You may feel that your long history should have given you wiggle room to make an occasional blunder, or you may realize that the infraction was simply a final straw that sealed her decision to end the friendship.

There's no harm in calling or writing a personal note to the woman who dumped you to tell her that you are sorry about the loss and to do what you can to repair the fractured friendship. If the friendship is important to you, it is always worthwhile to give her another chance to rethink her decision. She may have misunderstood or misperceived something you said or did. Perhaps she's waiting for an apology or just needs some time off to realize that she wants the relationship as much as you do. In some cases, you may actually be able to reconnect.

However, if you have tried to contact her repeatedly and she won't respond, at some point you need to back off and begin to accept that it's over, at least for the time being, and realize that there's nothing you can do to turn back the clock. If you came on to her boyfriend or husband, there may be no way she can forgive you. If you let her down or ditched her when she needed you emotionally, your transgression may be irreparable.

Speaking of the breakup of a significant friendship, one woman told me: "What has been a constant source of peace to me is that I left lovingly, even if she wasn't able to do the same. I think that has truly allowed me, all these years later, to deeply forgive myself and her."

Most breakups are difficult to get over because they are extraordinarily painful and uncomfortable for both parties. The precise reasons why someone wants out of a long-term friendship are often elusive, even to the woman who decided to end it. You can try to understand them in hindsight, which is sometimes helpful in working through the pain and avoiding a repetition of the trauma, but the reasons usually remain vague or even inexplicable. Overanalyzing the situation becomes an exercise in futility because you only know one side of the story: yours, not hers.

When long-standing friendships end, it comes as a shock not only to the person who experiences the unexpected loss, but also to people around her (other friends, family, colleagues, etc.). Believe it or not, it often rattles the life of the very person who precipitated the breakup and who may feel incredibly awkward about ending the relationship.

Many times, when the reason for the split is totally baffling, you have to entertain the possibility that it has more to do with her than it has to do with you. Something totally unrelated to you may be going on in your friend's life or consciousness, something you don't know about or couldn't possibly understand. She may be reeling from her husband's job loss or her own. She may be overwhelmed with caregiving responsibilities for a child or parent with a chronic and debilitating illness. She may be having emotional problems, like depression or anxiety, that aren't permitting her to function as she would like to but are too embarrassing for her to talk about with anyone.

I've personally been in this position, when a good friend simply had things going on that I didn't understand. I thought I had been dumped when she stopped returning my calls, but found out much later that my friend was struggling with a serious family health crisis. Her teenage daughter, Lee, was anorexic, out of control, and engaging in impulsive and self-destructive behaviors. She was absent from school more often than she was there, spending most of her days asleep and chatting online through the night.

Each morning was a strain for the entire family, who were left wondering whether Lee would make it out of the house. Her mother, my friend, also found superficial cuts on her daughter's wrists that were clearly self-inflicted. Obviously not having the energy or inclination to talk about her problems to other parents who might not understand, my friend distanced herself from friends and neighbors. She may have been reluctant to say anything to her small group of friends, hesitant to provide fodder for lunchtime gossip at school, because everyone's kids were all in the same grade. Only several years later, when her daughter was doing better, was she able to tell anyone about what had happened.

While not having her in my life hurt my feelings and made me wonder what had gone wrong in our friendship, I am grateful to have my friend back now. In retrospect, I understand that our friendship wasn't the problem, per se, because I realize the enormous stress my poor friend was under. Not only has my hurt and anger totally dissolved, but I wish that there was something I could have done at the time to let her know that I was there for her and to help her deal with her situation.

The stress and humiliation created by mental, emotional, or substance abuse problems of close relatives often take a silent toll on female friendships. Because of stigma and shame, it's hard for someone to tell you her sister was arrested for drunk driving or her husband was hospitalized for bipolar disorder. At times like this, people often feel so alone that their world becomes very narrow and their friendships are put on hold as they deal with a crisis. Sometimes you just need to accept the distance a friend puts between you and her even if you don't understand it.

When you can't make total sense of a situation logically, one plausible explanation is that you are missing a key piece of information. It's like being challenged to figure out a complex crossword puzzle without knowing the theme that ties all the clues together. For example, if your friend suddenly seems irritable and guarded, consider that she may be having personal or family problems that she doesn't feel comfortable talking about with you. Instead of sharing them, she maintains her privacy by cutting herself off from everyone. It isn't always about you!

Being dumped hurts and the path to acceptance is difficult, but it is better to befriend and lose than never to befriend at all. The good news is that most women get over the loss, and survive and even thrive afterward. Every single day, wise, wonderful women, who previously enjoyed spending significant amounts of time together become estranged from each other and rebound to find new friends again. They learn and accept the important lesson that friendships, more often than not, are vulnerable to change as we move through different stages and circumstances in our lives.

STAGE 7: RELIEF

It may seem paradoxical, but women say they experience a sense of relief after they have been dumped and have reached a state of acceptance. Very often, they look back and realize that the friendship wasn't as reciprocal or perfect as it seemed. The person who was jilted may have been the one who was always initiating phone calls or who was always trying to arrange dates. No one is completely comfortable in sustaining a one-sided relationship over the long haul. Randi ultimately realized that she desperately wanted a close friendship that was more reciprocal than the one she had with Nicole. After she accepted the loss and was able to see the limitations of that relationship, she felt a sense of hopefulness. I suggested that she look for a replacement closer to home. She may have had more in common with someone in her neighborhood (perhaps a mother of one of her children's friends) than she had with this expat. At different times in a woman's life, it may be more or less difficult to make and maintain female friendships. But before long, Randi's little ones will be older and she will have more time and options for female friendships than she does now. Since she currently has a very full plate, it might be worthwhile for her to reconnect by e-mail, at least on an interim basis, with some of her friends from back home.

As a friendship unravels, there may be great discomfort at first, but many women who had been reluctant to let go report a sense of closure by accepting the end of something they come to realize wasn't mutually satisfying.

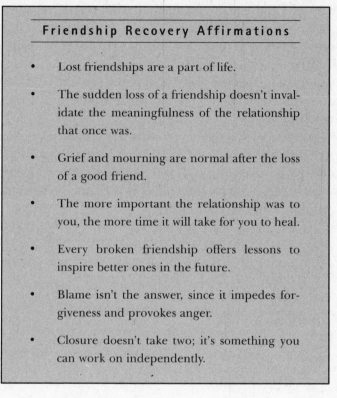

Friendship Recovery Affirmations

- Lost friendships are a part of life.

- The sudden loss of a friendship doesn't invalidate the meaningfulness of the relationship that once was.

- Grief and mourning are normal after the loss of a good friend.

- The more important the relationship was to you, the more time it will take for you to heal.

- Every broken friendship offers lessons to inspire better ones in the future.

- Blame isn't the answer, since it impedes forgiveness and provokes anger.

- Closure doesn't take two; it's something you can work on independently.

DO A REALITY CHECK

If you are the one who has been left, acknowledge the hurt and disappointment. It's very easy to feel dismissed, rejected, and as if you got the short end of the stick. You're probably mourning your loss at the same time as you are feeling miffed. Some research suggests that forgiveness is good for your health—so it's in your best interest to get over whatever is bothering you, even though it may take some effort on your part.

It isn't easy, but step back and try not to take it personally. Find new ways to frame what happened so you understand your friend's perspective and can hopefully avoid making the same mistake again. Remember that friendships usually don't last forever.

It's a mistake to think that the ending of a close relationship invalidates the authenticity of what came before. That is simply not true. At the time that you and she clicked, your stars were aligned. Try to think about the things you learned and gained from the relationship.

Taking an active role in allowing the friendship to end will help you start to heal. Most importantly: regain control of your own life by involving yourself with other old friends, cultivating new ones, and getting pleasure out of experiences with people and activities you enjoy.

CHAPTER 5

SPOTTING A TOXIC FRIENDSHIP

∞

"What do we live for, if it is not to make life less
difficult for each other?"

—GEORGE ELIOT (MARY ANN EVANS)

Some friendships weren't meant to be from the get-go, while others take a fairly disastrous turn along the way. It may be that one or both of you has never fully acquired the skills you need to be a true friend to the other, or that the two of you slowly began to grate on each other's nerves over time. Even the strongest friendships can ultimately become toxic.

It is important to remember that in the vast majority of cases, a "toxic friendship" refers to the friendship itself, not the people in it. That means two things: First, although your friendship might have been toxic and ended painfully, this does not necessarily mean your ex-friend was a toxic or bad person—it was something about the friendship that was failing one or both of you. Second, it means that it is important to reflect on your own role in the creation of the relationship, and where you might have been inadvertently contributing to its toxicity. Sometimes, when we are able to diagnose our own shortcomings, we are able to better understand those of our friends and ex-friends. If you're among the legions of women who have been dumped by a former best friend, reflecting on these possibilities sometimes helps heal the anger and distrust you suffered at the breakup.

Theoretically, friends can and should play an important role in reducing stress and providing support, but that's not always the case. You probably have heard the term "toxic friend"—*the stereo-typical mean, catty, unfaithful, judgmental, undermining woman*—from whom you should run, not walk, in the opposite direction. But things aren't that easy.

Even the best of friends have occasional conflicts and disappoint each other from time to time. However, a toxic friendship is one that is consistently, or more often than not, unequal, non-reciprocal, demanding, clingy, stress-inducing, demeaning, and/or unsupportive. Most of the time, toxicity is unintentional. Often, it is at least partly the responsibility of both parties. But that does not make it less harmful or frustrating.

A toxic friend could be the friend who makes you cringe each time you are with her. But just as you barely notice the surroundings in your own home or office after you have been there for a while, when a relationship is familiar to you, you may not realize how poisonous the person has become to your well-being. Or you may be so lonely you feel the friendship is better than nothing. Two sunflowers with their own stems and root systems can happily thrive in the same flowerpot. But a hearty sunflower can soon be overtaken when, instead, a strangling weed becomes firmly planted in the same pot.

When it comes to friendships, people are all a bit less than perfect, and their relationships are rarely all good or all bad. Even when you spot the danger signs of toxicity, they are usually subtle rather than glaring, especially at first blush, because they generally play themselves out within the context of a longer-term relationship. The friend who once seemed so caring and attentive may turn out to be extremely intrusive and possessive. Or you grow to recognize that the friend who once appeared to walk on water has more than her share of personality flaws, some of them fatal.

Because our friendships are laden with emotions, it's often hard to tease out fact from fantasy. Also, who wants to be the one to tell a friend that she is toxic? Or be the one to hear she herself is toxic from her friend?

COULD YOU BE A TOXIC FRIEND?

It's easier to recognize blemishes or faults in someone else than it is to take ownership of one's own imperfections. The psychological defense mechanism called "projection" is sometimes the culprit. Projection protects the ego from acknowledging its weaknesses because the individual "projects" these characteristics onto the person being criticized. But like Shauna, whose story you will read shortly, some of us eventually come to realize that we are the ones who are sabotaging, or even poisoning, one female friendship after another.

If you've been dumped repeatedly, you have to at least entertain the possibility that you have some characteristics or minor peccadilloes that have contributed toxicity to one or more of your relationships. This kind of self-reflection is always difficult, but being willing to acknowledge that you might have been part of the reason for a friendship falling apart may give you peace and help you learn for the future.

TOO NEEDY?

Shauna, 24, was shocked when her friend accused of her being too needy and dependent on other people. "I admit that it's hard to hear, especially since I can't stand that kind of behavior in others," she says. "But even more than that, it is hard to hear because I have a great fear of losing people close to me. This fear isn't that unreasonable because I've lost a few close friends recently to death and other complications of life, and now I'm more sensitive to the notion of losing friends. But somehow I allowed myself to believe that I needed to spend much more time than necessary with this person, and that's not fair for anyone," says Shauna. It's always good to have a strong support system of friends with whom to share life's ups and downs. However, it's never a good idea to dump all your problems on one friend. That's too much for anyone, and people have their own lives to deal with. "I realize now that I always have something physically or emotionally wrong with me, and those things are draining to hear or see all the time," she says. Sometimes, it's hard to recognize this unless one of your friends is brazen enough to gently tell you—because she cares, as Shauna's friend did. Yet, projection is a difficult defense to overcome because blaming someone else and externalizing suggests that self-awareness and reflection are lacking. An honest friend could gently confront the individual who is projecting and remind her that she has acted in similar ways before.

Shauna realized that she needed to set some limits. She began seeing a counselor once a week and kept a journal, writing down everything going on in her life so she could keep her friends in the loop to an extent, but save them from the drama of the deeper problems she was going through. With the help of the counselor, she was learning how to deal with a lot of her anxieties on her own.

TOO VOLATILE?

Gina, 24, had experienced a string of lost friendships with women. "We weren't able to communicate openly, resulting in unspoken feelings that erupted abruptly and ruined the relationships," she says. "I had come to expect this and felt I couldn't share my real feelings or be myself around other women. Why all of these friendships failed is perplexing to me," she adds. Gina wasn't aware that all the angry feelings she was trying to keep contained would find their way of spewing out.

If you find that there is a pattern in your fractured friendships, as Gina did, it may be because you are repeating the same behaviors over and over.

TOO MOODY?

If you have a special friendship that seems to be at risk or if you are distressed about the loss of multiple friendships, it makes sense to discuss the problem with a trusted third person; it might be another friend, a relative, or a counselor who can help you gain insight. Carol, 37, was in treatment for a mood disorder. It was her psychologist who pointed out the impact it was having on her friendships. "The reason I think my friendships ended was because of the bouts of depression and mania I was going through," she says. It seemed like one friend after another wanted to gain some distance from the symptoms of her illness, which became overwhelming to them.

Each friend was alarmed by Carol's neediness and by her threats of suicide, which were followed by an unsuccessful attempt. After speaking to her therapist, Carol realizes now that she was crying out for help to people who weren't properly equipped to respond.

If you have lost a friend or two in succession, it may not be anything to worry about. But when you start to recognize a pattern of lost friendships, one after another, intermittently, or very often, it's important to take notice. You need to consider that there may be some problem with your personality and behavior that is creating roadblocks in your ability to maintain close relationships. Or perhaps your standards and expectations are simply too high and your attitude needs to be adjusted.

Since the clinical reasons for this problem are so varied and particular to the individual, they are beyond the scope of this book. Yet it's important to say that engaging in psychotherapy or counseling doesn't necessarily mean that you're "sick." It has opened the door for many women to learn more about themselves and their friendships. In addition, relationship coaching, spiritual direction, or pastoral counseling may be other useful alternatives for taking a closer look at recurring friendship problems. Cognitive-behavioral techniques of looking at the ABC's—the antecedents, behaviors, and consequences—can be used as self-help tools to sort out the chain of events that lead one to act in ways which hinder viable friendships.

TOXIC BUILDUP

As I've mentioned, toxicity more commonly characterizes a relationship, not one individual, and tends to build up over time as two people get to better know one another. Toxicity in a friendship manifests itself in different ways, including emotional and physical exhaustion, or even headaches or other physical symptoms after you've spent time with the friend in question. Often, you may realize on some level that the friendship isn't making you happy, but you may experience guilt or fear at the idea of absenting yourself from the worsening situation.

Ellen was beginning to feel horrible for the negative feelings she had toward her good friend. "My friend Joanna called me every single day, and left really lengthy voice mails on my phone when I didn't answer," she says. They never had an argument and had been good friends for some time. How could she ignore her friend's phone calls? According to Ellen, she had good reason. "I'd try to talk to her about things that were going on in my life, and she'd listen, but as soon as I finished talking Joanna would say something like 'Oh, well the other day at work something really funny happened.'" Ellen realized that Joanna wasn't really listening; she was just waiting her turn to jump in with whatever she had to say. For Ellen, these conversations felt devoid of any give-and-take. No matter what the topic, it always turned back to what was going on with Joanna. "The thing I remember most was the day I had to put my dog down," says Ellen. "I called her and asked her to go for a walk so we could talk about things. The entire time we were together she talked about her ex-boyfriend, a guy she had broken up with a month before." It was as if a light bulb went off and Ellen finally realized why her relationship with Joanna was so unsatisfying. She wanted a friend who would listen to her, in the same way she would listen to her. "I am tired of always being the one who listens and gives support," she says. "I want a friend who can catch *me* when I fall." Ellen's needs were modest and not unreasonable but they were unattainable from Joanna, who was too narcissistic and self-involved to meet them. While Ellen worked for the friendship, Joanna seemingly wasn't able to.

In the case of Lily and Kate, recognizing toxicity took some time because of the natural tendency to overlook negatives in a relationship that offers rewards. Lily and Kate were both single moms when they met at a neighborhood gym. They felt so comfortable with each other that, almost immediately, they began revealing the intimate backstories of their lives. Kate's drug-addicted mother had given her up for adoption when she was less than five years old. Lily admired Kate's intelligence, savvy, and ability to converse about anything. Their friendship centered largely around their kids, who were close in age and enjoyed playing together, so the two women got together quite often. Over the years, Lily felt like an aunt to Kate's first son, who was like a cousin to her daughter, Missy. From the beginning of their friendship, Lily sensed that Kate had an uncomfortable edge to her personality. She was sarcastic and quick to anger, but Lily explained it away as a remnant of her traumatic past. "I knew she was headstrong and opinionated but accepted that," says Lily. There were times when she worried about her friend and even pitied her. She watched Kate go through female friends like other women go through cheap pantyhose. Lily would hear Kate say something mean or cutting, without any awareness that she was hurting another person's feelings. Noticing this trend caused Lily to gradually withdraw her total trust. "I realized she might turn on me one day, too," says Lily. It made Lily feel uncomfortable, but she continued to make allowances for her friend. Anyway, she didn't want to think about it because she enjoyed being with Kate more than any other friend she had met since she became a mom.

Now, after a decade of friendship, Lily says she could "write a book" about all the hateful things Kate said about her and the insults she heaped on her daughter, Missy. She feels that she overlooked and explained away the attacks for too long. "Kate was rude to me and her own family, and especially to waitstaff, baristas, and anyone in the service industry, as if she were a queen," says Lily.

Both women eventually remarried, first Lily and then Kate. That was when the gap between them grew even wider. "Kate married for money," says Lily. "She made it clear to her family and me that her plan was to marry someone with money, have a few more kids, and never ever have to work again. She called her husband a 'meal ticket' and began to cheat on him, saying she wasn't attracted to him," says Lily. Over time, the two women saw less and less of each other. Kate and her family relocated to another state and Lily felt a sense of relief with the increased distance between them. The factors that brought Lily and Kate together are understandable. Kate was engaging, fun-loving, and could be charming when she wanted to be. The two women were both single moms of kids around the same age in a community that seemed to be coupled-off, and Lily felt a sense of compassion towards someone who was dealt a bad hand early in her life.

Clearly, Kate's temperament was characterized by poor impulse control and a low tolerance for frustration. Although the warning signs were there from the start, Lily minimized them and focused on the positives because she wanted to keep the friendship going. After they each married, the vast discrepancies in their values of marriage, family, and friends became so stark that they could no longer be ignored. Lily finally allowed herself to see Kate as a total package: both the positives and the negatives. But letting go was more difficult than she would've imagined.

Setting Healthy Boundaries with a Needy Friend

- Change the nature of your friendship by learning to say "No." (For example, "Even though we are both single, I don't want to spend every Friday night together.")

- Tell her that you have to tend to your own needs (or those of others close to you) and don't feel guilty about it.

- Slip away and spend less time with her and more time acquiring friends who do not demand as much from you.

- If it's that bad, simply cut loose!

LOOKING IN THE MIRROR

As mentioned earlier, rarely is one person totally responsible for a toxic relationship. Like bacteria can only thrive in the correct medium in a petri dish, it's the combination of two personalities that allows for a toxic buildup in a friendship. In the examples above, while you might point fingers at self-centered Joanna or Kate, Ellen and Carol functioned as enablers who were too nurturing and accepting. Perhaps if they had been better about setting boundaries, the relationships wouldn't have derailed in the way they did.

If you are seeking to improve your friendships (or any other relationship for that matter), the place where you need to start is with yourself. As difficult as it is to recognize and escape from a toxic relationship that can be blamed primarily on the other person, the challenges are compounded when you are caught up in a consistent pattern of self-defeating attitudes or behaviors yourself.

You might say that Clare, a woman in her forties, has a case of foot-in-the-mouth syndrome. She always seemed to have problems keeping friends but she wasn't sure why. It was easy enough for her to meet people and develop friendships, but none of them seemed to last. "I'm one of those people who is always trying to make a joke and throws out a lot of one-liners when the opportunity arises. Unfortunately, sometimes the jokes unintentionally hurt people's feelings, and sometimes those people are my friends," says Clare. Clare never realized that her humor came off as cutting. "I only recognized it when the friend who I had hurt was visibly mad or not speaking to me," she says. "And even then, I have to wrack my brain to figure out what it was I said this time that pissed them off."

She is frustrated that people take it so personally. "Honestly, I'm not trying to be mean. In fact, the idea makes me cringe. I would never in a million years want to hurt anyone, let alone the people who are closest to me. While my friends know this about me, it seems that it doesn't matter; they get offended. I just wish people would lighten up a bit. I'm also frustrated that one bad joke can seem to nullify hundreds of nice things that I may have said or done. It doesn't seem fair. When I'm confronted with the fact that I said something mean, I do apologize," says Clare.

Recently, she had a run-in with a very good friend and colleague that made her feel awful. The two friends were at a conference where the speaker had not received his drink ticket for the cocktail reception. Her friend told another person within the small group in which they were standing, "I can give him mine." Without skipping a beat, Clare jokingly said, "Oh sure, suck up to the speaker!"

That was pretty much the end of it. Clare could tell her friend was annoyed with her because she barely spoke to her at work the next day, or the day after that. Clare finally said something. Her friend angrily retorted that she said she was through being nice to Clare; she didn't want to be seen as a "kiss ass." since Clare apparently thought of her that way.

Identifying the Signs of a
Toxic Friendship

- Does scheduling time together feel like an obligation rather than a pleasure?
- Is the friendship a constant source of irritation?
- Do either of you feel trapped when you are together?
- Do you feel tense in each other's presence?
- Do you feel like one friend is always trying to show off at the other's expense?
- Are you there for one another when needed?
- Are either of you self-centered, sneaky, deceitful, or disloyal?
- Do one or both of you show habitually bad judgment?
- Does one friend consistently feel like she is giving more than she is getting?
- Does the relationship feel curiously out-of-sync?
- Do you feel emotionally drained when you are together?
- Do either of you come away from one another feeling depressed?
- Is one friend always the "listener" and the other the "talker"?
- Do either of you dread each other's phone calls?
- Does either of you hate to see the other's screen name online when you look at your buddy list?
- Do your friend's emails feel too long to read?
- Given a choice, would one of you always choose to spend time with someone other than your friend?
- Have you done anything to undermine each other personally or professionally?
- Have you simply grown in different directions?
- Can you trust each other to keep confidences?
- Has one of you betrayed the other?

Because Clare's choice of jokes came off as mean-spirited, they impaired her female friendships. Since she realized she had that tendency, she should have been walking on eggshells, being particularly careful to not blurt out anything she would later regret. But, as was apparent from her repeated blunders, she has been unable to self-monitor. Friends felt for her the embarrassment she did not feel, which made them want to distance themselves from her.

Ironically, by nature, Clare was a quiet person who may have been using her humor to diffuse the tension and anxiety she felt when she was with other people. Having a quick wit and good sense of humor can be a gift because it is a powerful tool for connecting with people. But Clare needed to hone her social skills and channel her talent for humor in positive ways so that it enhanced her friendships rather than fractured them.

If you honestly review the signs of a toxic friendship discussed in this chapter, you may begin to think about your own role in a friendship that isn't working. Are you too secretive, competitive, or jealous of your friends? Are you asking, or demanding, too much of your friends and failing to maintain the boundaries necessary for healthy relationships? Or are you finding that you have so many more problems than anyone around you that you feel entitled to dump them on others?

Your answers will make the next steps you need to take clearer. However, female friendships are always complex. Just as the laws of friendship aren't cast in stone, neither can friends be categorized as either entirely healthy or wholly toxic. Friendships exist on a continuum and most fall somewhere in between.

If there is an upside to a toxic relationship, it is this: it will serve as a yardstick by which to measure future friendships that seem draining and, perhaps, help to avoid them.

THE RELUCTANCE TO LET GO

As women, we invest so much of ourselves in our female friends that it's natural to have a hard time thinking about losing them or letting go, regardless of who they are, whether we are the one who is dumped or the one who decides to dump someone else. Because of the sense of guilt, failure, and stigma associated with a failed friendship, there is no easy way to go about it.

Feminist psychologists have suggested that a toxic friendship is often one in which a woman's own personal growth and individuation is sacrificed at the expense of the demands of the other person. Sometimes choosing oneself rather than the friendship is important for future personal growth and individuation. But women have a difficult time separating from each other because emotional connection is so highly valued and broken friendships are seen as failures.

Like Carol, many women overlook subtle or even more obvious signs that something is amiss. They ignore and make allowances for them, focusing on the positive when signs of toxicity rear their ugly heads. These difficulties are compounded when there is a long shared history with fond memories and the boundaries of the friendship have expanded to encompass other friends or family.

The thought of tugging on the string that might unravel the friendship can be so unbearable that we deceive ourselves until the day when we have an *ah-ha!* experience. Suddenly, discomfort with the friendship becomes so apparent that we realize we just have to let go. That's what finally hit Carol. Kate's self-centeredness and impaired moral compass were always fatal flaws as far as Carol was concerned, but in the hope of preserving her friendship, she made excuses for Kate time after time.

THE SUBTLE SIGNS OF TOXICITY

Whether consciously or not, many women go through a weeding-out process, eliminating friends who turn out to be more trouble than they're worth. One woman called it "relationship-editing." By virtue of this process, some friendships end, others are dumped, and some relationships wither away ambiguously.

How do you know when it's time to cut the cord and let go of a friend? Unless you are grappling with a fatal flaw or heinous behavior (e.g., a friend who is sleeping with your lover, or a friend who strikes your child), the signs of a friendship gone sour aren't always readily apparent. Here are some clues:

1: THE FRIENDSHIP IS HIGH-MAINTENANCE

Like a seesaw, friendships tilt in one direction and then another. Sometimes we are on the giving end and sometimes the receiving. It's normal and expected for one friend to be needier at different points in the relationship—either in terms of time, exclusivity, or emotions. But with some friends, there's no sense of an overarching balance or reciprocity.

Does your friend always have something going on in her life that demands a shoulder to cry on? Does she intrude into your space unannounced? Is she always trying to control you? Is she always thrusting you into the role of a therapist, a role that you are ill-equipped or unwilling to play? Does she expect you to act as a rescuer and constantly see herself as a victim? Could you say the same about yourself?

It's not a beneficial situation when anyone, male or female, is totally dependent on another person. Maura's relationship with her friend Anna, both of them 35 years old, became so one-sided that it placed a strain on Maura's marriage.

The two women had kids who were born two months apart. "I went to Gymboree and met three other women who became my friends. I introduced Anna to them and she expected to become one of five, but I had a very special relationship with the other three," says Maura. "She would yell at me when I would go to a playdate at one of their homes, asking me why I didn't tell them to invite her."

When Anna's husband was diagnosed with cancer, she started leaning on Maura more and more, talking to her on the phone or visiting her for not one or two hours per night, but three or four. "My husband started saying things like, 'Why don't you go marry Anna?'" After hearing her husband's frustration, Maura finally realized that Anna had become too intrusive and needy, and that she had to establish boundaries to protect herself and her family.

For many women, there is a defining moment when they realize that a friend isn't there for them in the way they should be, or worse yet, that the friend is simply a self-absorbed taker who consistently is only out for herself. As women recounted their stories, they mentioned hurts that occurred decades ago that still haunt them. While not every relationship has to be fifty-fifty, it can't be totally tilted in one direction or the other, as happened to Rhianna.

Rhianna, 52, was living in Washington, D.C. when her close college friend, Leila, a travel agent, was living in Miami. Whenever Rhianna suggested they get together, Leila would always complain about how busy she was. "Admittedly, her job did entail a lot of travel," says Rhianna. When Rhianna returned from a vacation overseas, she found three voice mail messages waiting from Leila, who sounded desperate to get together.

"When I called back, Leila told me that her hubby, Henry, had a business meeting planned in D.C. and it would be great if they could visit and stay at my apartment," says Rhianna. "It took a lot of nerve for her to bird-dog me when I waited weeks for her to call me back," she says. "I'm not a hotel and taxi service," says Rhianna. "Leila only visited me when it made for a convenient layover." She realized that her friend was so self-absorbed that she probably didn't even know how offensive she had been.

When the two women and a third college friend planned a girl's weekend in Los Angeles, Leila brought her husband, who was happy to be chauffeured around and slept on their friend's couch. When the group went out for dinner, he asked for a separate check and made no offer to pay for their host. Rhianna finally put her foot down. Leila and her husband had mooched off her one too many times. "I wasn't going to put one more ounce of effort into the friendship," she says. "I was done and was sure I wouldn't feel a loss."

Rhianna's friendship with Leila may not have had a very strong foundation from the start—certainly, in recent years it was a relationship built primarily on past history and memories of their college days. But Rhianna wasn't willing to be used any longer. It was time to let go of something she sensed had been lost a long time ago.

A high-maintenance friend may be one who is unwilling to put energy into the relationship. She always expects the other person to be the one who initiates the calls and figures out a reason to get together. She breaks appointments and leaves her friend in the lurch when the next best thing comes along. When any of these behaviors become consistent patterns, it should make you stop and think about the worth of the friendship.

2: THE FRIENDSHIP FEELS SUFFOCATING

Some friendships feel like an emotional ball and chain. The friend is always in need of one thing or another: money, favors, help, attention, coddling, praise—or simply more time than you have to give. Like a wailing toddler, they can be so demanding that their friendship is exhausting.

She's a drama queen. No matter what you give, what you do,

how much, or how often, it will never be enough. Since character tends to endure, this person probably treats other people the same way. It's likely that many of her friends have probably already dropped out of the picture and that's why she is so demanding of you. One woman called a friend like this an "emotional vampire" who sucked up all her energy.

Who wants or needs that kind of friend? Many women do, actually. There are:

- those who like feeling needed—or once liked the feeling (even if they don't anymore).

- those who feel like they aren't worthy of healthier, more balanced relationships.

  or

- those who are stuck—either feeling angry or sorry for their needy friend—and feel unable to get out of it.

Once you have begun to recognize that a female friendship is a drag, you've taken the first step in relieving yourself of the burden.

Although most women would like to help their friends when they are down or hit bottom, at times a friend's needs can be so overwhelming that they exceed any one woman's ability to deal with them. For example: She's made it clear that she wants to be your best friend—and yours alone. She is so possessive that she can't stand the idea of you spending time with other people and is unable to tolerate a threesome. Or she expects to see you every weekend and your need for space is out of sync with hers. You would rather catch up on chores or do things with other people in your life. One woman called this a violation of her need for *me-time*.

She may be so controlling that she is resentful when you socialize with guys. Or she treats you like her child rather than her friend, acting bossy, condescending, and offering judgmental advice without being asked. One woman complained about a friend who was overbearing, constantly making critical comments about her weight and the unbecoming way she dressed. When any of these scenarios play out, a woman can feel smothered. Such was the case for Elizabeth, now 24, who cut off a high school friendship.

Although they were both smart and motivated students, Elizabeth and Kim were the two "alternative" kids at their school, requiring extra help. Their parents were friends and their own friendship came easily. "We saw each other almost every day, at school and afterward," says Elizabeth. But that closeness crossed a line and became suffocating when they stopped seeing any other friends.

"I would have liked to just cool off the friendship, but I was sixteen and impetuous. I simply ended it by not returning her calls or talking to her at school," says Elizabeth. "I felt guilty and bad about it, but I couldn't stand the thought of seeing her any-more—she made me feel as though I couldn't breathe—which, of course, intensified my guilt." Elizabeth recalls having a similar friendship during her freshman year of college. She ended that one much more quickly, because she could see—when this girl started calling her every day, multiple times a day, just wanting to "hang out"—that the friendship was headed in the same direction. As she matured, Elizabeth realized she no longer wanted friends who made her feel so needed that they overshadowed her life.

Some women seem to have a propensity for getting involved in suffocating relationships and are unable to see them for what they are. The first time they met, Karen, now in her early thirties, thought she had found a soul mate in her new friend Paige. Karen met Paige and her daughter at a children's event. The two women hit it off, and even though Paige's daughter was considerably younger than Karen's, the foursome got together for a few play-dates. Within a few months, Paige began calling Karen every day to complain about how hard it was to figure out naps and a feeding schedule for her daughter.

At first Karen didn't mind giving Paige advice because her own daughter was nap-resistant as well. "But calls every day about the same subject are overwhelming," says Karen. "Sometimes I want to go off on her because her daughter doesn't even act out or cry, despite being overtired. She is very mellow."

Karen had her share of problems that she could complain about. Her daughter was hyperactive, she had an infant son, and her husband had recently become unemployed. Karen says, "How come I can cope with all of this without wallowing when her life is comparatively easy and she couldn't even figure out a schedule for her child without daily support from me?" Karen has not cut off her relationship with Paige, but she has clearly reached the point where she feels the need to scale it back so she doesn't feel suffocated.

The relationship between Jen and Samantha, who are both 25 years old, also became overwhelming. The two women had been friends since childhood. Having no siblings of their own, they felt like sisters and spent much of their free time together. As Jen began dating, Samantha grew increasingly jealous, claiming that Jen wasn't spending enough time with her. "She would show up at restaurants, movies, sporting events, etc. while I was out with my dates, making them as well as me feel uncomfortable," says Jen. "It began to feel like I was being stalked." She told Samantha she needed more space, but her friend was unable to understand or unwilling to respect her needs. "She was even upset when I spent time with my family," says Jen. "The last straw was when she demanded that I set aside time for her each day."

Eventually it becomes intolerable to be with someone who has a sense of boundaries that violate your own.

Signs of a Suffocating Relationship

- She wants to be your one and only.
- She consumes too much of your time.
- She tries to control you.
- She always initiates get-togethers, calling, texting and IM-ing you.
- She contacts you multiple times a day for the slightest problem.
- You feel like you can't breathe on your own.
- She's dependent on you for everything.
- She's constantly seeking your validation.
- You feel like you are being stalked.
- She treats you like you and she are both the same person.

3: THE FRIENDSHIP HONEYMOON IS OVER

"If there is love at first sight, there is friendship at first sight, too," says one woman. Like a romance, it's as easy to be infatuated with someone at the beginning of a friendship as it is to be blindsided by a new friend's shortcomings. Over time, you may begin to see an unappealing side of your friend that you never noticed before and the stark reality of what you've gotten into hits you: you're really not that into her. This is reminiscent of the story at the beginning of this chapter that described what happened when Carol finally realized that she wasn't comfortable with her friend Kate's values and behaviors.

Crystal, 24, met her friend Margo in college. The two women were roommates who became fast friends. Crystal tended to be somewhat of a loner and Margo was a Queen Bee who attracted both men and women. She thrived on attention and being in the spotlight. She had a leading role in a campus production and was very active in her sorority. Through her association with Margo, Crystal was invited to pledge for the same sorority and became part of the same circle of friends. For the first time in her life, she felt popular, like someone on the inside rather than on the periphery.

By their junior year, the two were best friends. But Crystal had also realized that Margo was prone to picking petty arguments with people that would escalate into vendettas that consumed her waking life—and eventually Crystal's. She held grudges and obsessed about the injustices done to her, talking about them incessantly. Crystal took a very conciliatory angle in her relationship with Margo, always compromising and thereby saving herself from big fights. But even though Crystal avoided being cast as the enemy herself, she was now seeing an unappealing, abrasive side to her friend.

When they left college and both moved back to Los Angeles, the back-and-forth phone calls and blow-by-blow e-mails about these dramas were endless. Margo was obsessive about guys, only making time for women when she needed or wanted something. "I just couldn't stand these traits any longer," says Crystal. "Even though Margo wasn't at her worst with me, I couldn't take her anymore; it drove me nuts to be around her and I eventually bowed out by telling her I needed time alone."

Crystal learned that her Queen Bee friend had another side to her. Perhaps it had been there all along, but she never noticed it for what it was. At one point Crystal may have enjoyed being a sidekick but now that she had matured, she desperately wanted to be independent and make her own life.

4: A FRIENDSHIP FELONY HAS BEEN COMMITTED

It's easy to ignore little disappointments, but some are so big and hit you so hard that they are impossible to forgive or forget—sleeping with your husband, maligning your reputation, betraying your trust, or duping you. Author Florence

Isaacs calls these kinds of disappointments "friendship killers."

Although true friends don't ordinarily keep an accounting of who did what for whom, there are certain times when you want your good friends to be there for you—to understand, empathize, and/or offer concrete help. It may be when you are going through good times (pregnancy, childbirth, engagement, marriage, a milestone birthday, or promotion) or bad times (fertility problems, a serious illness, a divorce, a sick parent, a death in the family, or the loss of a job). If your friend is so self-absorbed that she has no ability to recognize the peaks and valleys of your life, the friendship is pretty much doomed, no matter how close you think you are.

Close friendships are also built on a foundation of trust. In order to remain close, a woman has to believe that her friend would never purposely undermine her—that her secrets will never go beyond her friend's ears. Jeanne, 21, fell prey to a disappointing friend, Maria, whom she met during her junior year of high school. Maria quickly became Jeanne's closest confidant.

Jeanne had gotten pregnant that summer and soon after found out that her boyfriend had been seeing her former best friend behind her back. She knew she didn't want to go through with the pregnancy. She no longer trusted her boyfriend and wanted to complete her college education before she became a mother. Fearful of disappointing her Irish Catholic family, she arranged for an abortion and told no one but Maria.

"When we got to college, I realized why everyone else seemed to have reservations about Maria," says Jeanne. "I found out she had shared my embarrassing secret with others. Everyone knew what had happened and it was like I was reliving that horrible time in my life. I was fearful it would get back to my family. I didn't give her a chance to explain and didn't want to discuss it." If she could no longer share intimacies with Maria, she no longer wanted her as a friend.

Cristina, 34, met her friend Rosa twelve years ago when they worked at the same bank. They became more than colleagues, eating lunch together each day and going shopping after work many evenings. Whenever they were together, they were never at a loss for words. When the branch office closed down and they found themselves working in separate locations, they still e-mailed each other and spoke every few weeks.

When Rosa became pregnant, Cristina (still seeing her boyfriend but not yet married) was thrilled to hear the news. She sent her mom-to-be cards before the baby was born and baby gifts afterwards. "When I got married and her baby was a month or two old, I never heard from her," says Cristina. A few months later, Cristina made it a point to e-mail Rosa, just in case she hadn't heard it through the grapevine. She wrote, "Did you know I got married two months ago?" There was no reply.

The silence was deafening. That she didn't get as much as an e-mail acknowledging her big day hurt Cristina deeply. "I was crushed," she said. When she confronted Rosa over the phone, her friend said that the stress of having a new baby justified her neglect. "I never forgave her, and that was seven years ago," says Cristina. Although they didn't see each other as often, Cristina still considered Rosa a very close friend.

Perhaps Cristina overreacted to what some might regard as a minor slight. But if a relationship is already tenuous, it's easy for disappointments to pile on until they tip over.

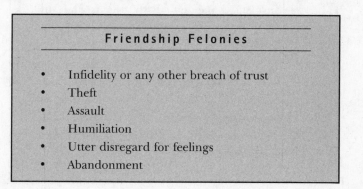

Friendship Felonies

- Infidelity or any other breach of trust
- Theft
- Assault
- Humiliation
- Utter disregard for feelings
- Abandonment

5: THE FRIENDSHIP SUCCUMBED TO ENVY

Because we are all different, it's a natural instinct to compare ourselves to others. We tend to gauge ourselves by how we stack up against our friends and acquaintances along a variety of dimensions—for example, looks, intelligence, career success, wealth, material possessions, and social standing. Most times, we realize that these things balance themselves out; while our friend may have the luck to never put on an ounce of unwanted weight, we have a keen sense of style.

Women with low self-esteem or those who are depressed, however, tend to focus exclusively on their shortcomings and are bitter about what they perceive as the advantages or good fortune of others. Taken to an extreme, such an individual tends to be self-involved, hostile, and cutting. It's natural to feel envy occasionally, but if this is a persistent pattern, it can signal a toxic friendship.

Jealousy vs. Envy

- *Jealousy* is an attitude of possessiveness when someone feels that a valued relationship is threatened. If your friend is possessive, she can't stand the thought of you having any other friends and wants you to spend all your time with her.

- *Envy* is a broader concept that can include coveting another person's characteristics or possessions. If your friend is envious of you, she is constantly comparing herself to you along material and non-material dimensions.

An excess of envy makes for an uncomfortable relationship because you can't be open and share your successes. If you do, you run the risk of making your friend feel worse. Each of us wants our friends to take pride in our accomplishments but this isn't always the case. Some women turn sour or become back-stabbers when it seems like their friend has more money, a better job, a bigger house, a richer family life, a slimmer figure, a more supportive mate, or has more girlfriends. Or it may be a case where a toxic friend is only content with a relationship that makes her feel superior. Why does this happen? Chalk it up to insecurity. Some women need to feel important by looking down on other women, even if they don't realize this about themselves.

Lori, 22, was best friends with Tara for several years. "Tara was always considered popular and cool and I was the follower-type," says Lori. When the two women left their private school for the public school system, Tara couldn't stand that their roles had reversed and her friend now seemed to be on a higher rung of the social ladder. Lori had a larger social circle, was more outgoing, became a leader, and was better liked than Tara, who was an outsider, a loner rejected by their classmates. "She got mad and ended our friendship on the computer by starting a fight about type fonts," says Lori. "We haven't spoken since." Obviously, the real upset wasn't about fonts; it had more to do with envy.

Another woman, age 25, described how her friend, whom she met in high school, began to put her down and compete with her over everything—from clothes to guys. "When I got into my dream college, instead of being happy for me, she told other people that I didn't deserve it," she says. "She went so far as giving me wrong advice so she could sit back and watch me squirm," she adds. When the woman eventually began to recognize this dysfunctional pattern, she knew that she had to end the relationship.

6: GUESS WHAT? IT REALLY ISN'T A FRIENDSHIP

The term *frenemy*, or sometimes *friendenemy*, has been used to describe people who are ostensibly your friends but who primarily are there to take advantage of what you can do for them. This is often the case when a friend is filled with ambivalence and jealousy. Such one-sided friendships tend to have short half-lives because they are so inherently painful and unsatisfying. Sometimes, money or jealousy is the root of these friendship evils.

Alyson, who is 31, says that her friend Nikki drives her nuts at times. "I'm not completely sure that she is a 'close friend.' Sometimes, she uses me for certain people I know. At the same time, she has been very kind," she says. She realizes that Nikki can be negative and toxic, but when she's not being snippy, she's interesting and original. It's hard for Alyson to let her hair down completely because she's never sure about how Nikki will respond.

It bears repeating that a toxic friendship can take many forms. A friendship that is toxic to one person may not be toxic to another. And a friendship can be bad for you without necessarily meaning that the other woman is a bad person.

To spot a toxic friendship, you need to objectively look at your friend's behaviors and your own, assess the problem, and determine whether it can be remedied. Sometimes this is hard to do and women dismiss the warnings and offers of help from other friends and family who are able to view the situation more dispassionately.

CHAPTER 6

FRIENDSHIPS IN FLUX

"Old friends is always best, 'less you can catch a new
one that's fit to make an old one out of."

—SARAH ORNE JEWETT

F riendships are inherently dynamic. Friends—even best
friends—find themselves in different orbits as their lives
change. One woman gets engaged and then married while
the other remains single, potentially creating a strain on their
relationship from either end. Two women may both be single,
but only one has the expectation that being single means spending every Friday night out with her best friend. One woman suddenly becomes widowed or divorced while her friend remains in
a stable marriage. One may have children while her friend
remains childless by choice or has trouble conceiving. One may
out herself as a lesbian; the other may react with uncertainty and
be unable to reconcile her lifestyle with their friendship.

As two friends grow and change, so does their friendship. If
their paths converge, it can strengthen the relationship, but if one
individual changes significantly and the other doesn't—or if two
people's lives diverge completely—it can signal doom. For example, if the basis of a friendship revolves around looking for men, it
may change when one friend becomes engaged or married. If two
friends graduate from college and one begins working for a small
non-profit and the other joins an investment banking firm with a

135

high salary, their preferred social circles and financial circumstances may change. One may want to take a ski trip to St. Moritz while the other is wondering how she will pay next month's rent.

There are many other reasons why two women who were once close might now feel like they live in different worlds. Sometimes fundamental differences between them have foreshadowed the end of the friendship. When a friendship is on the cusp of change, it often becomes eerily quiescent. The phone calls between you are more infrequent. You don't see each other for weeks or months at a time. You forget her e-mail address (which you once used constantly) or her cell phone number (which once was on your speed-dial), and you think she probably has forgotten both of yours.

She's no longer your go-to person when you need advice. You seem to have less in common and less reason to connect. There are other people to whom you pour out your heart. Even if there aren't, you can't imagine sharing the same intimacies you once did with her. If you needed to ask her for a big favor, you might summon up your courage to call her and ask—but it would take some mental gymnastics beforehand.

You wonder what went wrong. Then you push the thoughts out of your mind until some trigger reminds you of her again. When communication between two friends ceases, the status of the relationship is fuzzy. It's almost a "friendship coma," a relationship that is neither dead nor alive.

The longer the lapse in time, the more difficult it becomes for the former friends to reconnect. It's hard to be the one to call and try to explain the hiatus. When friendships reach this state, they usually wither away and die, sometimes beneath the radar of conscious awareness. One woman referred to the women in such relationships as "semi-friends," explaining that the bond was never actually broken. When this happens to you, you'll need to decide whether to let go, hang on, or do something about it.

The friendship of Chelsea and Erica fell into this category: their lives drifted apart as they followed two different trajectories. Erica, who is now 34, met Chelsea in grade school. Except when they had "serious boyfriends" during high school, they talked to each other constantly. Each woman knew she had a shoulder to cry on whenever a relationship with a guy ended.

Chelsea went off to college, but the two women kept in touch. By the time summers came around, they always picked up right where they left off again. They were maids of honor at each other's weddings. When Erica moved to another city after her marriage, they saw each other less, but they still felt close whenever she came back home to visit her folks. Whether or not her husband accompanied her on these trips, Erica always made time to reconnect with Chelsea.

"Then I began hearing from her less and less often," says Erica. "I got pregnant and found out about her pregnancies from other people, not her," she says. The last time Erica came to see her parents, she visited Chelsea and had the chance to meet her children. This time, she felt a distance that never existed before.

"I didn't have that feeling of connection I'd always had in the past," says Erica. "I still consider her a friend, but no one with whom I would share feelings and dreams anymore. Our lives were always different but now it seems as if we have nothing in common."

Almost every woman has had a friendship like Chelsea and Erica's: a friendship that was once very close but has grown more distant over time. There's a friend who probably is still in your address book; you may even remember her e-mail address or cell phone number by heart. If you saw each other you might still have warm feelings, but there isn't enough of a reason to get in touch or arrange to get together. There wasn't any disagreement or specific end point, but your relationship fizzled out. If someone asked about your relationship, you might respond: "We were friends some time ago." The relationship is ambiguous, seemingly on some kind of hold or hiatus, because neither of you know what to do with it. For reasons that you may not know or have never explored, you've drifted apart. Perhaps one of you changed or you both "outgrew" each other.

It feels puzzling, and sometimes uncomfortable, when a relationship with a best friend or a close friend starts to feel curiously out-of-sync for no apparent reason. Two friends who once meshed seamlessly move apart and are either bickering or feel bored when they're together. Yet there's no obvious reason for the demise of the once-close relationship.

Ironically, the same circumstances that make female friendships coalesce also make them vulnerable to dissolution. Women inevitably undergo a series of transitions over the course of their lives. At the same time, two individuals are maturing and changing, moving away or staying put, with no two lives following the same path. With all these transitions, there are lucky times when a friendship between two women sticks and other times, like a bad roll of the dice, when it falls apart.

Most times, once-close relationships fizzle or die a slow death unmarked by a confrontation or even a discussion. Some women describe it as a drifting away, with one or both friends lacking sufficient motivation to do anything to save the relationship. In essence, these friendships are seasonal, lasting only for a certain period of our lives when, metaphorically, all the stars are aligned. This does not, however, mean that they do not make a serious impact on the lives of the women involved, or that their passing will go unnoticed and unfelt.

As happened with Chelsea and Erica, drifting apart usually occurs slowly, almost imperceptibly. One or both women may feel like they don't have time for the other person anymore. But even if we deny it or make excuses, in truth, how we choose to spend our time and with whom reflects our priorities.

Another clue suggesting that friends are growing distant: differences that once were not only tolerated, but may have been enjoyed or admired, now become mildly annoying or even irritating. The friends may hang on to one another for quite some time or a specific change in circumstances—a graduation, move, pregnancy, career change, marriage, or divorce—may deliver the final death knell that provokes a convenient excuse for one of the friends to end the relationship.

Life Transitions That Affect Friendships

- Graduation
- Marriage or Coupling
- Motherhood
- Geographical Moves
- Pregnancy and Childbirth
- Infertility
- Career Changes or Job Loss
- Change in Socioeconomic Status
- Personal or Family Illness
- Mental, Emotional, or Substance Abuse Problems
- Major Caregiving Responsibilities
- Death of a Close Friend or Relative
- Accidents, Traumas, or Disability
- Significant Lifestyle Changes

THE INEVITABILITY OF CHANGE AND LOSS IN FRIENDSHIPS

The experience of two female friends growing apart is commonplace as early as childhood. Students cry on graduation day, whether in elementary school, middle school, high school or college, because everyone knows that these events herald the loss of at least some friendships. Geographical moves can also uproot a friendship. As easy as it is to come together when you are doing the same things in the same place at the same time, it's even easier to drift apart when you're headed off in different directions.

In high school, adolescent girls often leave friends behind as they fall into different crowds, have different interests, become boy-crazy, get wrapped up in competitive sports, or get involved with alcohol, sex, and/or drugs. Graduations from high school or college are also turning points when people move to different cities and develop their own lifestyles.

Research suggests that there may be a growing friendship deficit with people being less able to sustain the various relationships they make. A seminal study published in the *American Sociological Review* in 2006 reported that the circle of close friends held by Americans over the past two decades has shrunk markedly and that close ties are more family-based. The researchers also reported that the number of people who said that they had no close confidants had doubled.

Moving On

Kellie, 21, and Lauren were best friends who bonded over the many "firsts" they shared with each other. They entered high school at the same time, appeared in theater productions together, and took a cross-country bus trip over a summer vacation. They talked about their secret crushes, their close bond providing each other with self-confidence. They even both wound up in the principal's office because they were laughing so hard at a joke told to them by another student in English class.

"Then she just stopped putting forth any effort to maintain the friendship after we graduated from high school," says Kellie. Lauren went to college a few hours away and Kellie stuck closer to home. Each time Kellie called, Lauren would respond, "Yes, I'd love to hang out. I will call you later this week!" and never did. When this happened several times over three years, Kellie eventually gave up on her friend, but it still bothers her. She felt hurt and offended. "If she didn't want to hang out with me, all she had to do was tell me," says Kellie. "It just made me feel stupid."

Although Lauren provided Kellie with no clue as to why she distanced herself, it is likely that in college she found new friends whose company she may have enjoyed more at that point in her life than she did Lauren's. Moving away from home exposed Lauren to a new set of people and experiences that changed her as a person; she may have adopted a new set of friends with different values and interests.

When there hasn't been any discussion or closure, it makes it hard to understand, heal, and move forward, as was the case for Kellie. The pain can be long-lasting and emotionally consuming. Another woman who had grown apart from her best friend told me, "After it became apparent that we were no longer truly 'friends,' I was sad," she says. "That feeling lasted for several years and still remains today."

Another woman I met handled a similar situation in a different way, with a better outcome. She, too, decided to move on to greener pastures, essentially ditching a friend she had grown weary of, the timing coinciding with her move to another city, but out of respect for her once-close friend she called her and asked her to lunch before she left town.

She candidly told her friend that she really cherished all the good times they had together but she needed to concentrate on making new friends in her new city, as much as she was tempted to hold on to the past. Her friend was disappointed but accepted her decision.

Several months later, the woman realized that she really did miss her old friend and hadn't made as many new connections as she had hoped to. The two friends began to meet one weekend every other month for a relaxed lunch and shopping at a mall halfway between them. With less frequent contact, there was much more to share between them.

A former neighbor on my block told me in confidence that she was going to move at the end of the school year. She asked me to please not tell a soul because she was worried that other moms wouldn't agree to playdates with her and her son if they knew she was about to move. It seemed kind of far-fetched, but there are people who only want to have friendships of convenience. If you are not central to their universe, they lose interest in the friendship and are unwilling to extend themselves to make the friendship work.

Unless a relationship is toxic, it's prudent to maintain occasional or limited contact (e.g., infrequent phone calls or e-mails)

College Friendships

A study published in the journal *Personal Relationships* suggests that without an active effort to nurture them, college relationships are at high risk of falling apart. Professor Glenn Sparks, Ph.D., and his research team at Purdue University studied the friendships patterns of best friends who graduated during a nineteen-year period from 1983 to 2002.

On average, the graduates moved six times after college and the typical distance between friends was 895 miles. In addition to the geographic challenges, friendships were affected by blossoming romantic relationships, growing families, and increasing career demands.

Sparks offers a cautionary note based on his study: "Even if you have not spoken to a friend for three years, get back in touch," he says. "You may find a friendship that will last your whole life, and that is a great thing. Making friends is like managing a bank account. You must make investments, and it is never too early to start."

rather than to cut yourself off completely. You never know when you might be in the same universe again. This is especially true for your friends from high school and college.

While even very close and long-lasting friendships can unravel over time, the odds of a friendship fracturing are significantly higher when two friends don't know each other as well. One reason why is that early on in a relationship, friends are reluctant to reveal their true selves to one another with complete candor. When some secret or previously unseen character flaw seeps out, it may compromise their trust in one another.

One woman, Emma, 44, described such a breakup to me. Emma's close friend Carrie stopped calling or taking her calls. "I am comfortable that I didn't do anything to offend her. I truly didn't. But she let it slip in conversation once that her boyfriend of many years had asked her why she was never able to keep her female friends," Emma recalls. She eventually learned that Carrie had a troubled childhood from which she never totally recovered. "Although she was trying really hard to have healthy relationships, she just wasn't capable of keeping a friend," she says. As soon as she came close, Carrie withdrew without an explanation. Emma better understands Carrie's friendship difficulties by gaining insight into the past.

When women describe the reasons why their friendships fall apart, the losses are generally due to myriad reasons, including personal as well as situational or contextual factors. It's impossible to tease out precisely what went wrong, although women often mention how a life event or transition often gives one woman the "out" she is seeking, and that drifting apart ultimately brings one or both friends a sense of relief.

COUPLING

Marriage is another milestone that signals the strengthening of some friendships and the weakening of others. While the health and social benefits of friendship are great at every phase of life, most women find that it is harder to maintain one or more best friends when they are married, mothering, working, or caregiving due to competing demands on their time.

Some female friendships take an unexpected turn for the worse because boyfriends or husbands get in the way. When friends love spending time together, it's natural to want to extend the relationship to their significant others, but this doesn't always work out as hoped for. You may think: *wouldn't it be nice if the guys hit it off? We could go out to dinner together at that new Asian fusion restaurant. Or we could plan a vacation with both our families over the spring vacation.*

Just because there is chemistry between you and your girlfriend doesn't necessarily mean that the guys will feel the same way. Particularly if you don't have a long history with your friend, going out as a foursome is a little bit like going on a blind date. It might work or

Just Married: Keeping the Friendship Alive

If you are always a bridesmaid but never a bride, it may be tough (both emotionally and logistically) to maintain relationships with best friends who get married. Valerie Krause, co-author of *The Bridal Wave* with Erin Torneo, offers sage advice for a close friend of the bride who feels betrayed on some level, but wants to stay attached to her friend. Some of her suggestions are applicable to a variety of situations.

- *Be understanding.* Try to put yourself in her ballet slippers. Good friends have to understand that the bride's life and her priorities have changed. Her fiancé is her best friend (hopefully!) and everyone else has probably slid down a notch.

- *Get comfortable being a third wheel.* The bride is signing up for a lifetime with this guy so the good friend is going to have to get used to hanging with both of them. If invited, and without wearing out your welcome, be flexible about spending time as a threesome. As time goes by, there may be more time for you and your friend to spend alone.

- *Reset your watch.* Maybe she's busy on Saturday nights, but you can both sign up for morning yoga classes, weekly brunches, or both! Either way, the good friend should make some allowances for the bride. Don't punish her when she calls when her guy is out of town by refusing to hang out. To the contrary, seize these increasingly rare opportunities and go with the flow.

it might not. The men may bond and decide to meet each other at the gym, or they may find that they have precious little in common—in terms of their personality, style or interests—besides the friendship of their wives. The way to avoid problems is to go slowly and carefully, keeping your expectations realistic. (Much of the same holds true when introducing any new friend(s) to a twosome.)

Making New Couple-Friends

- If he doesn't already know them, prepare your partner for the meeting by giving him some background on the people he will be meeting.

- Prepare your girlfriend by explaining that just because you think the world of each other, the men may not hit it off, or you may find that their presence puts a strain on both of you.

- Plan the initial meeting at a low-key and neutral setting, perhaps a restaurant, and split the bill.

- If the men don't feel a spark for one another, make sure that any future couple get-togethers are infrequent and don't call for lots of interaction (e.g., catching a movie together followed by coffee rather than lingering over a long dinner).

- If the meeting bombs completely, talk to your girlfriend about it (without casting blame) and tell her that you hope it won't interfere with your friendship.

New mothers (whether in the workplace or at home), for example, who are responsible for one or more kids, often feel isolated, alone, and bereft of female friendships. In addition, they're often busy and exhausted.

When a woman gives birth, it changes the delicate balance between two friends. Even while they are pregnant, mothers fall in love with their babies and form an impenetrable attachment. The new mom may be more distracted and self-involved, leaving less time and emotional energy for her friends. After she gives birth, babies demand so much attention that Mom may be tethered to her new role and responsibilities, allowing even the best of her friendships to take a backseat to baby. She may think and talk about her baby continuously, not noticing that her childless friend is bored silly with her babbling.

The childless friend may feel like she has been knocked down a notch—and in reality, she has been! She may feel a sense of loss, and wonder when she can call or visit without being intrusive. She may feel hurt when the new mother says she only has a few moments to speak. Her friend is no longer as accessible as she was. If the childless mom is having difficulty conceiving, it can be particularly painful for her to spend time with someone who had no (or who overcame) fertility problems.

The Mother-Friend Connection

A 2002 survey in *Child Magazine* found that women who had previously spent fourteen hours per week with friends spent only five hours per week after they became mothers.

Friends need to recognize this dynamic in friendships and work around it. It may require adapting the friendship to the changed situation. The women may need to talk on the phone when the baby is napping or sleeping. They may need to plan girls' nights out when a spouse or relative can provide childcare. Getting together with a friend once a week or twice a month for a movie and dinner can be a nice break for the new mother, recharging her batteries and making her a better mother. If finances are tighter, they may need to think about planning a girls' night in.

The time friends spend together may need to be scheduled in advance and may have to consist of getting things done. For example, the friends can set up a regular appointment to have their nails manicured or their hair cut to maintain continuity in their relationship and have face-time with each other. Or they can use their time together to take care of chores, like grocery shopping and other things on the new mom's to-do list. In general, the friendship may not be as spontaneous, relaxing, or intense as it once was. The childless friend needs to be sensitive of the new strains on her friend, perhaps be less demanding, and even offer to help. She may need to broaden her circle of friends of she wants people to go out with on a day-to-day basis.

If the friendship is important, the two women need to make compromises so that it works for both of them. They need to recognize that this is a phase of life and roles may reverse at a later time. Flexibility and open communication are key. The new mother can find ways to meaningfully engage the childless friend in her new life by introducing her to the world of motherhood (for example, offering to let her hold and play with the baby or babysitting occasionally—making sure that she isn't burdening her or asking too much). In short, she can invite her to be part of her new life and that of her child rather than making her feel cut off from it.

She can initiate a conversation about how much the friendship still means to her. Realistically, with less time available, the new mother will need to be more strategic in carving out time for female friends—and in choosing the friends with whom she wants to spend her limited time. Unfortunately, there may be situations that are so rife with conflict and unmet expectations that the friendship becomes unsatisfying to one or both women. If either of them is rigid and unwilling to alter the nature of the relationship, it can lead to constant tension and disappointment. In that case, it might be better for the friendship to take a hiatus.

In contrast to married moms, younger women, single women, and older divorced and widowed women generally have more time and emotional energy to cultivate and nurture best friends. Hopefully, simply being aware of these natural ebbs and flows in the friendship cycle enables women to better understand their own needs and to be forgiving of their friends. When a friendship is important, women need to find a way to renegotiate its terms as changes in the lifecycle occur.

EXPERIENCING LOSS

Unexpected losses can alter many aspects of a woman's life, including her friendships. As a result, some bonds of friendship are strengthened while others come unhinged. Women may find themselves thrust into sisterhoods new to them—depending on the circumstances, it may be groups of breast cancer survivors, divorcees, widows, or the unemployed—that offer new opportunities for friendship and support.

When my friend Mickey Goodman lost her husband, it threw her friendships into a tale spin. "There are books, pamphlets, and Web sites devoted to practical matters that must be dealt with following the death of a spouse: advice on attorneys, wills, insurance policies, retirement, social security, bank accounts—ad nauseam," she says. "There is no advice on dealing with people who crush your spirit." Couples that were her friends for years stopped calling and one insensitive friend suggested she would be more comfortable with a women's group rather than a couples' book club she had belonged to for years. Fortunately, others reacted differently. "So many friends soared with the angels," she adds. They brought "mountains of food" and called to check in on her regularly and express their concern.

Divorces, specifically, can lead to unexpected "long good-byes" between friends. During the months or years preceding the divorce, the friend experiencing marital problems may not be herself. Understandably, she can be edgy, depressed, or preoccupied. It may be difficult for her to focus on anything but her own desperate situation. She may not care to share her time or feelings with certain friends, as some begin to drop off her radar. Some of her friends may not understand and step away on their own, leaving her feeling misunderstood or unsupported. In couple friends, dividing lines may be drawn if a female friend opts to side with one spouse over another. It can be devastating when a close female friend and her husband opt to take your husband's side.

Even the aftermath of divorce has a profound impact on friendships. With one friend married and the other divorced, two woman's lifestyles may become more disparate. They may no longer share the same interests or social circle; the divorce may entail a disruptive move or change in financial status; the divorcee may find that she has to devote more time to her children or to her work to make ends meet. The divorced woman may prefer to spend time with single, divorced, or widowed women who have more freedom to travel or go out together on weekends. More importantly, she may feel that they are more in tune with her emotions. If a friend is in a tenuous partnership, she may find the divorce threatening and seek distance.

Fortunately, disruptions like these, while common, aren't always the rule; many women going through painful separations and divorces say that they have been able to rely on their female friends (and sometimes their friends' husbands) to help them survive through this tumultuous time in their lives.

Serious illnesses can also separate the wheat from the chaff when it comes to friendships. In her book *Cancer Is a Bitch: Or, I'd Rather Be Having a Midlife Crisis*, author Gail Konop Baker writes: "I'm part of a club I didn't mean to join." Baker, a mother of three and wife of a doctor, was a self-professed health nut. She ran marathons, practiced yoga, and ate organic foods. Like many of us, she believed that she could keep breast cancer at bay. Then, at the age of 45, she was the first in her circle of friends to be diagnosed with breast cancer. She describes the instant bond she felt when she met other survivors. "It's like we share a secret language," she says.

While her old friends were supportive in every concrete way during her treatment, bringing her food and taking care of her kids, she sensed their own dread and fear. Some women were able to transcend that. "Just before my surgery when I was in a very funky funk, one of my best friends came over and told me, 'If you have to shave my head, I'll shave mine in solidarity.' Luckily I didn't have to but her words made me feel like she would walk through the fire with me," says Konop Baker. Her illness, she says, turned out to be a defining event in terms of her friendships. "Cancer brought clarity to my life and gave me license to declutter my life. So yes, some friendships, the ones that were draining me, fell away. I felt like I didn't have time to waste on relationships that weren't mutually enriching. But it also made me aware of the depth of some of my friendships and deepened those bonds."

Whether a woman is single or married, losing a job can be an assault on her self-esteem as well as her finances. So if your friend gets a pink slip or you do, it can upset the precarious balance of a friendship. This is likely to be an awkward and uncomfortable situation, riddled with embarrassment for the person who has just become unemployed, even if it is through no fault of her own. At such times, even close friends can be at a loss for words.

Friends: Just What the Surgeon Ordered

Every year, about 15 million Americans undergo surgical procedures. Whenever anyone goes under the knife, even for an elective procedure, it is likely to be a time of great stress. Whether the surgery is for breast cancer, an ovarian cyst, or a cosmetic procedure, female friendships can help ease an otherwise difficult journey. Friends can provide physician referrals, listen when you need a second set of eyes and ears to interview a doctor, and provide a potent dose of caring and cheer at your bedside.

A 2008 study published in the *Journal of the American College of Surgeons* confirms that a strong network of family and friends can even ease postoperative pain and anxiety, and speed recuperation. "Strong social connectedness can have a tremendous impact on patient recovery by helping blunt the effect of stress caused by postoperative pain, as well as ease concerns about health, finances and separation from family members," says Allison R. Mitchinson, MPH, was one of the co-authors.

The researchers studied more than 600 patients undergoing major thoracic or abdominal operations at two Veterans Affairs' medical centers. Prior to surgery, the patients responded to a questionnaire that elicited the numbers and frequency of their social contacts. Patients with smaller social networks reported significantly higher preoperative pain intensity, unpleasantness, and anxiety.

Friendships in Flux

Yes, it's always tricky to know how to console someone after a loss, just as it is difficult for someone to depend on her friends, to be able to ask for their help, or to show her appreciation. But everyone needs a little help and nurturance from their friends, especially at times like these. Think about what you would want if you were in the same situation.

SEEING THINGS DIFFERENTLY

Sometimes two friends see things differently—based on their respective upbringing, experiences, backgrounds, personalities, race, ethnicity, sexual orientations, or a host of other factors—and must work to understand each other's points of view for the friendship to last. Jewel, 28, described a sensitive racial issue with her friend Charlene that could easily have threatened the relationship if it hadn't been addressed head-on.

"Charlene is a woman of color and kind of ambiguous ethnic origin to people who don't know her," says Jewel. "Perhaps because of our young age when we met, this had never been a topic of conversation or concern between us." A couple of years ago, the two friends were together when a third person asked Charlene whether she was an American. Perhaps unwisely, Jewel jumped in to defend her friend and said Charlene was more American than Jewel herself because Charlene's family had been in America for more than four generations. (Jewel is white, but her mother was an immigrant)

That remark triggered an intense discussion between the two friends. "She said my comment hurt her, because she felt that for as long as we had been friends, I had tried to 'whitewash' her so that she better fit in my world," says Jewel. Jewel was shocked because the thought had never crossed her mind. "I thought I was defending her, not hurting her," she says. Then Charlene brought up at least five other instances when she felt like Jewel had tried to "treat her as white" and ignore her heritage.

Although it was exceedingly uncomfortable at first, this conversation turned out to be very productive for he friendship. If

151

Helping a Friend Who Has Lost Her Job

Be there for her
Listen to what happened. Let her tell her story. Don't pry unnecessarily. Don't recite all the grim unemployment statistics she's already been bombarded with by the media. Tell her that you're sorry and will do what you can to help.

Follow her lead
Losing a job is a little like losing a loved one (or losing a friend). People go through stages from anger to acceptance. Don't try to talk her out of her feelings. Don't tell her you know how she feels because you really can't put yourself in her shoes.

Reach out
If she hasn't told you about her job loss directly, give her a call or send her an email acknowledging the loss. True friends don't pretend not to know about bad things. It may be hard for her to repeat the same story to everyone she knows.

Offer concrete help
Do you have networking ideas to share? Job leads? Can you help her brainstorm?

Don't be cloyingly annoying
E-mail or call regularly but don't come on too strong or too often. There's nothing more annoying than being constantly asked if you've found a job yet. Wait for her to tell you.

Distract her
Remind her that there are other parts of life beyond work. Offer to take her to dinner or a movie. Invite her to a Girls' Night In with a small group of close friends.

Offer her a bridge loan
Many people say that friends and money don't mix, but if you can afford it and she really needs it—and she's a close friend— offer a modest loan to help tide her over this rough period.

Watch for signs of (emotional) depression
Recognize that extended unemployment takes an emotional toll. If your friend seems very distressed, tell someone close to her (perhaps a relative) and/or suggest that she seek professional help.

they hadn't had it, Jewel would never have known Charlene had been feeling the way she did, and the resentment might have built up and had a negative impact on their friendship. "I was able to address all her specific worries and we both felt better (and closer) afterward," says Jewel. Since then, Jewel is especially sensitive to not homogenizing other female friends of color and unintentionally robbing them of their identity.

GOING IN DIFFERENT DIRECTIONS

Money can also create a tremendous divide between good friends. If one friend suddenly inherits a huge amount of money, marries a very wealthy man, wins the lottery, or is catapulted to an executive position, it may change the way she leads her life and place her in a different social circle. Even though she may still cling to old friendships, the friends she left behind may feel jealous, resentful, or inadequate. On a more practical level, they may not be able to eat in the same chic restaurants or order expensive wines. Yet it can also be uncomfortable for them if the well-heeled friend generously offers to pay their way. Of course, both friends can be work out this problem sensitively, making sure that money doesn't get into the way of the friendship. Perhaps, they choose to dine out less lavishly so they can split the bill.

As mentioned previously, substance abuse or mental disorders like schizophrenia, bipolar disorder, anxiety, and depression can set the stage for unanticipated tensions in a friendship. In some instances, these disorders make it extraordinarily difficult for a woman to sustain healthy relationships.

Mindy and Faith became close friends about a year ago. They lived in the same small town and hit it off right away, becoming "super close really fast," as Mindy described to me. They had remarkably similar interests, desires, and goals. Their toddler daughters were born two weeks apart and the women, with kids in tow, spent many hours together each day. When they weren't together, they phoned, texted, and e-mailed each other. They took a memorable trip to California together with their respective families over the summer; they rented a van and drove along the Pacific Coast Highway from San Francisco to San Diego. They felt and acted like one big family; Mindy considered Faith the sister she'd never had.

Mindy noticed that off and on, her friend would shut down and ignore her for days at a time, not returning any of her calls or messages. "I thought it was odd," she says, "but I wasn't especially concerned about it at the time." When Mindy asked her friend about it, Faith would always have an excuse, claiming she wasn't feeling well or she was having an argument with her husband. "Faith's marriage had been rocky since day one," says Mindy. "She'd only been married for less than one year and was already pregnant with her second child. Her husband and she went to marriage therapy every other week. Their communication was horrible, from what she told me."

Then another disturbing pattern emerged. Faith started accusing Mindy or yelling at her all the time. "She blew up at me over the phone one night. I was shocked," says Mindy. It was devastating to hear Faith's accusations, especially since Mindy had no idea where they were coming from. She never knew precisely what was going on with her mercurial friend. She could only presume that she was either having a bad day or not feeling well.

Mindy felt like she was walking a tightrope. "I kept my distance, but at the same time tried to reach out in case she needed anything," says Mindy. But Faith continued to ignore her for days at a time. When she did finally contact Mindy, Faith would act like nothing had happened; there was no mention of the unreturned calls. "She brushed things under the mat," says Mindy. "She never let on to her true feelings. She bottled everything inside and finally blew up at me. I was crushed, disappointed, hurt, and angry," she says.

Although she can't be sure, Mindy suspects that Faith has bipolar disorder because her moods cycled from one extreme to another. Either she was really happy or despondent and not wanting to talk to anyone. Despite the roller coaster ride their friendship became, Mindy had a hard time giving up on her troubled friend, even after Faith eventually severed all contact. Mindy repeatedly tried to call. Faith wouldn't answer her phone. She sent Faith an e-mail asking her

Recognizing the Symptoms of a Mental Disorder in a Friend

Everyone has their ups and downs but some women suffer from serious and persistent emotional problems that can't be resolved by hugs, long talks, and the support of caring friends. According to the National Institute of Mental Health (NIMH), about one in four Americans, ages 18 and older, suffers from a diagnosable mental disorder in a given year

The odds are good that most women will encounter female friends with problems ranging from mild to severe. Diagnosing a mental disorder isn't as straightforward as taking an X-ray of your arm to see if it's fractured or doing a throat culture to see if you have a strep throat. To the contrary, there are no specific laboratory tests or X-rays to diagnose mental disorders.

To the casual observer, different mental disorders have similar and overlapping symptoms which may include: depressed mood, disorganized thinking, loss of contact with reality, suspiciousness, excessive energy and decreased need for sleep, loss of interest in activities that were once satisfying, anxiety, impulsivity, and impaired judgment. To make a diagnosis, a mental health professional needs to take a detailed history, conduct a clinical interview, speak to family members, and to observe the individual's behavior and symptoms.

No one should ever attempt to diagnose a friend. However, if you see behaviors and symptoms that raise concerns, talk to your friend about them directly (without using labels) and encourage her to seek professional help. In addition, if the person isn't able to function (e.g., take care of her child, maintain her home, or get to work in the morning), these may indicate deterioration in functioning associated with a mental disorder.

forgiveness, even though she really felt like she hadn't done anything wrong. "I'm happy with my life the way it is," Faith responded.

One of the hardest things for Mindy, aside from her concern about Faith, is worrying about the fallout of their breakup; she and Faith have many friends in common. The two women are the coordinators of a local moms' group and people have started to notice that they no longer talk to each other. "What am I supposed to tell our mutual friends?" says Mindy. "I am not trying to get girls on my side, but it has been extremely difficult to keep this from them. I truly care about her. I loved her and her family. I gave her everything. I think about her every day. I wonder how she is doing, but can't contact her anymore. She truly slapped my face and acted like she doesn't need someone like me in her life."

Mindy is hurt and doesn't understand what happened to the friendship even though she realizes that Faith is overwhelmed by her emotional and marital problems. It took time for her to accept that their split wasn't caused by anything that happened between them, but Faith's overwhelming problems made for an unstable and unpredictable friendship. The two women knew each other for a relatively short period of time, so Mindy did not know enough about Faith to realize the potential pitfalls of the friendship until it was over.

It is important to mention the inordinate difficulty and guilt women experience when they recognize that their friend may have a serious emotional problem that is affecting the relationship. Sometimes the problem is relatively new and arises during the course of the friendship; other times, it was there all the time but wasn't previously recognized. In both cases, the situation feels so overwhelming that it has poisoned the friendship.

Marcie, now 25, met her friend Vikki when they lived together during their senior year of college. At first, Marcie enjoyed her friend's antics; Vikki was the life of any party. Then, Marcie realized that her friend's moods were like a roller coaster; she was either depressed or over-the-top. "She was difficult to be friends with because she experienced such extreme emotions and mood swings. She constantly tried to steal my boyfriends. At times, her

Helping a Friend Who Is Depressed

If your friend is depressed, here are some ways in which you can help and possibly make a difference:

- Listen carefully, provide support, and offer to spend some time doing things you enjoy together (taking a walk or bicycle ride, or going to a movie).

- Offer to help her with concrete tasks she can't accomplish on her own because she feels overwhelmed or has no energy.

- Try to be patient—and never be pushy. Don't dismiss her feelings. Show that you understand them but encourage her to realize that these feelings are only temporary and will eventually pass.

- Don't dance around the issue. Tell your friend that you think she is depressed and needs help. Remind her that depression is a treatable illness and encourage your friend to seek treatment.

- If she resists your initial suggestion, try again but don't nag. Don't make demands or set ultimatums. Many depressed people need time to find their way to treatment and some people just want to be left alone.

- If you worry that your friend may be harboring suicidal thoughts, you have certain ethical obligations. Be direct and ask her if she feels suicidal. If she does, remind her that she is important to you and that she needs immediate professional help. Never allow the burden of having a depressed friend be yours alone. Be sure to inform someone else (for example, her partner or closest relative.) If you're her partner, tell her doctor.

- Recognize that you can only be a friend, not a mental health professional, and remind your friend of that too. There is just so much that friends can do and give. You may need to reluctantly cut loose and be there for her when she begins to recover.

wild energy was tiresome, embarrassing, or dangerous—but ultimately, she became so jealous when I made friends with another girl that she drove me away. It clarified what a negative relationship it was," she says.

Marcie suspected that Vikki had an untreated mood disorder. Each time she suggested that her friend talk to a professional, her pleas were ignored. Vikki responded by saying that she didn't really need someone to talk with as long as she had Marcie. Marcie decided to opt out of the friendship because she could no longer handle it and knew she couldn't substitute for the help she thought Vikki needed. "I keep that in mind now and don't have time for relationships like that one," she says.

Although Vikki's mood swings were pathological, it can also be a downer to have a friend who always seems to be blue or who suffers from low-grade depression. One barometer you can use to tell if a friend is depressed is to spend time with her and to see how you feel. One woman realized that her friend was becoming increasingly negative about everything in her life. They would meet for lunch and she would leave feeling blue, not renewed. She was going through a separation and didn't have the emotional energy required for such a downer relationship.

Many women have friends who suffer from an addiction. Whether it is using drugs or alcohol, shoplifting or gambling, it can be taxing to see your friend engage in self-destructive behaviors with little regard for the people they are hurting.

Bridget, 39, had a friend named Jan who was in recovery for drug addiction for many years. "Though Jan continues on her path of sobriety and self-discovery, a lot has changed over time," says Bridget, who feels she can no longer handle the relationship. "I think one of the main things for me was her lack of reciprocity," says Jan. "I went through so much with her, was always there for her emotionally—put up with many relapses, lots of drama, and in the end, when I got married, she couldn't deal with my happiness." Although Bridget still feels pained by the loss, in the end she feels that the relationship was unfair. She has decided that she will no longer befriend people who aren't "in control of their demons."

One of the complications of having a friend with emotional or substance abuse problems is that in addition to problems with judgment these disorders are often characterized by lack of insight. Sharon, 43, and Kate were close friends whose friendship also extended to their families. Everyone joked that they did everything together—vacations, dinners, and birthdays. It was clear that they enjoyed each other's company immensely. But a couple of years into the relationship, Sharon found out that Kate had a serious problem with alcohol and drugs. As the problem went unchecked, Kate began taking more risks to hide her habit and seemed to care little about the consequences.

"She stole from us, lied, and put our son in danger while driving under the influence without a license," says Sharon. "We did everything we could and more for her, including making efforts to get her help when her husband couldn't face up to the problems she was having. But our efforts failed and we realized we could no longer sustain the relationship."

Sharon stopped taking her friend's calls and told the rest of her family the reasons for her decision. She felt that it was useless to talk to Kate, who was in total denial about her problems. "For about a year and a half, I thought about her every day. I couldn't stop crying until I became very angry," she says. Sharon suspects that if Kate ever gets her problem under control, the two women could easily get back to where they once were. But addiction is a medical problem that is difficult to resolve.

This isn't to say that people with problems are incapable of strong and enduring friendships, but their illness can impact their friendships in ways that are often difficult to handle or understand.

THE SIGNIFICANCE OF SHARED HISTORY

With the inherent vulnerability and volatility of friendships, it's hard to predict with any certainty why one challenged friendship will survive and another fall apart. But often a history of shared experiences provides the glue that enables friends to stick together and to keep their relationship cemented during rocky times. Such was the case of the remarkable friendships chronicled by Jeffrey Zaslow in *The Girls from Ames: A Story of Women and a Forty-Year Friendship*.

When misunderstandings, disappointments, or disagreements occur, they are easier to overlook or to get over in the context of a friendship that has history and longevity. Being able to reminisce about past events and experiences, knowing many of the same people and places, and having a long-term investment in another person enriches a relationship and gives it more depth.

Women who have known each other since childhood, who have experienced firsts in their lives together, share common ground—and a greater chance of overcoming rough patches than those with fewer ties, who come from disparate vantage points.

CHAPTER 7

MAKING THE TOUGH CALL: MEND IT OR END IT

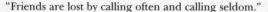

"Friends are lost by calling often and calling seldom."

—Proverb

Friendships—even best friendships—invariably change and evolve as the people in them change and evolve, and sometimes these friendships veer off course. Should that situation arise, you need to be poised to take stock and decide whether to mend them or end the friendship. If you are certain a friendship is toxic and beyond repair, you should trust your instincts and let go. But friendships, like most of the rest of life, are rarely black-and-white; they are almost always shades of gray. Even in scenarios where it is clear that the relationship should come to an end, there are ways to make the break easier both on your soon-to-be-ex-friend and on yourself—not to mention the people who are close to you both.

No Turning Back?

Just as opting for major surgery without exploring all the options and possible outcomes isn't wise, making decisions about excising a friendship should never be made lightly without thinking through the consequences. In some sense, ending a friendship is likely to be a one-way street, so you need to assess your feelings and the significance of the friendship before you act in haste and say or do things you wish you hadn't. Ending a friendship is always emotionally charged and often very stressful—no less stressful than ending a romantic relationship with someone you still care about.

Based on the data I've collected over the past two years, fractured or fracturing friendships are only salvageable about 50 percent of the time. When these friendships are renewed, they are often only partial successes; many women say that the second time around, the friendship is "not nearly as close," "not like it used to be," or "never back to where we were." Others used qualifiers to describe their reconciliations; they have "somewhat" reconciled, they are "sort of" friends again, and they are able to confide in each other "to a degree." One woman summed it up, saying: "Once trust is broken, relationships are more fragile and more at arm's length."

You may be able to resume the relationship with your friend on some level, but it will be unalterably changed. The truth is that while some close friendships can be mended, they almost never reconstitute with the same degree of intimacy and intensity. Thus, it's important not to burn bridges prematurely or unnecessarily.

It's equally important to remember that once you have brought up this often difficult conversation with your friend, in all likelihood neither of you will be able to forget it or fully put it behind you. So choosing words and timing wisely is crucial to causing both your friend and yourself as little pain as possible. In some cases, the best decision is to never have the conversation at all.

So how do you decide what's best in your situation? Start by asking yourself the following questions:

- Do you understand and accept the potential consequences?
- Do you owe your friend the courtesy of being direct and honest with her?
- Is a confrontation likely to cause a knock-down drag-out fight that makes you both miserable?
- On some level, are you hoping that a confrontation will lead to your friend's changing her behavior?
- Are those hopes and expectations realistic?
- Are your complaints or disappointments ones that she could remedy?

- Being honest with yourself, on some level, do you want to cause her pain to punish her for the pain she's caused you?
- Do you genuinely believe that being honest with her might help her or serve as a wake-up call for fixing her own life or other relationships?

As you think through these questions, try to be as honest with yourself as possible. Write a list of pros and cons on each side of each question—sometimes seeing your thought process in writing helps you be less emotional and wiser about making a decision.

ASSESSING THE COLLATERAL DAMAGE

Monica, 40, is married with three kids who are involved in sports and other activities that consume most of their free time. Over a period of four years, Monica and her husband developed a group of friends with kids the same ages. Her closest friend in the group was Susan.

Monica's and Susan's families also became close, and took two very pleasant vacations together. When the two families went to the beach together for the third time, another family joined them. "It was a terrible trip," says Monica. "Jenny, the other mother, was a bore and ruined much of the weekend. She ganged up against me and, afterwards, my best friend Susan ignored me for an entire month. I finally confronted Susan at a baseball game. She called me names and said she was tired of defending me to everyone."

Susan tried to patch things up, and eventually Jenny started being friendly. But when summer was coming around, Susan asked Monica if her family would think about a "separate" house at the beach. Making that comment drew a proverbial line in the sand between Monica and her "friends."

"I wish these people didn't bother me, but I feel terribly betrayed," says Monica. "Our kids are all in the same activities and I can't get away from them. I'm even considering moving our family to another state." Just because these women are behaving like girls in junior high school shouldn't mean Monica needs to play in a different playground.

When a couple breaks up, there is often forethought about the division of properties they once had in common. In considering a divorce, parents usually think first about the consequences for their children. One common oversight women make when ending their friendships is considering those kinds of collateral losses, and how they might be dealt with.

One potential loss to think about if you are considering ending a friendship: not only will you be ending the relationship with your friend, but you may also be cutting yourself off from other collateral connections you have made through your friend—her family, her friends, and her acquaintances—which, to some extent, may now have become yours. You need to consider the spillover or damage of the breakup to all the other relationships you share—mutual friends, children, spouses you thought of as friends, or coworkers who will be dragged into the drama.

If you have a circle of friends in common, will they feel the need to align themselves with either her or you? Will she be likely to trash you to the other women? Will you have to explain the falling-out? Can you handle the gossip that may ensue? If you are mothers and your children are playmates, will it make the kids feel uncomfortable that their moms are no longer talking? Will you be able to go with your friends on that girlfriend getaway to Vegas if you just ditched a friend who is going on the same trip? How will you feel about going to your high school reunion if you know she will be there, too?

If you are couple friends (two friends who are friends as individuals as well as couples), what effect will it have on your partner's relationship with his or her friend? Will you be inadvertently destroying other people's friendships? If so, is the breakup worth sacrificing your partner's friendship as well? It's probably worth discussing this as a couple beforehand so you know in advance if your husband, boyfriend, or girlfriend feels their relationship is too important for you to risk or if they'll be able to sustain it without you.

Making the Tough Call

If you're contemplating ending a friendship with a colleague at work, whether she is a peer, supervisor, or subordinate, you need to be certain you don't unintentionally provoke her (or any special allies she might have) to undermine your role at work. You may also risk creating a hostile work environment, or an awkward one. Will it seriously impact your productivity or career track? If there is a possibility that it will, you should carefully consider your options, and whether there might be a less confrontational way of loosening yourself from the friendship. Sometimes, subtly downgrading friends to acquaintances—distancing yourself quietly, without sitting down to hash out grievances—reduces the fallout not only for you, but also for other family, colleagues, and friends.

GIVING UP SHARED HISTORIES

There is also the collateral damage of your shared history to take into account. Why would a woman give a second thought to a friendship that seems to be offering little at the moment? One important reason is that friendships, particularly long-standing ones, are deep and rich in terms of their memories and connections to our past.

I have a few recollections of my days in college, but when my friend Vikki comes to visit, the shared memories come pouring out. Similarly, when my friend Diana comes, she reminds me of the strange antics of my first husband during that ill-fated marriage. And my friend Judy reminds me of when our children were playmates before they could even walk. Our friends are like memory books that document and archive the different passages of our lives. We need to clearly assess the likely gains and losses of writing off those irreplaceable friends.

"I have many lovely friends I've walked through life with," says Erica, 42. "We do not talk daily, weekly, or even yearly, but when we do meet or speak it is as though no time has passed and we are brought back to the time when we were ladies of the past, only now we are older and wise."

Sometimes, this means giving your friend (and yourself) the benefit of the doubt: for example, by overlooking, saying no, or holding back. Another option is to put the friendship on hold by taking a relationship break or sabbatical. You can make an excuse, tell a white lie, or make a gentle statement such as, "I'm so overwhelmed these days that I really need some time for myself. It has more to do with me than it does with you. I hope you'll understand."

Conversely, there are some friendships that are definitely not worth saving because they are fatally flawed. It takes wisdom and insight to be able to discern the difference between those that are keepers and those that aren't. Sometimes—in fact, often—we are too close to our own situations to exercise that wisdom and insight on our own. It may be helpful to try to talk through your feelings about the friendship and how it's affecting you with a very neutral outsider—your partner, perhaps, or another female friend who is not a mutual acquaintance and so won't be dragged into gossip or personal judgment calls. Another good potential listener is a family member, who may be less biased toward your friendship—sometimes, a sister, aunt, or cousin who cares about you but doesn't know your friend can react most candidly to your story. Hopefully, this third, unbiased person can help you vet the ramifications of your decision before it is set in stone. But making the call is always difficult.

Some women view a failed friendship philosophically and don't look back at all. "If the friendship has failed, there was a real reason," says one. They may be reluctant to get hurt or disappointed by the same person twice, and feel that it is more important to focus on looking forward than looking back. "The failure of the original relationship casts a dark shadow over the renewed one," says another woman.

"Friendships are supposed to be positives in your life," says author Florence Isaacs, one of the first people to match the term *toxic* with *friend*. "There's only so much time, and time spent in a negative friendship is time you could be spending on a more rewarding experience. If the friendship is draining, something needs to be changed," she says.

CONDUCTING A FRIENDSHIP AUDIT

As you might think of doing when making any important decision that isn't clear-cut, it's often helpful to list the pros and cons of various scenarios on a piece of paper. Divide the paper into three columns. In the first one, list all the positives the friendship brings to your life. In the second column, list all the negatives of the relationship as it currently exists. In the last column, think through and list some of the consequences of ending the relationship. One woman I spoke to did this regularly for all the friendships she felt ambivalent about. She aptly called it a "friendship audit."

Less-than-satisfying relationships that aren't toxic can still be out-of-sync and upsetting. Every friendship goes through ebbs and flows, and the relationship may simply be in a low period. Friendships are similar to marriage: both require hard work to keep them going. Before you give up on such friendships, one option is to try to mend them. By making small changes, there may be a way to modify an imperfect friendship so it becomes more rewarding for you as well as your friend.

One way this can be achieved is by adjusting your expectations of the friendship so it better conforms to your needs. Maybe you are expecting too much of one friend and need to add others to your inventory. Or perhaps you are spending too much alone time with one person and need to invite other people to join you when you are with your friend. Or perhaps you and your friend get too wrapped up in talking and need to add some activity to your get-togethers to buffer the intensity of her moods or her questions of you, which feel like an interrogation.

Depending on the miscommunication, disappointment, or transgression, the fixes may be minor or the relationship may require a major overhaul. Salvaging the friendship may demand not only an attitude adjustment but also behavioral changes. One thing is essential to keep in mind: you can only control your own behaviors, not those of your once-close friend.

MENDING A FRIENDSHIP

If one of your current friendships is tattered but feels too precious to lose, here are some tips to get it back on track:

OPEN THE DOOR

Summon up your courage to start a dialogue. Don't make assumptions about what you think your friend is thinking, because they may be totally erroneous. If there is any hope of mending the relationship, you need to communicate. "Don't ignore the elephant in the room," says Felicity, who knew deep down that her friend was unhappy and depressed but could never bring it up with her. Now, she rues her decision. "If she had felt able to tell me what was going on, maybe she'd still be in my life," she says. Sometimes people are reluctant to talk about their personal problems, even to good friends, but given a window of opportunity, they're only too happy to share.

If it's been some time since you've connected with a friend and you wonder what's going on, don't ignore it. Begin with a letter, phone call, or e-mail, depending on how you are accustomed to relating to each other, and suggest that you speak or get together. She may be waiting for you to make the first move. E-mail or snail-mail correspondence offers the advantage of making sure your friend isn't caught off guard.

"When you come to a bump in a friendship, be understanding and evaluate if the friendship is worth continuing," says another woman. "If it is, speak up and don't let it grow into a great divide." Once you connect, be candid but sensitive about your needs and any perceived failings of the relationship. If there's been a transgression that is relatively minor, talk about it.

"Suppression and accommodation only lead to anger and resentment," warns life coach Debbie Mandel. Just as good marriages require work, so do good friendships. When two people communicate and make adjustments as they go along, they are less likely to create emotional schisms between them. Don't ever let things build up to the point that you're furious and ready to lash out in anger at your friend at the most minimal slight.

You may need to explicitly redefine the boundaries of the relationship. If you withdrew because you felt suffocated, tell her that you care for her a great deal but simply don't have enough time or energy to be her only friend in the way you once were. Stick to your guns.

BE THE FIRST TO OFFER THE OLIVE BRANCH

A friend may have been insensitive to your feelings, forgotten your special birthday, failed to be there when you needed her, or put you at a distance without an explanation. Girls and women of every age typically have such high expectations of their female friends that even relatively minor snubs or transgressions can make them feel like they've been attacked.

Eventually the pain subsides, but it is still hard to forgive or forget. If you are like me, you'll obsess about what happened, replaying the hurt without getting over it. Yet it is in our best self-interest to practice forgiveness. It is healthier, both physically and emotionally, to forgive rather than to harbor grudges. Remaining angry can wreak havoc on your heart and nervous system, leaving you feeling anxious, tense, and depressed.

Forgiveness usually doesn't occur spontaneously, so here are some steps you can take:

How to Forgive a Friend

- Replay the event in your mind and admit you feel hurt.
- Consciously decide that you want to forgive. It may be helpful to write it down and say it aloud.
- Try to understand what happened from her perspective instead of yours.
- Instead of thinking that the infraction was purposeful, reframe it as having to do with her rather than you.
- Give it time. Sometimes, the passage of time makes it easier to forgive.

Practiced well, forgiveness improves physical health, provides a sense of emotional relief and closure, and has the social effect of teaching us to be more compassionate and empathetic with others. You may find that you are able to resuscitate the friendship. If the transgression was a serious one, your friendship may not survive, but forgiving will allow you to move forward feeling more whole.

Many women are pleasantly surprised when they find that their friendships are reborn, with tincture of time. Paula, now 36, and her friend Olivia had been best friends since first grade. After they had a falling out as college roommates, they didn't talk for more than a year. "Her sister invited me to her wedding and I showed up at my friend's workplace one day just to tell her I was coming and to chat about the wedding," says Paula. "I was nervous because I thought she hated me! But she was glad to see me and we just picked up where we left off. We are still close today." Paula and Olivia's tiff occurred so long ago that its substance was no longer memorable—yet their fondness for one another had remained.

After some time has passed, if you are aware of something you did that might have created a split between you and your friend, even if you aren't sure it was wrong, don't be too big to apologize. "Even if you don't know how or what to say, the symbolic gesture of trying goes a long way," says one woman. Swallow your pride and explain how sorry you are and how much the friendship means to you. Admitting your blame may open the door for her to take her share of responsibility for the misunderstanding as well.

Depending on the transgression, the timing, and the state of mind of your friend, she might or might not be able to accept or even hear your apology. Just because you are prepared and ready to reconcile doesn't mean she is. If you fall upon a deaf ear, chalk it off to bad timing or circumstances beyond your control and leave it be for now. Think about whether and when you should try again. "You can't make the other person more vested in the relationship," says one woman. Your gesture may be rebuffed or ignored, but rather than feel angry or frustrated, try to forgive your friend for not being ready for a reconciliation. Hopefully, it will ease your mind considerably to know that at least your side of the street is clean, and that you are not the party perpetuating bad feeling.

Adriana, 27, moved some distance away from her friend Susan. After Adriana married and gave birth, their relationship just seemed to fade away. Through a mutual friend, she heard that Susan also had gotten married and had a child. "This past July was her thirtieth birthday, so I called to wish her a happy one," says Adriana. "I expected to get her answering machine, but we actually spoke. I invited her to my baby shower in August and she came and brought thoughtful gifts." The two women talked late into the night after all the other guests had left and Susan went home the next morning.

"I sent her a thank-you card and a birth announcement, and then she sent a card with a gift card tucked inside as a 'wedding present.'" It was particularly moving because Adriana had already been married for two and a half years. To her, it signaled that their friendship really hadn't missed a beat.

BE FLEXIBLE

Many friendships fall into patterns, regardless of whether they are workable now. For example, it's easy for one friend to become the talker and the other the listener. Even in a circle of friends, it's natural for different friends to assume different roles because they each have different personalities (e.g., one may be the perennial hostess, another may be the mother, and a third may be rabble-rouser). But sometimes friends outgrow these roles, becoming bored or impatient with the storyline of their friendship. Here are some ways to salvage your friendships:

Steps to Save a Dying Friendship

- Get in touch with your feelings. Present the "new you" to your friend(s) rather than relegating yourself to your old role.
- When you are feeling uncomfortable, learn to say "'No" and to set reasonable boundaries.
- Take a break and skip getting together for a couple of weeks; see if it feels better the next time you're together.
- Shake things up. Do different things than you customarily do together. Do them in different places.
- Spend less time with this friend and expand your friendships so you depend less heavily on this one.
- Try to figure out if something outside the friendship is making you more impatient than usual (for example, work-related distress, marital discord, or personal health).

Making the Tough Call

You may find that it is too difficult to maintain a close friendship at the same intensity or frequency as you once did. If your friend is asking to see you too often, overstays her welcome when she visits, or spends too much time on the phone with you, you may need to be honest and say something like, "Although I'm always home, I work at home and get easily distracted. I really need to get better about scheduling our time together." Or you might say, "Being a new mother is overwhelming to me. If I cut you short on the phone, please understand that I'm trying to find my way in this new role." If the friendship is starting to annoy you, don't be afraid to set realistic boundaries and stick to them.

As opposed to writing off the friendship completely, allow your friend the opportunity to change. She may not realize that something she is doing could potentially jeopardize the friendship. "Friendship is a school of correction," write sociologists Terri Apter and Ruthellen Josselson. Consider whether you may be a magnet for needy friends because you've allowed yourself to play the role of a confessor and counselor for people around you. If you redefine the boundaries of your relationships, you may find that some of your neediest friends rise to the occasion and become more self-sufficient.

Alternatively, you may be the one who wants more time, companionship, or emotional support than your friend is able or willing to give. Instead of rejecting the person completely, see if there are some adjustments that would make your relationship work better. You may simply need to adjust your expectations. One woman calls this strategy downgrading the friendship. "Sometimes, our expectations go beyond what normal human beings can deliver," says another.

If you feel like your friendship is dying because of too much emotional intensity, you can make small changes that limit opportunities for intimacy. Instead of always meeting your friend one-on-one, suggest that a third person join you or make it a group for a change. You can also diffuse its intensity by planning the friendship around mutually enjoyable activities (making plans for a monthly movie, or a trip to a museum).

BEST FRIENDS FOREVER

Some friendships are resurrected against all odds. Shani, 53, told me about her high school friend Marla, who dropped her like a hot potato many years ago. "She was going through a divorce and she willingly gave custody of her kids to her ex," says Shani. "I had just gotten married a year or so before and was having my first child." Marla wanted to live a party life and saw Shani's life as a criticism of her own choices. Feeling persecuted by the friendship, she cut Shani off entirely. "She never talked with me about it but I put two and two together—and her sister confirmed my suspicions," says Shani.

A few weeks ago, Marla called Shani out of the blue after twenty-three years! "I delayed calling her back, thinking, 'Who needs the drama, explanations, or whatever? Maybe she's just doing the twelve-step thing or something,'" Shani says. Then she told another dear friend that she didn't have time for this. Merely uttering those words sounded "so stingy" to Shani that she realized she owed her friend a return call.

When she finally made the call, both women were happy beyond words. "I did ask why she waited so long, and she told me she had thought of me almost every day," says Shani. "She responded: 'Just chicken, I guess'—which was a good enough explanation for me!" Since that time, the two women have had good, long phone calls—as if no time has passed between them—and they're making plans to see each other soon.

Very often, relationships become inconvenient because two women's lives take different paths—in terms of geography, availability, or a host of other reasons. One respondent explained the collapse of a terrific friendship by saying, "Life got in the way." Even best friendships can be derailed by situational circumstances. If the problems are truly situational, it is often possible to get the friendship back on track by making relatively minor adjustments on one or both sides of the friendship equation. Remember that no friendship is perfect, and that each one may require slight changes.

EXPRESS YOURSELF

Sometimes your friend is involved in something she can't change or get herself out of on her own. It could be a bad relationship, or an alcohol or drug abuse problem that's destroying your friendship. Cases like this may demand that you speak out and say something for her well-being and the sustainability of your friendship.

Carole, 19, watched her friend Wendy start dating William, who seemed like a great guy. "Then, he started taking up more and more of her time until he had her skipping school and sneaking out of her house for him," says Carole. "We didn't see Wendy for about eight months and called her a POW—Prisoner of Will." Then we decided to do an 'intervention.' We told her how sad we were that we were no longer friends because of him." Wendy eventually came around to her friends, broke up with the guy, and now the women are back to being the "bestest" friends.

Jessenia, 24, was spending more than her paycheck each week, despite the general turndown in the economy, and eating up her small savings account. When they went shopping together, several times, her friend Freda saw her buy expensive handbags and shoes that she knew Jessenia could ill afford. Jessenia was on a shopping high, maxing out her credit cards. When Freda raised the issue, Jessenia blew up at her. But when Jessenia asked to borrow money when they ate out, Freda realized that it was an opportune time to "have the talk" again. To her surprise, Jessenia agreed to see a financial counselor to help her with budgeting.

It isn't always easy to say what's on your mind, particularly when you think it is something your friend doesn't want to hear. But it may be worth the risk—particularly if the friendship is close and important to you, or if your friend's physical or mental health is at stake.

Your friend may need the nudge or push from someone who cares about her to make a positive change. Too often, women worry that giving someone unsolicited advice may turn out to be a friendship killer. Although this can be true, the most likely outcome is that advice will fall on deaf ears if your friend isn't ready to change. For example, you can tell a girlfriend who is dating a man who has been marrried for many years that she will likely experience heartbreak before it ends. If she isn't ready to end it, she will simply ignore you. Even if she gets angry initially, she may later come to appreciate the honest gesture you've made.

GIVE IT TIME

While technology has changed our lives and offers new opportunities to sustain friendships that transcend geography, there really is no substitute for face time when it comes to friendships. Yes, everyone is busy, multitasking, and stretched to the limit. But if having close friendships is important to you (as it should be), you need to figure out ways to fit friendship into your schedule. Instead of saying "We should really talk again soon," or "Let's get together," pick up your calendar and make a date right away while you have your friend's attention. If you put it off, it will likely never happen.

Juggling multiple roles simultaneously (for example, wife or partner, mother, daughter, worker, caregiver, or several of these), often without much control over the demands they place on you, can strain relationships with friends. New responsibilities, especially caring for children or aging parents, can topple the precarious balance and rhythm that friends adopt as a way of relating to each other. It's important to be aware of these challenges so you can creatively address them.

If you are single, maybe you can join your friend and her husband for an evening out. Or perhaps you can visit your friend at her home while the baby is napping. Electronic technology like cell phones, text messages, and social media (such as Facebook or MySpace) can help you transcend some of the gaps. Perhaps you can't see your friend after work anymore, but you can catchup on your cell phones as you both commute from the office.

Although friendships while married or mothering are more complex than when you're flying solo, it's important to remember that even the closest couple benefits from having outside relation-ships and spending some time apart. The same can be said for moms having adult time with friends, separate from their kids.

My friend Susan has a close friend in Canada who is about fifteen years older than she is. When her friend called after they hadn't seen each other for quite some time and invited her to visit, Susan put down the phone, immediately called the airline, booked a reasonably priced flight, and spent three days across the border reconnecting with her friend. Had she let the opportunity slip, the two women might have grown further apart.

Amy, 56, found a novel way to kill two birds with one stone. She exercises—virtually—with a friend who lives hundreds of miles away. Amy lives in New York and her best friend lives in Boston. They've known each other for more than twenty years. Their friendship began as colleagues but they weren't really close until four years ago, when they reconnected and started exercis-ing together every day.

"We talk on the telephone while we work out on our respective elliptical machines," says Amy. "It is an incredibly wonderful, satisfy-ing, and mutually rewarding relationship. We spend more time interacting with each other than we do with our husbands or chil-dren, not because our relationship is more important, but it's hard to find together time when everyone is busy with their own schedules." Thanks to their unlimited long-distance calling plans, they can talk for hours and hours without worrying about the cost.

With a "watchful waiting" attitude, some friendships are renewed against all odds. Linda, 59, told me such a story. "My friend Kathy was going through a difficult time for a period of eight years," says Linda. Because they had lost contact with each other, Linda was-n't at all sure what was going on. She would vacillate between worry and anger at her friend. "She stopped visiting, didn't return phone calls, and showed no signs of wanting any contact," says Linda.

But because the relationship was important to her, Linda sent Kathy holiday cards each year and invitations to special events that they had attended together in the past. "Recently, she took me up on two invitations and mentioned that she was able to do this because she knew I was there waiting for her," says Linda.

Make allowances and be patient. You never know what's going on in another woman's life and when she'll be in a position to boomerang back to you.

FORGIVE AND FORGET

If the friendship is meaningful and the fracture was relatively minor, make a conscious decision to get over it. There are bumps in every relationship. "We are all human, after all, and no one can be perfect all the time," says one woman. It's easy to get angry when you were looking forward to eating lunch out with your friend at the office and she tells you that she can't go because she forgot about her lunchtime meeting with her supervisor—this, after recently breaking a date to go to the movies together because she realized she had to babysit for her niece that night. You know that your friend was never very good at planning and scheduling, but she's proven that she's as loyal as they come and would do anything for you. You swallow and buy her a leather-bound calendar for Christmas.

Unintentional hurts are one of the risks of close friendships. Because you are close and respect each other, you both become more vulnerable and exposed. So when small hurts occur (as they often will), you need to talk about them, forgive, and move on. If you've had a falling-out or even if you haven't seen someone for a very long time, you don't want to wait too long before you do. As one woman says, "Fresh wounds are easier to heal than scars." Many other women agree that apologies are more difficult with the passage of time. "If you want to save the relationship, do it fast," says another one. Hopefully, relationships with once-close friends are flexible and forgiving enough so both parties can adapt to change and recognize the other friend's constraints.

Tips for Making Your Apologies Work

- **Step back and think about what happened.** You can't sweep it under the carpet and pretend it never happened because it will affect your friendship. Examine your own motivations, the consequences, and how you can undo it.

- **Take responsibility for what you did wrong.** It doesn't help to offer feeble excuses if what you did was hurtful or offensive, in both your opinion and your friend's. Make a clear-cut apology.

- **Acknowledge the effect of your mistake.** A plain-spoken but sincere apology—without qualifiers—is often the best strategy. For example, "I'm so terribly sorry that I wasn't there for you when you needed me. I wish I had been by your side."

- **Explain your motivations, assuming they were well-intended.** We are all prone to making errors in judgment, and sometimes we simply fail to predict how our friend will react. But if she is interested in hearing your thought process, try to explain to her what went wrong. Make an effort not to be defensive—remember, you are doing your best to win her back.

- **Try to find some way to make amends.** Perhaps you can treat her to dinner, bake her a cake, take her for a massage or pedicure. Small gestures may seem, well, small, but often they add up into something meaningful.

- **If your friend doesn't immediately forgive you, follow up with a personal note, restating what you said in person or by phone.** This gesture will allow your friend time to mull over what happened and hopefully come to the decision that she wants to save the friendship too.

- **Be sensitive to timing**. While you might be ready to apologize, your friend may still be seething or feel too hurt to respond. Give her time before you attempt to apologize again.

- **Don't let too much time pass so that the friendship drifts apart.** Ask her to get together to talk or to go to the movies to show her you hope for reconciliation.

APOLOGIZE AS SOON AS POSSIBLE IF YOU WERE AT FAULT

If you made a big blunder or blurted out something regret-table, all you can do is try to apologize—although it may take some work to turn things around. Remember that no friendship is con-flict-free and even good friends may say the wrong things at the wrong times or make mistakes occasionally. If your friend is unwill-ing or unable to forgive you, don't lash out in anger. Instead, step back and learn from the experience. At least you've done what you could to clear your conscience. On the other hand, if you aren't able to understand what you did wrong, it is difficult to apologize and whatever you say won't come across as sincere. You will need to talk to your friend about what happened so you can better understand what role you played in making her unhappy.

When there's been a big hurt—even if a heartfelt and appropri-ate apology is accepted—there's been a breach of trust. Because of this, you will need to make renewed efforts to strengthen the friend-ship, but it often can be done.

When you and your friend share a reservoir of goodwill based on history and trust, minor missteps are usually forgivable with an appropriate apology—unless the missteps have been repeated once too often. However, when the hurt you've caused is big, apologies generally require more effort.

"My 'friend' wants me back in her life desperately but doesn't want to talk about what happened to us; she does not want to own up to the things she did and they were so devastating to me that there is no way I could be friends with her again by simply pretending none of it happened, and sweeping it under the carpet," says one woman.

TAKING A BREAK

Some women insist that they would never formally end a friendship; they would just back off. Others aren't philosophically opposed to ending one, but aren't ready to make the decision. One option that works in both situations: you can consciously decide to place the friendship on hold and take a friendship sabbatical, even setting up a specific time frame to wait and reevaluate its merits. It can be explicit, where both parties mutually agree they need a break, or one-sided, something you decide and implement yourself without making it overt.

This option is more likely to work if there hasn't been an argument or disagreement between the two of you. The sabbatical may give one or both of you the time you need to defuse negative feelings and work out the kinks in your friendship constructively.

Sue, now 24, and her friend Fern were close friends with another girl in high school. "I honestly got sick of the third friend," says Sue. "We were very similar and it drove me crazy." So while away at college, Sue stopped talking to her and saw her only on rare occasions when the three women came home for visits. During their senior year of college, Sue and the third friend started to hang out together and became closer again. "We discussed our 'time off' and how we just needed some space," says Sue.

Sue was wise enough not to alienate the friend, which paved the way for her to be able to befriend her later on. Sometimes a relationship becomes so strained over time you feel like dumping the friend completely, but backing off can be a viable alternative.

Lori, 47, had such an experience. Lori had been single and unattached most of her life while her friends always seemed to be in relationships that worked. Once those progressed into marriages and eventually children, she had less and less in common with these friends, so the dynamics changed considerably.

"Some of my friends had acquired lavish lifestyles that were far different from my own," says Lori. At some point, it became difficult for her not to be jealous of both the emotional and material riches of one particular friend. She says, "While I was sitting on a pity pot of a lonely life in a job I hated, I took a sabbatical from the friendship—I didn't phone to say hello or make any plans. Part of my MO was to find out if she'd walk away completely, which she didn't."

Now the two women seldom see each other, but they have come to accept the differences in their current lifestyles, treasure their shared past, and enjoy each other in small doses. "Bottom line, though, the friendship is stronger than ever, just different. I trust and value my friend more than I did twenty years ago," says Lori.

By taking a break, you may realize that some of the rifts in your friendships are just a matter of timing or a temporary incompatibility.

You as Portfolio Manager

It's important to remember that you need to play an active role in managing your friendship portfolio. You can identify "keepers," work hard at keeping them, forgive and ask forgiveness, downgrade the duds, and take a break if you still aren't sure which is which. If you do find that you need to end a fractured friendship, a little advance planning will make the passage easier for you, your friend, and the people around you.

CHAPTER 8

TIME TO SAY GOODBYE: ENDING A FRIENDSHIP THAT CAN'T BE FIXED

"I have lost friends, some by death . . . others by sheer inability to cross the street."

—VIRGINIA WOOLF

I t is frightening for us to imagine that, in all probability, the most likely outcome of any friendship—even a very good one—is that it will end. Yet women still feel guilty and ashamed about a failed friendship. Because these breakups tend to be shrouded in secrecy, we only hear of those that end because of an egregious blowup or betrayal, which adds to their shame and stigma.

When supermodel and TV host Tyra Banks focused one of her shows on the topic, "When Good Friends Go Bad," her message board was overwhelmed with close to two thousand comments from viewers who reported that their best friends had crossed the line by doing something so terrible that they were unable to forgive them. Yet most of these women were reluctant to cut the cord and end the friendship.

Typically, when a woman begins to realize that a friendship is falling apart or isn't worth saving, she may not even be aware of her feelings. Some women begin to feel increasingly edgy and uncomfortable being with the friend, talking on the phone, or making plans. Others get headaches or stomachaches in anticipation of a get-together. Most women assume that their friend doesn't know or have the same feelings, and perpetuate the deception that the friendship is still alive.

One woman told me that the hardest part of the whole thing for her was the month or so when she knew she didn't want to be friends with someone anymore but spent time with her acting like nothing was wrong. Once you decide you need to end a friendship, it's not uncommon to feel edgy and uncomfortable until you do it, and you may even feel that way afterwards for some time.

Understandably, kissing off a once-close friend—closing a door—is always difficult. But in the end, when a friendship truly isn't worth saving, you need to cut your losses and make the ending as graceful and painless as possible. "At first I felt the loss, but as time passed, it was like a burden being lifted from my shoulders," said one woman who ended a toxic friendship. Another said she felt a sense of liberation and freedom upon extricating herself from a bad relationship.

Amber told me her story. She and Pia, both 41, met through mutual friends more than twenty years ago in high school. When they came home from college during the summer between their sophomore and junior years, they bumped into each other again at a friend's party and started spending more time together. "We enjoyed shopping and dancing and, for the most part, each other's company," says Amber. "We were young and attractive and would go out to clubs, having a great time meeting other people."

One thing that bothered Amber was Pia's persistent negativity. Given the chance, Pia complained about everything and everyone. The two women fell into almost stereotypical roles in their relationship. Amber was the funny, outgoing extrovert and Pia was the cool, blasé sophisticate. Somehow the two personalities seemed to mesh, and Amber introduced her friend to her family and included her in their rituals and celebrations, as Pia had always had troubles with her own family.

But Pia had incredibly bad judgment about men and sex; she

loved to shock people with her language and actions. This was tolerable when they were young, but grew increasingly uncomfortable and embarrassing as they got older. "After all, a thirty-five-year-old in revealing clothes, obviously trying to seduce a family friend can be mortifying!" says Amber.

Many times, Amber tried to encourage Pia to get into therapy to work on her "issues." However, Pia was resistant, insisting that she wasn't the "therapy type." "She preferred using me as her therapist—something I was ill-equipped to handle," says Amber. "She would unload her problems and I would listen, trying to make her laugh while I offered suggestions." The rare times when Pia's life was going well, she had a habit of taking on other people's problems as if they were her own. It became exhausting for Amber to listen to Pia's problems and those of everyone else Pia knew. The few times that Amber needed someone's ear or shoulder to lean on, she was typically met with Pia's "Well, life sucks. What did you expect?" attitude, which only made her feel more upset and depressed.

Amber began confiding in her friend less and less. When Amber married and had children, Pia grew extremely jealous and bitter rather than happy for her friend. Pia felt abandoned and resented the time Amber was lavishing on her family, time that once was hers alone. "She hated spending time with my son and resented my husband," says Amber. "I began avoiding her because she would openly swear and talk about her sexual conquests in front of my child, despite my repeated requests that she not."

When Pia's fortieth birthday rolled around, Amber felt responsible for making the day special for her friend. Ironically, that effort turned out to be the final straw in their already strained relationship. Amber threw a surprise party, and rather than being appreciative, Pia reacted angrily, telling her friend that she hated surprises. "She had to be coaxed back into the event," says Amber. Her behavior was reprehensible: she was rude to the guests and spent a lot of time on her cell phone. Pia opened her gifts and made negative comments about almost every one of them. She opened a beautifully wrapped box with perfume from one of the guests and actually uttered out loud, "The last time I wore this, I gagged." Amber was incredibly embarrassed.

After the party, Pia wanted to go out dancing and was furious that Amber wouldn't join her on her birthday—even though she knew that a babysitter was waiting for Amber at home. Lashing out at Amber, Pia told her that she needed to work on finding new friends who didn't have children.

Suddenly, it was as if a light bulb had been switched on in a dark room. "I realized she was right," says Amber. The two women haven't spoken since that night. They gave each other a perfunctory hug before they parted but Amber couldn't wait to get home and must have looked upset.

Pia e-mailed her once after that night, to find out why Amber was so mad at her. "I explained that I wasn't mad—that I thought that she behaved badly and that I was sorry she was so unhappy with her life," says Amber. "She e-mailed back a two-page rant about what a terrible friend I had been. I read part of it, then hit 'Delete.'"

When Amber first met Pia, the two women were single and at similar points in their lives: pretty carefree with a shared, age-appropriate interest in dancing and attracting men. Although their personalities were vastly different, it didn't much matter because of the superficial nature of their relationship. When Amber got to know Pia better, she recognized her friend's fatal flaws: self-centeredness coupled with bad judgment. Pia was narcissistic, exhibitionistic, and foul-mouthed. The relationship started deteriorating as Amber began to realize she was at the short end of a one-sided friendship.

It's always hard to end friendships—even if they are toxic and one-sided. This was certainly the case for Amber, with her fierce sense of loyalty and compassion. It almost took a blow to the head for her to gain insight and admit her negative feelings about the friendship. Amber finally realized that she had little respect for her friend and didn't want her to be part of her life anymore.

"I don't wish her ill," says Amber. "But I was enabling her to be the person she was, someone who was hurtful to me and my family." Amber says she put up with Pia for so long because they had so much history, and she felt sorry for someone who had alienated virtually everyone else in her life. "I felt responsible for her," she says. "At the end of the day, when someone meets love and caring with bitterness and selfishness, a decision has to be made. It freed me up to have the courage to draw new boundaries with other relationships and end those that were becoming unhealthy," she adds.

Amber still wonders how Pia is doing. "I was about to call her last Christmas when I received a card," says Amber. "It was her handwriting—no return address. I opened the card and it read like an itemized list of the bad things going on in her life." That brought back memories of all those phone calls that never started with "Hello" but with something along the lines of "I hate my life. You'll never believe what happened to me." The card reminded Amber that she had made the right decision.

Sometimes the task of ending a friendship is so difficult that it takes more than one try. We romanticize the relationship, remember the good times, and tend to give our friends multiple chances. But personality endures, and rarely changes in the ways we would like it to. Annie, now 48 years old, told me such a story.

Annie met Liz while the two were traveling as singles in Europe. They bonded instantly. Liz wanted to visit the United States, so they kept in close touch after their trip. When Liz arrived in San Francisco about a year later, she was able to get a work permit and Annie found her some work through a friend.

"She lived in my place for months, but once she found a boyfriend, she moved out without giving me any notice," says Annie. Annie was peeved at her ungracious visitor because getting a replacement roommate wouldn't be easy or quick. "I stopped speaking to her until her mom visited and begged me to forgive her, explaining how insecure her daughter was and that she sometimes did stupid things," she says. Annie forgave her and they grew closer.

But the apartment abandonment was far from Liz's last infraction. "Over the years she did some awful things to me," says Annie. But she always succumbed to Liz's pleas for forgiveness out of compassion. She knew Liz was self-centered, unhappy, and had low self-esteem. Then Annie found out that Liz lied to her boyfriend, stopped using birth control, and got pregnant. "She was dying for a baby," says Annie. "I despised her attitude about making the decision despite her guy not being ready for fatherhood. Again, it was all about her."

Then Annie's mom died suddenly in an accident. Liz said the right things that day, but her own mom arrived for a visit while Annie was sitting shiva. "She disappeared into self-absorption when her mom arrived. I'd just lost my mom and she didn't call or pay a shiva call," says Annie, who felt that she would have liked Liz and her mom to be there for her at that time. "She never liked to share her people with me because she was too greedy."

A week later, Liz went into early labor. Her mom called Annie, who immediately called Liz. "She began to speak, but visitors arrived to see her and I could hear her delighting in the attention they gave her about possibly losing her son (he survived)," says Annie. Liz got off the phone as quickly as she could, telling Annie to call again at a more convenient time.

"She didn't call when I lost my mother, but now was acting like a princess who expected to be courted," says Annie. "We never spoke again, and I have no regrets." It's been several years since then. Annie was recently rushing to an appointment and heard her name being called. It was Liz. The two women exchanged pleasantries but Annie rushed off.

"We could have reconnected, but I chose not to. I always say, 'Close one door and another three open,'" she says. After closing that door, Annie was able to meet some healthier, more reliable friends.

Annie and Liz were friends for fifteen years before Annie realized she needed to end the relationship. She had to endure the same types of hurts over and over until it finally sunk in. Sometimes we cling to friendships that should be over because we are waiting for the "right" time. When a relationship has proven itself to be wrong for you over time, there isn't ever likely to be a good time to end it. In fact, things could get worse.

Maintaining friendships that no longer work is like having a closet cluttered with clothes of all different sizes. Some of them fit and some of them don't. Some are in style and others clearly look like they're from a bygone era. My closet is filled with clothes that are so squished together that I can barely see them. There's no room to hang new outfits I would like to add to my inventory. Admittedly, many of the pieces are just taking up space. If only I had the discipline to organize my closet, it would be a lot easier and more rewarding to get dressed each morning.

Similarly, if you are spending your time on friendships that don't fit, you are keeping yourself from developing new ones that might be more fulfilling and better fitting. There is certainly a feeling of guilt attached to getting rid of someone who needs you and depends on you—but you have to evaluate the friendship and make sure it is balanced in terms of meeting the needs of two people, not just one. There's no denying that such a decision might entail a real loss of the familiar or giving up of shared history for you, but you need to weigh the losses against all that stands to be gained.

CLOSING THE DOOR WITHOUT SLAMMING IT

It always feels awkward to end a friendship, and it's extremely difficult to find the right words, the right way, or the right time to do it. You should never break up in haste, without carefully thinking through the repercussions, unless you've been the victim of a terrible betrayal (e.g., finding your girlfriend has been having an affair with your husband or has inflicted undue psychological or physical harm on your child), in which case, you may need to act more precipitously.

Here are some thoughts to help you determine the best way to end a female friendship with grace and kindness in your own particular circumstance:

CHOOSE THE BEST MODE OF COMMUNICATION

There are at least four methods you can use to end a friendship. These include: handling it in person, online (through email or IMing), on the phone, or by snail mail. Unfortunately, none of these approaches is perfect and each one poses its own unique problems. The approach someone chooses will vary based on the nature of the friendship, the nature of the breakup, and the personalities of the people involved.

One important thing to keep in mind is that you have been very carefully preparing for this moment (unless the relationship ends in a blowup). You've thought long and hard and have made a decision that hasn't come easily. But, in most circumstances, the other person is caught off guard—if not by the decision, then by its timing.

If you are dealing with a very sensible person who isn't likely to care about the loss of the relationship, you can probably have a low-key, candid talk and it will be over. (But would you really be planning this conversation at all if you were dealing with a very sensible person?) Since the breakup is one-sided and will appear as if it is coming from left field as far as the other person is concerned, this generally won't be the case.

Face-to-face confrontations are among the most painful and difficult to execute successfully. Delivering the news in person, telling your friend that it's over and you want out, is likely to embarrass the person who is being dumped and put her in the position of feeling attacked and defensive. The same is true of phone conversations, but at least the person has the option of hanging up until she gains her composure.

A phone conversation, as opposed to an in-your-face conversation, permits some distance and also allows your friend the chance to express herself in case there is a minor misunderstanding that could possibly be cleared up when you speak. This is especially important if the relationship was a significant one that you think still holds out some hope for saving.

But in-person and phone breakups can lead to unnecessary arguments about who was right and who was wrong. It's preferable to have a no-fault split that doesn't cast blame on one person or the other—this is more likely achieved when the other person has time to recoup and isn't put on the spot. You want to avoid insulting the person unnecessarily or getting back at her verbally if she insults you. You have your own feelings about who is to blame for the breakup but it's pointless, and probably hopeless, to try to convince your friend to agree with you.

E-mail or snail mail aren't perfect options either, simply because it isn't prudent to put anything in writing that can be duplicated, forwarded to mutual friends, or could later come back to haunt you. If you do choose to take that route, you should spend a great deal of time obsessing about what to write, the precise words to use, and whether a handwritten note or e-mail is better. Remember that your friend will likely spend a great deal of time reading what you wrote, over and over again.

Sending a note, whether e-mail or snail mail, is particularly helpful if you feel very angry, are fearful that you'll lose control when you deliver the message, or if you think you'll back down from your decision when your friend is upset, either feeling hurt or acting confrontationally. Again, the important caveat about a "Dear Jane" letter: make sure that you don't write anything down that you would worry about anyone else seeing. This can be achieved by being fairly general in what you write, keeping it brief, and refraining from blaming her. The risk of an e-mail being forwarded or even distributed to a list is probably greater than that of a personal note being read by others.

PREPARE AHEAD

As you are deciding what to say and how to say it, it can be helpful to use a journal (not to be shared with anyone) to write down your feelings and vent your frustration. It is also a way to develop a brief written script to help you make sure you don't forget the one or two points you need to tell your friend.

Taking the time to compose, organize, and write your thoughts down, especially on paper, helps clarify your thinking before you blurt out something you'll later be sorry for saying. Be sure to wait until your initial anger subsides. If you are so angry or uncomfortable that you can't handle it on your own, you may want to convey the message through a trusted third party.

If you choose to deliver the message by e-mail or snail mail, don't send it immediately after you write it; wait at least until the next day when you can read it more dispassionately.

CHOOSE YOUR TIMING

If you decide to use the phone, try to avoid catching the person at work, while she is driving, during dinner, or at some other equally uncomfortable time to talk. Instead, try to figure out a time when she is likely to be relaxed and at ease. The conversation is bound to be tense without added distractions.

If possible, don't dump on your friend when she's besieged with other problems that will ease over time. For example, if she just lost a parent, try to hang on until she's recuperated a bit emotionally. It's just a matter of being considerate and not hitting someone when she is down.

BE AS HONEST AND DIRECT AS YOU CAN WITHOUT BEING HURTFUL

It is best when people can be as honest as possible in relationships. However, the way a friendship ends is likely to be remembered for a long time, so carefully consider what to say, what not

Defriending on the Internet

The rules of defriending on social media sites like Facebook, MySpace, and LinkedIn are even murkier than in real life. Before you defriend someone in cyberspace, consider carefully whether it will be worthwhile or helpful, because the consequences can come back to haunt you. Depending on the nature of your relationship, it can be as volatile as jilting a friend in real life. If the friendship was once meaningful and you change your mind after you've defriended someone, your relationship will never be the same.

Might it be easier for both of you to just let her go on sitting on your friend list? Perhaps seeing her there regularly may be painful to you, or perhaps if you are particularly distrustful of her you don't want her to have access to your personal information or profile anymore. But if neither of these cases is true, consider just learning to ignore her on your social networking site without taking the fairly confrontational action of deleting her from your friend list—because she is bound to notice. On the Internet, there's always the danger that your fingers will work more quickly than your brain.

If you decide not to defriend, consider the possibility that your former friend may still be curious about you—even to the point of "stalking" you—and may be keeping up with your life. Be aware of privacy settings and don't write things on your homepage or in messages to others that she might see and consider a personal attack on her.

to say, how much to say, and how you can get your message across so that you leave your ex-BF emotionally unscathed to the extent that it is possible.

Always start off acknowledging something positive that you both gained from the relationship. Don't be too effusive or you won't be credible. That said, try to figure out a benevolent explanation for your decision. It should be somewhat reality-based, even though you may choose to leave out unnecessary details. It's unkind to jilt someone without any explanation. Try to think about how you would feel if someone did that to you.

If you really are certain you want to end it, be clear that you are telling, not asking, and that your decision is firm for the time being. If you have already seriously considered your options, you don't want to open the door for further discussion, anger, or a confrontation—and you want to be as kind as possible because this is someone that you once cared about, confided in, and trusted—and probably vice versa.

DON'T PLAY THE BLAME GAME

This is your decision to end the relationship, so take responsibility for what you are doing. Don't use this as an opportunity to be vindictive. Instead, act like a grown-up and take ownership without assigning blame. After all, you are the decider; it's what you want, not what she wants, no matter what led you to the decision.

You don't need to heap blame upon your friend to deflect blame and guilt from yourself. Simply think of it as a no-fault breakup that happened because the relationship didn't work for the two of you. Remind your friend, and if necessary, remind yourself that rifts in female friendships are commonplace.

TELL A WHITE LIE

If your relationship is intense, it's okay to tell a little white lie. (Yes, "honesty is always best" was another myth your mother taught you!) You can tell your friend that you have some problems you need to work out privately; that you need to focus on school, your work, or family obligations; that you need time for yourself; that you need some respite from the relationship; or whatever else feels comfortable and believable to say.

"It's easy to think that friendships are going to last forever, but they sometimes end. If it happens abruptly, try to mend things so they don't end with bitterness on either side," says one woman. When people are jilted and left upset, you face a serious risk of their breaking your confidences, gossiping unfavorably about you to people you both know, or undermining you in a work setting. If you've told your once-best friend everything about you, she is in a position to write your unauthorized biography! That is why a benevolent white lie—one that might not give your friend an honest understanding of why you can't bear to have her be a part of your life any longer, but which will hopefully spare her feelings and not provoke her to lash out at you—can often be the most graceful solution.

This approach might backfire if your friend is very persistent and demands an explanation, but at least you tried.

LET IT FIZZLE

Another perfectly legitimate way to extricate yourself from a less intense friendship, especially if the contact is infrequent, is to simply let the relationship fizzle by making yourself unavailable until your friend gets the message. Ignore her e-mails, phone calls, or text messages. (Of course, this won't work if you and your former BF are used to speaking in person, on the phone, or online multiple times a day.) When you do see each other, just tell your friend that you've been preoccupied or busy with other people.

One woman and her friend were in an uncomfortable situation where they continued to see each other every day so she just kept her distance, being cordial and friendly but nothing more. Over time, the two women became more estranged and it was easier for both of them to eventually let go.

THROW HER AN ANCHOR

If your friend is in a challenging life situation—battling depression or addiction, reeling from a divorce or other loss, or recently diagnosed with a serious illness—extricating yourself from the relationship may be extraordinarily difficult because you feel guilty. You may rationalize that she needs you, has no one else, or that the timing isn't right. Or you may recognize that your friend has moved away from you and wants nothing more than to crawl under the covers.

Before you cut the cord, it might be useful to suggest other resources to your friend that can substitute for, and perhaps be even more helpful than, your friendship. There are numerous organizations that sponsor support groups and/or online forums that provide an opportunity for people to connect and share a sense of community based on similar experiences.

You might also want to confide to a third party that you feel drained by the friendship, need a break, and aren't able to provide all the support your friend needs. You can identify a spouse or other relative and make them aware of the situation so your friend has someone else available to her.

While there's no universally accepted etiquette or protocol on how to break up with a friend, if you unilaterally decide to end a friendship without leaving room for discussion, there are some precautions you can take.

PREPARING FOR THE AFTERLIFE

You need to prepare yourself psychologically for the possibility of bumping into your ex-friend somewhere: in a supermarket, at the park, at the hairdresser, at the post office, or even at a restaurant or hotel when you are on vacation. In an essay in *New York* magazine, author Amy Sohn talks about the ubiquitous fear woman have of running into an ex-best friend.

It's normal to worry about such encounters but your worries can be quelled if you are prepared to handle such a scenario should it occur. What should you do and how should you behave when you run into her? Act appropriately. This means acknowledging you know the person by saying hello, smiling, or nodding—but not engaging in a conversation or more than that. Once you are mentally prepared and have rehearsed your role, you no longer have to fear it happening.

Even if you are the decider who dumps your friend, the emotional fallout of a lost friendship shouldn't be minimized. It doesn't heal easily or quickly. Women are left singed or even scarred by their losses. Some refer to it as one of the most difficult situations they have ever been through. One woman described having panic attacks every time she saw someone wearing a coat that looked similar to that of her ex-friend. Others are obsessed with how their friend looks, what she is doing, or what she is thinking.

Breaking Up Is Hard to Do

- Think through what you will say, when, and how.
- Take responsibility for your decision rather than blaming the other person.
- Be as honest as the circumstances allow.
- Make every effort to leave the other person as emotionally whole and unscathed as possible.

When two women go from speaking ten or more times a day to silence, the sense of estrangement can be unbearable. As a result, many women hunker down to protect themselves and become socially isolated. It may shatter their self-confidence, and make them fearful of other women, or even mistrustful of relationships in general. Experiencing the disappointment of an ended friendship—which we are taught to think of as a personal failure—often makes us wonder whether we are worthy of being someone else's friend at all, and what we have to bring to the plate. Will we be able to keep other friendships over the long term?

One result is that many women make a concerted effort to find substitutes, to replace the friend that was lost. That's what happened to Meg, 25, who was tortured by a blowup with a friend. "I spent the next six months in a state of constant anxiety, obsessed about what had happened, guilty beyond belief, replaying the whole thing in my mind again and again, trying to figure out whether I was wrong or she was wrong," she says. "It gradually got better but still, three years later, it's hard to talk about it without getting upset."

Leah, 23, broke up with her girlfriend at the same time she broke up with her boyfriend. "It affected me terribly, and the two losses became integrally confused," says Leah. "To lose the two people closest to me—through what at the time felt like two acts of betrayal—was too much for me to handle." She experienced feelings of anger and sadness for almost a year after she first cut things off with her friend and says she still experiences such feelings now, although to a lesser degree. "I am still especially wistful when I think about how we had envisioned our future—two neighboring houses where our children would play together in the lot between. Letting go of that was as hard as getting dumped by my boyfriend," she says.

Give yourself the gift of time to mourn and get over the loss, but don't allow it to poison other relationships. Oddly, some women come away feeling grateful after losing a friend. They have gained a heightened awareness of how precious and how fluid female friendships are and how important it is to make them a priority in their hectic, multitasking lives. They learn that they can't take their good friends for granted. They recommit to being there for them, and to devote the time they need to keep up relationships.

"It's taught me that it's okay to love your friends as fiercely as you would a partner," says one woman. "A friend is a different kind of partner. And while not all friendships will last a lifetime, that doesn't mean that they aren't truly valuable."

CHAPTER 9

GETTING OVER THE MYTHS: LEARNING FROM LOSS

∞

"It's the friends that you can call up at 4 A.M. that matter."
—MARLENE DIETRICH

The search for perfection and permanence in any relationship is usually elusive. But when a friendship was meaningful and fulfilling, and you thought it would last a lifetime, it's difficult to accept that it's ended. This is especially true the first time it happens. The person to whom you poured out your heart and soul, told all your secrets, and with whom you forged a presumed sisterhood, is gone.

Find solace in knowing that you're not alone and that millions of women have experienced this pain. As painful and disappointing as these breakups are, they make us wiser and make our friendships much stronger and more resilient. So here are some last words of advice for dealing with these breakups:

ACCEPT THE INEVITABILITY OF CHANGE

Most friendships are bound to a specific time, place, or season. Some women characterize these relationships as having expiration dates or shelf lives, because friendships tend to run their natural course. "I realized that friendships do come and go as you get older and your interests change. So now, I simply accept that fact," says one woman.

A best friend who once had a starring role in your life may reappear once again, only this time as a cameo. "Some things and people come into your life for just a short period of time, some for a bit longer, and some for a lifetime," says another. "People come into your life for a purpose." If you sense that a friendship feels too strained for comfort, perhaps it's time to let it go. But do so with grace. The loss of one friendship makes an opening for another.

Pain after loss is normal. Recognize that you feel hurt because you lost something that was important to you. Give yourself the gift of time to mourn and heal from your loss. Think about the positives that you were able to take away and be grateful that you are no longer compelled to maintain a façade of a friendship that drifted away or turned sour. "A failed friendship isn't really a failure. It's about life changing and people moving on. Sometimes a friendship dwindles but that can be appropriate and right. It is not a failure," says another woman.

DON'T GIVE UP ON FEMALE FRIENDSHIPS

The traumatic loss of a close friend undermines a woman's self-confidence and trust. One common response is to be wary and suspicious of friendships with other women (or even relationships with men). The image of a friendless woman with a cat may not be as stereotypical as it first appears.

Whether the choice was hers or yours, it is an unsettling loss and a disappointment in terms of what the friendship was or what the friendship might have been. It leads a woman to question what she did wrong and whether she's capable of maintaining relationships. "I blamed myself for the whole thing and felt for the longest time that I wasn't worthy of a close friendship," says one woman. "When you put everything into a friendship where you feel so secure, and for no apparent reason things start to fall apart, it's hard to trust again," says another.

The ending of a friendship doesn't necessarily mean that one person or the other is at fault, that someone did something wrong, or that the friendship never had any significance or value. Even previously wonderful relationships between friends can later turn out to be a poor fit. Look at breakups as no-fault events (which they usually are) and stop blaming yourself or her. Certainly, don't give up on your other female friendships, present and future, because that would only compound your loss.

Find ways to regain control of your life. Nurture other friendships. Spend more time with family. Do things you enjoy and that give you pleasure. Don't inadvertently punish anyone, including yourself.

THINK CAREFULLY ABOUT WHETHER YOU WANT OR NEED ONE BEST FRIEND

"Sometimes we see people as we want to see them and not as they really are," says one woman. She recognized this after several years of disappointment, finally realizing that her friendship with her best friend was largely a construct of her own imagination.

It's unlikely that any one individual can meet your needs and it's more likely that you'll need friends for different reasons and seasons of your life. The same people with whom you enjoy exchanging parenting tips in a mother-child playgroup may not be the same women with whom you want to shop, share stock-tips, or talk heart-to-heart. Having just one friend with whom you are close and intimate is a big risk to take, no matter how solid the friendship.

When one young woman was dumped by her one and only friend, she was heartbroken. "I would never have a BFF again," she says emphatically. She realized that having more than one could protect her from that desperate heartbreak she had experienced.

Not every woman wants or needs a best friend. Consider whether you would prefer to surround yourself with a small number of meaningful friendships. It's important to strive for quality friendships rather than large numbers of superficial ones that aren't rewarding. "For the most part, I [now] focus on nurturing a small number of really close friendships," says another woman.

HANG ON FOR THE RIDE

Expectations of any friendship often need to be adjusted. We need to think about whether we are expecting too much or too little from friends, or whether it's a case of too much too soon. Especially with new relationships, we need to be able to communicate and establish sensible boundaries between our new friends and ourselves.

Maybe you shouldn't place all your trust in a person until you know her well over time. And perhaps, says one woman: "It isn't a good idea to tell some friends some things, no matter how long you know them." Exercising greater caution in whom you befriend and how quickly you do so can be a good thing in the end. "I'm far happier to let my friendships grow over time," says one woman.

Another woman learned that honesty isn't always the best policy. Some friendships fracture because one or both friends are too judgmental and outspoken. "I was very vocal with my friend and told her exactly what I thought of a situation, because I didn't want to see her hurt. I now realize that I can't control someone else's decisions about whom they want in their life. I just need to be supportive and, if it doesn't work out, be there when she needs me. It [the friendship] definitely taught me to bite my tongue."

Some friendships tolerate long breaks; others require constant contact. It's always useful when two friends are on the same wavelength, or at least understand what to expect. "My other friends understand that we can go for long periods without communicating and still be friends," says another. "I've learned about the kind of friend I am and the kind of friends I want to surround myself with."

Every friend has her individual quirks and to maintain relationships you may need to simply be more tolerant and forgiving. "I realize now that no relationship is immune to problems," says a woman. "I try to focus on making new friends and strengthening the friendships I have—trying not to be judgmental and to be more accepting of people's flaws," says another. "If I judged everyone by their flaws, I wouldn't have any friends." Close friends need to be able to let each other know how they are feeling and give each other the opportunity to make corrections in the friendship as they go along.

Ultimately, Amanda, 25, decided that she was no longer willing to tolerate a friend who wasn't dependable. When Amanda met Linda, she felt an automatic click, like they instantly understood each other. "She was sweet and understanding, and we shared a lot of things and interests," says Amanda. "She started spending so much time with her boyfriend that she would constantly flake out of plans and make up shady excuses instead of being up-front." It happened so often over such a long period of time that Amanda eventually distanced herself from Linda. "I was really upset; it felt like a betrayal as it was happening," she says.

Amanda concluded that just clicking with someone isn't good enough. "Reliability, trustworthiness, and dependability are important as well," she says. "When this girl was around, she was great. It's just that she wasn't around most of the time and couldn't be depended on.

YOUR WOMEN FRIENDS ARE AS
IMPORTANT AS THE MEN IN YOUR LIFE

We need to delicately balance the males and females in our life in a way that works. An all too common scenario, as described by Donna (who was suddenly ditched when her friend Gayle met a dashing globetrotter) is that of a best friend who suddenly falls head-over-heels in love with a man and totally abandons the woman whose shoulders she cried upon before she found him. It's not cool, and it is downright rude to repeatedly cancel dates with female friends to accommodate a man.

Another sure relationship killer is the friend who comes on to the man (or woman) who is her friend's romantic interest. Sadly, some women recognize that they need to be very cautious with friends who are jealous of them. "I don't think women are loyal to other women the way I see men being loyal to one another," says one woman scorned. "Women are more likely to stab each other in the back, especially for a guy. My mother always told me, 'Don't tell your girlfriends who you like.' I have learned this lesson several times . . . no matter how close I am to my girlfriends, I don't tell them my true feelings about a guy unless I'm already dating him."

"I'm very cautious about introducing my new boyfriend to my friends," says another woman. "I'm reluctant to share my feelings about my boyfriend if my girlfriend doesn't have a significant other." Yet these women are a minority. For most women, the takeaway message is that many male-female relationships—and even marriages—don't last forever either (and even when they do, aren't always totally fulfilling). Thus, women need to realize the significance of maintaining intimate relationships with female friend regardless of their relationships with men. "I will never again push my friends aside for a guy," says one woman.

Women can talk to each other about hopes and dreams that most men can never understand. "I have many childhood friendships that have lasted for years and a guy I know for two weeks shouldn't come between that," says another. If your boyfriend is unable to tolerate and get along with your female friends, that should raise a red flag of its own.

A caveat: taken to an extreme, some woman don't recognize that one of the reasons why they are making unrealistic demands of their female friends is because they are sublimating their needs for romantic companionship. "It made me realize that I wasn't exploring my need for male relationships, and instead was living with unrequited feelings that were destructive to my friendships," says one such woman.

CHOOSE FRIENDS WISELY

Making meaningful and satisfying friendships requires wisdom and experience. From loss often comes a better knowledge of what we are attracted to and what we need to stay away from. The lost friendship becomes a marker by which women can compare and judge subsequent friendships. It reminds us to be selective and alerts us to red flags when they appear.

"I don't like to make friends with women that are very close-minded, because that's how I view the followers of the religion that I left," says one. Another says that she stays clear of women who play the "victim role." Even the experience of having a relationship with someone who is habitually late can make the individual seek out someone who is habitually on time. Another woman recognized that there wasn't any room on her dance card for relationships that were relegated to "phone and text" only. She was interested in building friendships with women who could give her "face time." Another made the conscious decision to seek out friends "who are positive and upbeat." Yet another sought out "people who are physically active with a passion for at least one thing in life."

Because friendship comes in so many flavors, you need to be open to people who don't immediately fit your stereotype of someone who looks best-friend-worthy. "I've learned that you should not judge people or choose your friends only based on commonalities," says one woman. "You should learn to allow differences and love people for who they are."

Many women feel that they regretted becoming enablers for friends who abused drugs or alcohol or got into trouble with the law—and refused to accept help. For them, these situations eventually became friendship killers so they became increasingly cautious about making the same mistakes. "I decided to rethink the people I hang around with and what kind of influence they would have on me. One bad night with my friend who was an abuser scarred me for life," she says.

One woman described her close friend as extremely controlling. Apparently, both felt comfortable with the relationship until the submissive one "attained more balance in her life" and became more secure and assertive. When that happened, her friend's efforts to control their relationship turned into seething anger that destroyed it.

Unfortunately, you can't hope to redesign a friend or radically change her personality. When it comes to people, women or men, character endures. "It's like that old saying about choosing a boyfriend based on how he treats a waiter in a restaurant," says one woman. "I saw how this person treated other friends—many times, she slept with someone a friend was involved with or interested in—and she tended to flip out on people when she got angry. I just thought because we were so close and had shared so much it would never come around to me. Now I know better."

DON'T BECOME A REPEAT OFFENDER

Feeling totally gun-shy about making friendships after that one? It's not surprising but there are ways you can protect and cushion yourself from people who will cause you continual pain. Have you noticed a pattern in your relationships? Are you consistently attracted to people who use and disappoint you? Are your relationships unbalanced or one-sided? Do you find yourself attracted to people who have insatiable needs, or who are selfish in terms of their demands of your time and understanding? Are you prone to befriending users and takers? Have you been dumped too many times? Remind yourself to look out for, avoid, and downgrade toxic relationships.

Friendless: Common Problems of Repeat Offenders

• **Trouble prospecting.** You may be making bad choices when you choose potential friends. The odds are better that a friendship will "stick" when two people have a common thread, perhaps a shared interest (e.g., hobby or membership in a club or gym) or shared circumstances (e.g., neighbors or coworkers). Think about the people with whom you are trying to connect and whether there is any natural glue that could keep the friendship going. Think out of the box as well: resist the temptation to stereotype who looks like she would be a good friend and who doesn't. You may be eliminating a potential friend without giving her a chance. For example, someone who looks shallow may have more depth to her than you think.

• **Trouble bonding.** Some people say they simply don't have a "knack" for making friends. In some cases, they are coming on too heavy, too soon. Friendships unfold gradually as women share intimacies with one another—this takes time. You need to be willing to let your friends know the real you, but you don't want to spill your guts out the first time you're out to lunch.

• **Something else.** There may be something off-putting about your behavior. Is there someone (perhaps, a family member) whom you trust—and who knows you well—who might tell you what it is? If not, it might be worthwhile to seek advice from a counselor.

On the other hand, you may learn that the toxicity in the relationship is your doing rather than your friend's. Some women commented that a good friend lets you know when you seem to be veering off course. Are your problems and neediness too much to handle, even for the best of friends? "I'm very careful now not to burden my friends unduly with my problems unless I just can't bear to keep it inside," says one woman. "I try to take those feelings to a therapist," she added.

One woman said she's learned that she can't and doesn't want to fix all of her friends' problems. She stays away from too much "drama" in a relationship. "I feel like I have the power to choose my friends, not have them choose me; I deserve better," says another. Similarily, another says: "I now choose people who have resolved their lifelong issues, or who are in control of their demons. No gossip. Solid people only. With a major sense of humor."

To be without close female friends can be extremely isolating and lonely. If you are in this situation, it's always difficult to pinpoint the precise reason(s) for your dilemma.

Recognition of this problem is, of course, the first step in solving it. If having no friendships or having toxic friendships is a persistent pattern that you can't avoid on your own, speak to a counselor or other mental health professional who can help you determine why you are doing this to yourself and how you can stop. If you are still in high school or college, you may be able to get help from someone in the school counseling office.

REBOOT

I'm busy. You're busy. Everyone's busy, but friendships take time. If you are pressed for time, find ways to do things with friends that you normally do alone—exercise, shopping, eating lunch. With the availability of the Internet and low-cost or no-cost long-distance phone calls, no matter how far away your friends are, there really is no excuse for losing touch with the ones who really count. Without some type of contact, friendships are memories without currency.

Taking Advantage of Technology

The average young person who is connected to digital technology has 94 numbers on her cell phone, 78 people on her instant messenger list and 86 friends in her social networking community. There is no reason why you can't nurture friendships over the miles or over oceans.

The bottom line: call her, text her, write her, or e-mail her and set up a time to meet before too much time elapses, even if it is just for coffee. Think of it as an investment in your physical and emotional well-being.

CHAPTER 10

MOVING FORWARD

"I have a chosen family of friends."

—GLORIA STEINEM

After you've inventoried the friends you have, assessed the quality of those relationships, and determined what you need to do to purge yourself of relationships that are emotionally draining and destructive, you may feel a nagging sense of emptiness. To return to the cluttered closet analogy, it's that same feeling you're left with after you finally get around to organizing and disposing of the clothes you're tired of or that no longer fit. There's a lot more room, but it feels like you suddenly have nothing to wear. The actual holes in your wardrobe haven't changed; they've just become more obvious.

When you lose a good friend, for whatever reason, it's common to find yourself in the doldrums. Because most women juggle multiple roles and lead busy lifestyles, their days and evenings filled with responsibilities and activities, they may not even feel the impact of the loss right away. Instead, they experience a gnawing feeling that something is missing and don't know precisely why they feel that way.

After a significant loss, even when surrounded by people, you are likely to miss the intimacy of a close friendship that felt easy and familiar. In a quiet moment, you feel like phoning someone— to complain about the promotion you got passed over for at work, or the argument you had with the receptionist in the gynecologist's office—and you can't think of whom to call. Or you may miss her regular calls, calls about nothing, but nevertheless reassuring in terms of their regularity and playfulness. A wave of loneliness comes over you. "For weeks or even months, I would look at my cell phone," says one woman. "It was so weird not having it ring all the time, just to talk about nonsense or things that made us laugh, especially gossip. I would drive up to my house, past her house, and try not to look that way—sort of trying to make-believe she didn't exist."

This situation has variously been described as a "friendship deficit" or "friendship shortage." It isn't that you don't have any friends, but you don't have enough of the right kind of friends—women to whom you feel very close. There's no one with whom to share your joys, your sorrows, or your day-to-day hassles and frustrations.

Now the good news: if you are bemoaning a friendship deficit, that awareness should motivate you to replenish your inventory. And now you have the time and space you need to develop friendships of the very best kind.

THE CASE FOR REPLENISHING THE STOCK

A number of research studies suggest friendships are essential to good health and longevity. Loneliness and lack of social supports are linked to an increased risk of heart disease, viral infections, and cancer as well as to higher mortality rates. One popular theory is that friendships serve as a buffer against stress.

Not only do friendships enhance our health, they bolster our confidence and self-esteem. They also serve as an antidote to depression and loneliness and help ward off psychosomatic illness.

As part of its Chain of Confidence campaign to promote self-confidence through female friendship, Tupperware, the plastic

Rx for Better Health: Friendship

According to a research team at the University of California, Los Angeles (UCLA), social isolation is linked to gene alterations that drive inflammation, the first response of the immune system. In a study funded in part by the National Institutes of Health (NIH), the researchers found that "the biological impact of social isolation reaches down into some of our most basic internal processes, the activity of our genes."

"We found that changes in immune cell gene expression were specifically linked to the subjective experience of social distance," said said Steve Cole, MD, of the UCLA Cousins Center for Psychoneuroimmunology In other words, people in the study who felt more closely connected to other people had stronger immune systems. "The differences we observed were independent of other known risk factors, such as health, age, weight, and medication use. The changes were even independent of the objective size of a person's social network. We found that what counts at the level of gene expression is not how many people you know, it's how many you feel really close to over time."

Another study confirms that good friendships and a good number of them are associated with better health, a combination of the two being the best prescription of all. The study of four thousand people in California showed that survival was linked to the size of one's social circle. Women with fewer than six friendships had significantly higher rates of coronary artery disease, obesity, diabetes, high blood pressure and depression, and were at two and half times greater risk of death over the course of the study.

A study that followed 1,500 Australians for more than a decade found that a network of good friends was more important than close family ties in conferring longevity, irrespective of other profound changes (such as death of spouse or relocation of family) in an individual's life. In addition to helping ward off depression and decreasing stress, close friendships can play a role in discouraging unhealthy behaviors (such as smoking or drinking too much).

container company, commissioned a study that polled over five hundred women across the country, ages eighteen and older. The survey results revealed that 85% believed that a supportive network of friends is more vital to self-confidence than good looks.

Friendship and Self-Confidence

Findings of the Chain of Confidence poll:

- 88% of women would rather give up shopping for a year than give up their female friends for a year.
- 89% of women feel that they are able to succeed after hearing how a friend overcame a challenge to reach her goal.
- 67% of women say they feel more confident when they are able to help someone solve a problem.
- 63% of women feel more confident when they relate better with their peers.

It isn't easy going from that initial friendly glance to making a true friend. How many times have you wanted to befriend someone and felt uncertain about how to go about it?

MAKING FRIENDS

When you're a kid, making friends is easy. There's a new friend to be found wherever you turn: at school, next door, or on the playground. But once you graduate high school or college, making friends doesn't come as easily, and women need to be more proactive. To make new friends, you need to actively engage with other women. For some people, this comes naturally. For others, especially if you tend to be shy, the idea of finding and making new friendships can be daunting.

Moving Forward

I tend to be shy, so I challenged myself to experience the discomfort of signing up for a Scrabble course at my local library without knowing anyone who would be there. I enjoy playing whenever I can muster up a partner. Although I am nowhere near the level of a tournament Scrabble player, I play well enough that no one I know likes to play with me. I was hoping I could find a compatible player at the library on that Thursday afternoon.

When I entered the meeting room off the main section of the library, I momentarily worried that I would wind up being the only person in the room sitting at a table by myself. Intellectually, I knew I would probably connect with someone; but viscerally, for those few seconds, it was chilling to think about when and how that would transpire.

I took a seat across from an attractive woman who smiled at me. After that, the rest of the interaction flowed. I realized that she had taken that proverbial first step. A simple smile, a warm welcome, or a sincere expression of interest in another person are little steps that lay the foundation for friendships.

Depending on your age or stage in life, you can find fertile fields for cultivating friendships at school, at work, at the gym, volunteering at a community organization, attending an event in the local library, or shopping at a supermarket picking out tomatoes. While initially we don't seem like we are cut from the same cloth, Donna, my hairstylist for the last decade, has turned into one of my closest friends. Each of these environments offers opportunities if you leave yourself open to them. Befriending usually starts with that smile and a "pick-up line" that defines some commonality between you and another person. For example:

In school: *Are you in my intro psych class on Thursday afternoons?*

In the library: *Don't I recall seeing you at the library last Friday?*

In the grocery store: *Do you take the same train as I do in the morning?*

At your child's school: *My daughter is really excited about the class trip next week; is yours?*

At the gym: *This patch of rainy weather is really getting to me. How about you?*

At the party: *I love your purse. Where did you find it?*

At the PTA meeting: *Was your son in my son's third-grade class?*

At work: *Let's go to lunch so I can hear more about your trip to Ireland. I've always wanted to go there.*

At the Scrabble course: *Have you been playing Scrabble for a long time?*

Some women desperately want to make friends but are held back by their own anxiety. "I don't have any female friends," one woman says. "I say 'yes' to plans and then start panicking about what to do, say, and wear, and ultimately think of an excuse so I don't have to go. I suffer from severe anxiety and it really cripples my ability to trust."

If you feel like you are always being evaluated by others and it's standing in the way of your friendships, you may have a treatable condition called social anxiety. The National Institute of Mental Health describes some of the hallmark symptoms. (See box on facing page.)

Thinking that they are merely shy, some women with social anxiety go undiagnosed and untreated for years, unable to sustain relationships, yet social anxiety is eminently treatable.

> ## More than Shy: Could It Be Social Anxiety?
>
> - Anxiety being around other people
> - Feeling self-conscious in front of other people, and worrying about how you will act
> - Being afraid of being embarrassed in front of other people
> - Being afraid that other people will judge you
> - Worrying for days or weeks before an event where other people will be
> - Staying away from places where there are other people
> - Having a hard time making friends and keeping friends
> - Having physical symptoms when you are with other people, such as blushing, heavy sweating, trembling, nausea, or having a hard time talking

FRIENDS AT SCHOOL

Clearly, adolescence and young adulthood are a prime time not only to hone your skills in making and keeping friends but also to make what may turn out to be long-lasting friendships. Never again does someone have as many choices and the advantage of proximity. During elementary school, middle school, high school, and especially the college years, women are surrounded by same-age peers, who are at a similar stage in their lives sharing many of the same experiences.

Social media like MySpace and Facebook are facilitating college friendships. For example, incoming college freshmen can identify and connect with their peers prior to leaving home. Using IM or e-mail, roomies-to-be can introduce themselves and learn about each other before they come face-to-face (with cell phone cameras, webcams, or uploaded pictures on Facebook—allowing them to even see one another online). Once on campus, students can identify and connect with others in campus organizations or groups, or with students in their classrooms or dorms.

If you are still in school or are a mom of someone in school, the message is simple: take advantage of these years as a unique opportunity to cultivate friendships and, afterwards, hang on to the ones that are satisfying. They are valuable investments in your social future.

The Economics of Friendship

A study in the *Journal of Socio-Economics* suggests that friends are more important than money when it comes to achieving happiness. Using "micro-economic life satisfaction equations" and the "shadow pricing method" (methodologies more commonly used in economics), Dr. Nattavudh Powdthavee of the University of London's Institute of Education found that increased interactions with friends and relatives resulted in an added value of £85,000 (or about $127,000) a year in life satisfaction. Ironically, increases in actual income bought very little added happiness.

Since nurturing relationships and careers both take time and effort, the research suggests that career-driven individuals who work excessive hours at the expense of their social relationships may be putting their eggs in the wrong basket if they are searching for true happiness.

FRIENDS AT WORK

The adage "never mix work with friendship" has become relatively obsolete. As more women are joining the workforce and spending more hours at work, the workplace (whether it is an office, a retail shop, a factory, or a virtual office) has become a fertile meeting ground for making female friendships. Your friends at work share their passions and understand your ambitions. They make the daily grind more pleasurable and may even be help you advance in your career. If you are fortunate, work friends become plain old friends.

As I think back, some of my longest and closest relationships after college are the ones I made with women I met in the course of my work, either directly in my office setting or more peripherally as colleagues in my profession. When I first joined the National Institute of Mental Health (NIMH), I shared a space with a woman named Risa, who became a best friend. The same thing happened at my next job when I met Linda. These women have all continued to be friends, both personally and professionally, as the years have passed. As a freelance writer, I've developed close bonds with other writers and editors I first met online and later met in person. There are even some people that I've never met who live in far-flung places that I still consider friends. I know that the next time I travel to Atlanta, there will be at least one room waiting for me, that of a friend.

One cautionary note on workplace friendships: Women are often worried about getting involved with workplace acquaintances that might later betray them. Yes, this is a situation that calls for some extra caution. While friendships at work generally "work," they can sour quickly when two people are at different levels of responsibility, particularly if one is supervising the other; if the two are coworkers, and one of them isn't doing her share of the work; or if two colleagues are very competitive.

At the same time, taking a calculated (and small) risk to get to know someone at work is usually rewarding. A Gallup poll showed that employees with best friends at work not only are happier, but also more productive. Women help us understand and anchor our feelings, expand our networks, learn nuts and bolts, and generally enable us to do a better job. Of course, you need to be certain that the individual you are befriending is truly someone you can trust—which can only be determined with time and experience.

MARRIED AND PARTNERED FRIENDS

It is often far more challenging for women to maintain female friendships when they are coupled than when they are single. Issues crop up about how to balance single friends with a married life and how to make a third person (your friend) feel welcome with a couple. The degree of a woman's self-sufficiency and the possessiveness of her spouse or partner often dictate the nature and depth of her female friendships.

Sometimes, women forsake their friendships in favor of their marriage, only to later feel sorry about it. Abby, 70 years old, shared her late-in-life experience. Prior to meeting Barbara about two years ago, Abby and her husband were "glued together." After the two women met and began spending time together, Abby realized how much she missed female companionship. "To this day, I believe she was the best friend I ever had in my life," says Abby.

One day Abby came home from a movie and dinner with Barbara just before midnight and her husband was waiting up for her, quite incensed at the hour. "He said he didn't like me spending so much time with my friend and that it wasn't 'normal.' It upset me very much, and I told Barbara how he felt," says Abby. After that discussion, the two women began to see less and less of each other.

"Our friendship was never the same," says Abby. Her husband was retired, had few interests of his own, and was extremely possessive, making it extraordinarily difficult for Abby to make or maintain female friendships. She was afraid to question his demands, and because of his anger, simply acquiesced, giving up on meeting her own needs.

Sometimes, the loss of friendships is more insidious and just seems to sneak up on a woman. A woman more than thirty years younger than Abby also gave up many of her close friendships when she got married because she chose to devote time and energy to her husband and growing family. Their social relationships as a couple were exclusively with couples her husband introduced her to through his work. There was no time for her to see her old friends or make new ones. Now she says that she is trying to "pick up the pieces" of female friendships that she let fall by the wayside.

Because of the importance of friendships and because married couples or committed partners benefit from spending time apart, it's important to find ways to balance the roles of partner and friend. While you can control your own behavior, it's harder to crack the personality of a spouse or partner. In an extreme case like Abby's, it might be worthwhile to consult a counselor or mental health professional to work through problems of jealousy and possessiveness that interfere with friendship.

MOTHER FRIENDS

Having infants or young children can be isolating due to the intense demands of mothering, but children provide an easy entrée for connections to other mothers at the park, on the playground, at the library or at the gym. It is estimated that more than four million parents attend parent/child playgroups on a weekly basis.

Activities for parents and kids include playgroups, mornings in the park, and special Moms & Tots events. Single moms can join organizations like Parents Without Partners to meet friends in similar circumstances. It's important to recognize that even mommies need friendship and support—and that the roles of mother and friend aren't incompatible. In fact, they can be synergistic if you play them right!

Playgrounds for Young Moms

An organization called Mommy & Me maintains an online database of playgroups for parents and children to interact with each other while they meet other parents facing similar challenges.

Mothers & More is a non-profit organization dedicated to improving the lives of mothers through support, education, and advocacy. There are currently 2,170 chapters in 34 states, accessible through an online searchable database. The organization provides opportunities for moms to socialize and connect both online and in person. For example, the Rochester chapter of Mothers & More hosts twice-monthly meetings for grown-up conversation, members-only on line chats, meal delivery for mothers who are sick, a monthly mom's night out, and special interest clubs (including crafts, scrapping, and a book club).

There are also many online forums where mothers can connect during the day (or the wee hours of the night) to share experiences and get advice. While most women no longer live with large extended families, having access to the Internet makes parenting far less isolating than it might otherwise be.

INTERGENERATIONAL FRIENDSHIPS

One less obvious way to replenish your stock of friends is to look for people older and younger than yourself with whom you share something in common. No matter which side of the equation you're on, intergenerational friendships offer pluses for both people.

In the introduction to this book, I briefly mentioned my longest relationship, which happens to be intergenerational. I met Dr. Rita Dunn when I was just eleven years old. She was a kindergarten teacher and I was her class monitor. I stood at the end of the line as she took her little ones to the playground, and I helped pick up their blocks and clean the messy jars of finger paint after play period. I loved the time I spent with her. She was beautifully attired, stunningly attractive, and had a knack for making an awkward preteen feel special.

Also the school drama coach, my older friend coaxed me to try out for the role of Ado Annie in *Oklahoma!*—and ultimately gave me the part. I never could imagine another circumstance under which such a shy young girl would ever find the self-confidence to appear center stage and belt out, "I Can't Say No." She told me I could do it and I did. In the audience, my startled parents beamed with pride. From time to time, I still hum the lyrics in the shower and look back at the cast photos in my closet.

Over the years—through junior high school, high school, and college—my favorite teacher sent me lovely handwritten notes and gifts, and I kept her up-to-date about the changes in my life. She invited me to her home and introduced me to her family. When she became a college teacher, I took a graduate education course with her. When I wrote my dissertation, she was by then a full professor and graciously served as one of the advisors on my doctoral committee.

Even during the decade when we lived in different states, I in Maryland and she in New York, we found ways to talk and get together. When I was poised to remarry after my divorce, I asked my mentor how I would know when and if I found Mr. Right. "When you find him, you won't need to ask," she counseled wisely with her voice of experience. It was wonderful to have someone to turn to who was so possessed of wisdom and cared about my success.

Without even realizing when the change occurred, "Dr. Dunn" became my dear friend "Rita" and the age gap between us disappeared. Ironically, I live not more than ten miles from her home, so we go to the theater together (we even saw a revival of *Oklahoma!* on Broadway), celebrate birthday lunches whenever we can, and share dinners with our spouses. I realize how special this friendship is. Without her, I would not be the person I have become. And I know she takes great pride in that as well.

In a similar vein, I read a quirky article in *The Charlotte Observer* that told a story about an intergenerational friendship with an unusual beginning. Five years ago, a then 17-year-old high school student named Millie received a rambling email from someone she didn't know. It stated that Harriet and Esther and Tubby were "doing great in a nursing home."

Perplexed by the message, Millie returned the e-mail to its sender. She soon learned that the email she received was sent, by mistake, by a retired farmer named Bonnie who lived in South Dakota. Yes, it was one of those emails that got lost in cyberspace and wound up in the wrong mailbox—maybe it was providential— but it started a dialogue between two unlikely friends that you might see as an Odd Couple.

This awkward beginning resulted in a close friendship that has lasted for more than five rather eventful years, as young Millie finished four years of college and became an art teacher, and Bonnie's husband passed away. The two women are fifty-five years apart in age; Bonnie is childless and old enough to be Millie's grandmother. But as sometimes happens with friendships, the two clicked and found that there was much to share between them. They even planned to meet in person.

One woman told me that her most successful relationships were with friends, both male and female, who were almost a decade older than her. "Their wisdom and maturity is something I value," she says. When she expressed her opinions or sought advice from these older friends, she felt that they were more genuine, responsive, and sensible than most of her peers. They also had more time to devote to friendships. In turn, her older friends must have been thrilled with the energy and openness that she brought to their lives. When the relationship works, it doesn't take much time for two good friends to become completely unaware.of the years between them.

There probably is a larger lesson that women can learn from friendships like these. All of your friends don't have to be "just like you." When we first meet someone, we are often put off by differences between us, whether it is age, race, ethnicity, or lifestyle. But if you are open to people and cast a wider net, you may find new friendships in unlikely places.

Nostalgia as an Antidote to Loneliness

A study published in *Psychological Science* (November 2008) suggests one instinctive response to feelings of loneliness and isolation is nostalgia. In four different studies, psychologists at the University of Southampton and Sun Yat-Sen University in Guangzhou, China looked at people from various walks of life, including schoolchildren, college students, and factory workers. They found that lonely people used nostalgia as a coping mechanism, drawing upon their sentimental memories of the past. The more lonely people were, the more nostalgic they tended to become as a way of increasing their self-perceived feeling of social support.

"Our findings show that nostalgia is a psychological resource that protects and fosters mental health," says Dr. Tim Wildschut of the University of Southampton. "It strengthens feelings of social connectedness and belongingness, partially improving the harmful repercussions of loneliness. The past, when appropriately harnessed, can strengthen psychological resistance to the vicissitudes of life."

One implication of these research findings: If your current situation doesn't lend itself to making new friends or connecting with the ones you already have, take a brief trip down memory lane and relive the peaks of your past friendships. Then, resurface and find ways to have face-to-face contact.

If you smile when you look at old photographs of friends or have an older mother or grandmother who gets tremendous joy from telling you stories about the pictures of friends in her high school yearbook, then you've had a chance to observe this phenomenon up close.

FINDING YOUR SISTERHOOD

Whether you are a caregiver, recent widow, breast-cancer survivor, newly diagnosed with another chronic disease, divorced, gay, in recovery, or a victim of domestic violence, there may be times when you feel like you are alone—the only one in your situation. You may even feel that you don't have the energy for female friendships or won't be accepted by other women.

To the contrary, there is a sisterhood of women willing to embrace you, to hold your hand on your journey, and to offer you their friendship. You can contact your local library, religious institution, or hospital to find formal support groups. In addition, you may be fortunate enough to develop long-term friendships with women who have walked in your shoes.

When we face life's most difficult challenges, there is a natural tendency to hunker down and become isolated. You need to guard against that and allow yourself to befriend and to be befriended. There are also many online chat rooms and support groups that can help you feel less alone, making your burdens feel lighter.

> ### Recent Novels about
> ### Female Friendships
>
> In addition to the growing number of non-fiction books about female friendships, recently there has been a spate of terrific novels that tell the stories of sisterhoods of women who come together for support and friendship. They inspire us to think about our friendships and compare them to the ones we read about. Some of my favorites include:
>
> * *The Wednesday Sisters*, Meg Waite Clayton (2008)
> * *The Professors' Wives' Club*, Joanne Rendell (2008)
> * *Friday Nights*, Joanna Trollope (2008)
> * *The Friday Night Knitting Club*, Kate Jacobs (2008)

FINDING FRIENDS BY LOOKING TO THE PAST

With all the advances in communications technology, it's becoming easier to find that best friend from high school whom you haven't heard from for ages and rekindle friendships from the past. You can Google her, search for her on a reunion site like Classmates.com or Reunions.com, or perhaps find her on one of the popular social networking sites like MySpace or Facebook. Because school friendships are built upon common experiences—family, neighborhood, social and academic ties—these friendships remind us of our roots and the people we once were.

Last year, Kendall, 38, got a note on Classmates.com from an old friend from junior and senior high school. The two women hadn't spoken to each other in nineteen years. Her friend reached her by e-mail and they reconnected even though they lived almost a thousand miles away from each other. "I went to visit her in

Florida, which was a great decision," says Kendall. "Now we stay in touch via phone or e-mail. It's wonderful."

Every attempt to reclaim an old friendship doesn't turn out as well as Kendall's did, but many do, and there isn't much to lose by giving it a try.

SIX DEGREES: MAKING FRIENDS OF FRIENDS INTO YOUR FRIENDS

Another approach to making new friends is when you make a new acquaintance to try to figure out what you have in common or whether you know any of the same people.

Psychologist Stanley Milgram conducted a landmark experiment at Harvard University in the 1960s that looked at the "small world phenomenon." Using snail mail correspondence, Milgram asked his study participants to forward an information packet about the study to the person they knew—who was mostly likely to know the person ultimately targeted to receive the correspondence. Although the majority of the mailings never reached their destination, among those that did, the average length of the social path from the first person to the target recipient was 5.5 or 6 people. Based on this research, others later coined this phenomenon the "six degrees of separation" between people.

One very practical take-home message from this research: When you are in a classroom or at a cocktail party, conference, or other social event where you don't know anyone, it's always fun to try to figure out who or what you have in common. For example, by asking a few questions about where the person was raised or where she went to school, you may find the link. With any degree of luck, you may be able to strike up a new friendship based on shared history, values, interests, or friendships.

More recently, author Malcolm Gladwell wrote in *The Tipping Point* about the "funneling" that underlies the small world phenomenon. Gladwell pointed out that some people serve as social

Buried Treasure: 8 Tips for Finding a Long-Lost Friend

- Try finding the person using Google by putting her first name and last name in quotes.

- See what comes up. If you know the city and/or state where she lives or last lived, you can refine the search by putting that after her name in quotes.

- Check out groups from your high school or college on social networking sites like Facebook or MySpace.

- Search for former classmates on sites like Reunion.com or Classmates.com—or e-mail or phone the alumni office of your school.

- Let your fingers do the walking—use the white pages directory on switchboard.com.

- No luck finding her in a directory? Are her parents or other relatives findable? Chances are they may still live in the same town she did. Try finding their phone numbers or e-mail addresses.

- If you don't know any relatives, you could try the friend-of-a-friend route. Do you know someone who knew her that you are still in touch with and who may be easier to find?

- Any clue to the kind of work she is doing? Perhaps, you can find her through LinkedIn, a professional association, or the human resources office of her former place of employment.

Even better than digging: If you develop a blog or personal website, your old friends may come out of the woodwork looking for you. I was so delighted to hear from some of my childhood friends who serendipitously found me when I started to blog about friendship.

connectors. These individuals have large networks of friends and a talent for bringing otherwise loosely connected people together. It's nice to know someone like that because by virtue of your friendship with a connector, you are likely to develop connections with some of their friends and social contacts.

The practice of making friends of your friends' friends can be tricky; you may inadvertently offend your original friend. Looked at through one lens, "friend poaching" or "social poaching" (as it is nicknamed) can be viewed as the ultimate betrayal, akin to "friend-napping." Through another, it can be seen as a reasonable way of networking or making new friends through vetted introductions.

The key is to think about the consequences of what you are doing, to make sure it isn't done behind your friend's back, and to try to make efforts to be inclusive rather than exclusive.

"Our Mutual Friend," a 2004 essay by Lucinda Rosenfeld in *New York* magazine, expressed the jealousy and hurt the author experienced after she had been poached. When she learned that her two friends were planning a ski trip together—without her—she felt excluded (even though she had no interest in skiing). It harked back to the days of junior high school.

I've been poached, too. I had two close friends, let's call them Marcie and Hayley, whom I decided to introduce to one another. I knew they would instantly click because they had so much in common: neither worked outside the home, both loved competitive tennis, and had two kids around the same ages. It was a good hunch because they soon became best friends with each other as I drifted into the background.

Admittedly, the first time I bumped into them at Starbucks having coffee without me, I felt a bit strange and awkward, even hurt, but as soon as I regrouped mentally I realized that I didn't have as much time or motivation to spend with either one of them as they did with each other. Now we get together as a threesome occasionally. Rosenfeld also found that being poached could be a blessing in disguise. Prior to the treachery, she had found herself in the unpleasant role of constantly ministering to one of the women who was needy and always crying on her shoulder. It gave her a way out.

With the booming popularity of social network sites like Facebook, MySpace, and LinkedIn, the ethics and etiquette of friend poaching may be turning upside down. In cyberspace, becoming a friend of a cyber-friend is not only socially acceptable, but is actually one of the raisons d'être of participation.

Being poached offline isn't necessarily a bad thing, either. Because friendships change over time, a friendship that is "stolen" may have long been gone. It may offer the poachee an opportunity to change, take a break from, or get rid of a friendship that was draining, all-consuming, or toxic in other ways.

For this reason, don't feel guilty about poaching. Unlike family or marriage, friendships have no blood or legal ties; the good ones are totally voluntary relationships that enhance our lives. Feel guilty? Remember that your new friend has the free will to add, subtract, or realign her friendships.

One other caveat: friend poaching is unacceptable, and maybe even pathological, when an individual consistently tries to derail friendships and hurt people around her.

PREVENTING UNNECESSARY LOSSES

Given the fluidity of our lives, it is often challenging to hang on to female friends, no matter how long or how well two friends are connected. A relationship is at risk if two people lose the common ground between them, no longer being in the same place at the same time or sharing the same circle of intimates.

The past two generations of women have become more mobile, picking up and leaving the cities and towns where they were born for educational, career, and social opportunities. These relocations and other life transitions challenge women to find ways to add continuity to their relationships.

The Concept of Triadic Closure

Now researchers at Harvard and UCLA are using the Facebook social utility to learn more about triadic closure, or how friends become friends of friends. More than a century ago, a sociologist named Georg Simmel first described the concept of triadic closure, but there have been few empirical studies on the topic.

Using Facebook as a laboratory, social scientists hope to better understand how friends befriend their friends' friends—which one day may shed light on the exclusionary social cliques that draw circles keeping some people in and others out. Given the importance of friendship in our lives, used well, Facebook and other such social networking sites could potentially yield important information on how to build and sustain healthy relationships.

If best friends live across the country, they can plan a weekend getaway on one coast, the other, or somewhere in-between. If a best friend at work is retiring, she can make arrangements to see former colleague, regularly outside the office. If she's a young mother, she can make time to get away for an evening or afternoon movie with her single friend.

Emily told me about her friend Robin, who sounded like a poster child for keeping connections and maintaining friendships: "I think friendship takes serious commitment and a lot of time," says Emily, 59. Robin, whom Emily met in high school, is "very gifted" in that regard. Robin is a great letter writer and a fabulous hostess. In the summer, her old Victorian house is like a B&B, with friends coming and returning because she makes their stay so pleasant and relaxing. Thirty years ago, she met a French couple in a restaurant in Toulouse. They struck up a conversation, and she's kept in touch and invited them to the United States, and she still visits them in France.

"Robin is amazing that way," says Emily. She knows that Robin's Christmas letter list must be endless, but she is always glad to be included on it. "I marvel at her efforts to stay connected and think of all the wonderful people I've lost touch with," she says.

While preserving friendships comes almost instinctively to Robin, other women have to work at it, making conscious efforts to retain friendships they cherish that seem to be drifting away. This may entail finding better ways to communicate with your friends. Dana, 46, told me that she regretted not having the communication skills and courage to tell her former best friend that she missed her and to ask her why she was drifting away. "I think I was too shy, stoic, and immature to do that in high school," she says.

When my dear friend Linda left New York and moved to Washington, D.C. (to marry the man I introduced her to), I thought the move might signal the end of our friendship as we knew it. (To a degree, my matchmaking had already altered my relationship with her husband.)

My fears were unfounded because Linda is as tied to her cell phone as a baby is to an umbilical cord. She calls me during her commute to and from work—and whenever else she is in transit. I do the same. We also text each other back and forth several times a day. Ironically, our long-distance friendship has brought us closer than we were previously. Of course, we also make it a point to connect in person multiple times a year, both as girlfriends and as couples.

Advances in technology have created a plethora of opportunities for friends to click, literally and figuratively, resulting in a seismic shift in how women befriend, defriend, and maintain connections. The ubiquitous use of cell phones, text messages, emails, instant messages (IMs), and social media (in some cases added to, and in other cases supplanting, conventional telephones and snail mail) have redefined friendship. They have also removed most of the alibis once available for failing to maintain a relationship. If it is important to you, you can keep it.

Phone Friends

Researchers at the University of Notre Dame and Pontifical Catholic University in Chile examined 8 million phone calls made by 2 million people and found that if two friends make contact with each other at least every fifteen days, they are more likely to have an enduring friendship.

People around the world send out billions of e-mails each day. The Internet provides another tool for women, even those who work at home, to meet new friends from around the world and to nurture existing connections. For example, e-mail has enabled women to maintain friendships that allow for close communication even when their respective schedules are out of sync.

For example, my friend Patricia is an early bird. After purging my accumulated junk mail from the night before, I love to read her e-mail messages each morning. She tells me what she is writing about, sends me interesting web links, asks advice, or lets me know about the latest sales at Chico's. As a night owl, I tend to respond to her late at night with all the stories of my day. We both met online through a writer's organization and arranged a face-to-face meeting about a year after we met. Although we live too far apart to shop together or have lunch, our online friendship remains strong. When my father died, Patricia and her husband made the sixty-mile trip to visit and offer her condolences to my family and me.

One woman I know keeps a package of note cards in her glove compartment so when she's waiting to pick up her kids from school she can write a personal note to an out-of-town friend.

Moving Forward

There are so many ways to stay in touch with friends. The many women I interviewed over the course of writing this book offered their advice about how to enhance the odds of your friends making you a keeper too.

How to Make Yourself a Keeper

- Be yourself. If a friend can't take it or doesn't like you for being yourself, then she isn't a true friend anyway.
- Be human. Smile whenever you are so moved. Try not to moan too much.
- If you make a promise, live up to that promise.
- Be punctual, dependable, and reliable.
- Show up. If she's having an event or a party, be a body for her— she'll appreciate you for it.
- Learn as much as you can about a friend before telling your entire life story.
- Make yourself a better listener and try not to interrupt. Pay attention and tune in to what your friend is saying or not saying before you chime in and talk about yourself.
- Let your friend know that you are interested in her feelings and opinions. All of us want friends who allow us to feel understood.
- Express your needs. Even close friends aren't mind-readers.
- Be there with your fire extinguisher when they crash and burn.
- Give each other space. Don't box each other in.
- Be a comfort blanket but don't smother her.
- Remember that she detests olives in her salad.
- Abandon judgment and resist saying "I told you so."
- Be willing to make sacrifices and compromise; if everything always has to be your way, you will be one lonely person.
- When she has three kids and they're sick, go clean their bathtub or something.
- Don't sleep with your best friend's boyfriend.
- Assesss the friendship periodically to see if it needs adjustments on either side.

235

KEEPING FRIENDSHIPS FRESH

Here are some additional tips for keeping the friendships you've made:

BREAK THE SILENCE

With the ubiquity of cell phones and computers, there is no reason to be incommunicado with friends, no matter how busy you are! Take a few minutes to say hello, tell your friend what is going on in your life, and to show some interest in what is going on in hers. Oral communication, whatever form it takes, has helped forge friendship since the time of tribal cultures.

One woman told me she always makes a point of checking in with her friends if she hasn't heard from them for a few months. She's done this over thirty years and says it's worth it, even if she is always the one to make the call. Don't ever let more than three months elapse without contacting a dear friend.

MAKE TIME FOR FACE TIME

This cannot be understated: making and keeping friendships takes time, and there's no substitute for making time in your life for friendships. Schedule time for friendships just as you would schedule any other task or event that is important to your health and well-being. As you age, making friends becomes more difficult, so it is extremely important to nurture relationships along the way.

If you live near each other, find ways to coordinate chores and other things you have to do: schedule your mammograms or manicures together, go food shopping together, or take an exercise class together.

While friendships, like romance, can be nurtured with occasional phone calls and flowers, there is nothing like face time to remind you why you both became friends in the first place. If you really want to mend or preserve a friendship that appears to be fizzling out, make time for coffee or a walk in the park with just the two of you alone.

Even if the friendship is separated by the miles, find a way to get together at her place, yours, or in-between—even if it's only once a year.

CELEBRATE MILESTONES

In some ways, little girls never grow up. It always brings a smile to a woman's heart when a friend remembers her birthday or anniversary with a phone call, e-mail, or card.

If you've been disconnected, use the opportunity to reconnect. You might send a note acknowledging the milestone and write, "I've missed you. I've been thinking of you and hope that we can get together. I'll call you before the end of the month." If one of your friends has achieved something special—a promotion, a role in a play, or written a book—send her a note supporting her success.

Several of my neighbors have established a nice tradition. We make plans to have a special lunch together each time one of us has a birthday. Although our lives have taken different paths over the years, it's a pleasant way to catch up and renew our friendship.

CREATE NEW RITUALS

Girlfriend getaways are increasingly popular options that friends are using to renew their spirits and their relationships. Some women meet one or more times a year at the beach, in the city, or at a golf resort. Whatever the ritual, find something that you both enjoy doing and use it as an excuse to come together periodically. It can be a movie once a month or a trip to the beach each summer.

If you are short of time and/or money, you can plan a "girls' night in." Rent a movie and be prepared to pause the DVR each time one of you can't wait until the end to chat. Themed dinners, Oscar parties, and watching the finales of your favorite TV shows of the season are also perfect excuses for all-girls get-togethers.

KEEP UP YOUR END OF THE BARGAIN

Friendships take work and it takes two women to make a friendship last. No one likes to have plans fall through at the last minute. Try to follow through on what you say you are going to do and keep appointments. Don't always wait for invitations; take your turn in being the initiator. Attend her parties whenever possible. Don't be vague about when you will see each other next. Schedule it on your calendar, in pen.

PRACTICE UNEXPECTED KINDNESS

Do something unasked for just because it's nice. Send her a note on your prettiest stationery telling her why you treasure her friendship. When one woman recently asked her friend for the recipe for chocolate fudge that her three-year-old daughter loved eating at her home, her friend whipped up a batch and left it on her doorstep with the recipe as a surprise. She wanted to let her friend know how much she meant to her.

MAKE HEROIC EFFORTS TO CONNECT WHEN IT DOESN'T HAPPEN ON ITS OWN

Sometimes two paths don't cross unless we go out of our way to make the connections. One woman described her friendship with someone whose life was far different and busier than her own. "She has six kids; I have zero unless you count my three pets!" she said. But she thought the woman was "amazing" and went out of her way to find commonalities that would bring them together.

If you feel like a valuable friendship is slipping away, do what you can to reel it back in. If face-to-face contact is impossible, arrange a way to maintain regular contact by cell phone or on the Internet so you can keep up with each other's lives until you meet.

"Facebook is an amazingly wonderful thing," says one woman. "It enabled me to talk more often with a friend who now lives many states away from me." She uses the social network to contact friends who are important but are more peripheral to her day-to-day life: friends she met vacationing, at overnight camp, and from middle school. "If you think someone is special to you, let them know exactly how you feel whether they reciprocate or not."

One woman said that when she meets someone with whom she really connects, it's worth the effort to make the relationship work. She called it "taking extra steps" and explained it like this: "I make sure I go the extra mile to stay close to her (e.g., calling her frequently, making the 1.5-hour drive to see her often, paying attention to her birthday as well as her two kids' birthdays.) We've had some bumps in our relationship but I've learned not to take this one for granted."

Why do some relatively strong friendships fall apart while others endure? Certainly, the duration of the friendship has some bearing. The less you have invested in a relationship, both in terms of time and emotion, the less likely you are to make a Herculean effort to save it.

A history of shared experiences often provides the glue that enables friends to stick together and to keep their relationship cemented during rocky times. When misunderstandings, disappointments, or disagreements occur, they are easier to overlook or to get over within the context of a friendship that has longevity. Being able to reminisce about past events and experiences, knowing many of the same people and places, and having a long-term investment in another person enriches a relationship and gives it a special dimension.

Two women who know each other since childhood, who have experienced firsts in their lives together and who have similar socio-cultural backgrounds have more common ground—and a greater chance of overcoming rough patches—than those with fewer ties, who come from disparate vantage points.

Personality counts, too. Every relationship has rough spots. But if two friends are able to communicate with tact and sensitivity, there is a better chance that their needs will be met and that the relationship will survive. When friends are relatively inflexible and unwilling to communicate, they are less likely to weather difficulties.

One woman says: "Your best friend is the person who not only knows all the important stories and events in your life, but has lived through them with you. Your best friend isn't the person you call when you are in jail; most likely, she is sitting in the cell beside you." Your best friend is the person you could call if you had to get rid of a dead body on your living room floor.

On the other hand, rather than a pointed disagreement, many times there are profound and fundamental changes that occur in a relationship over time as two people grow and change in different directions. This is as likely to happen in female friendships as it is in marriage. If a friendship becomes so weak that there is only history, there is less reason and motivation for both parties to try to preserve the relationship. In essence, no one is at fault or has precipitated a unilateral change, but the loss can be just as painful.

∞

A woman needs close friends whom she can turn to every day (and night) of her life. It may not be the same person each day because, like our lives, friendships are dynamic. But I hope that your best friends—even if the list is serial—offer you the unique sense of intimacy, trust, and reciprocity that will allow you to feel loved, understood, needed, supported, challenged, and inspired.

Yes, these relationships are complicated, some even bordering on mysterious, and creating them and making the meaningful ones stick takes some work. But they are as essential to our happiness and well-being as are nutritious food, clean water, and fresh air. Female friendships have their ups and downs—and most of them don't last forever—but we are very fortunate when best friends are a constant in our lives.

ABOUT THE FRACTURED FRIENDSHIP SURVEY

∽

The *Fractured Friendship Survey* was designed to be brief and easy to complete, with a mix of quantitative (numerical) and qualitative (open-ended) questions. Female respondents were asked to provide information about themselves, their friendships, and about one meaningful friendship in their lives that had ended.

Seven quantitative questions asked information about:

1. The number of women a respondent considered to be her "best" or "very close" friends;
2. Looking back at one such meaningful friendship that ended, how the respondent met that friend (at school, at work, as neighbors, through mutual friends or other);
3. The respondent's perceptions of how the fractured friendship ended—her decision, her friend's decision or a mutual one;
4. The approximate length of the fractured friendship—in terms of years and/or months;
5. The frequency of communication in that relationship;
6. The approximate number of hours spent communicating with the friend per week; and
7. The respondent's chronological age when the friendship ended.

The heart of the survey consisted of seven open-ended questions designed to elicit information about each woman's experience with a fractured friendship, including:

- What made the friendship special
- Her perception of why the friendship ended;
- The nature and duration of the emotional impact created by the loss;
- The effect of the loss upon other friendships;
- The respondent's view about the meaning of a "best friend" relationship;
- Any experiences the respondent had or ideas she has now about renewing failed friendships;
- General advice about maintaining viable friendships

Finally, four optional questions asked for identifying information that was used to clarify ambiguous responses or follow up with lengthier interviews. These included: Name of the respondent, her age, her phone number, and her email address I designed the 18-item online *Fractured Friendship* survey using design and analysis software available on www.SurveyMonkey .com. Volunteer respondents were recruited through notices I posted on *Craig's List* ads (in several major cities); on the social networking sites *Facebook* and *My Space*; on writer forums to which I belong (www.ASJA.org, www.freelancesuccess.com); and on my own website (www.irenelevine.com) and my blog (www.fracturedfriendships.com also accessible at www.thefriend-shipblog.com).

More than 1500 women responded to the survey between April 2007 and April 2009, with more than 85 percent of them completing all the questions. Some of the limitations of the survey:

- The sample was a convenience sample rather than a random one, so certain groups of women may have over- or under-represented compared to the general population, e.g., certain age, race or ethnic groups; lesbian and transgender women; women from different geographic locales.

About the Fractured Friendship Survey

- The survey was conducted online rather than in-person; online surveys have become a predominant form of survey research but its validity is still questioned.

- Individual women, rather than dyads (pairs) of friends responded, so the information may be biased and subjective.

- Much of the information solicited was retrospective, relying on the respondent's memory of the past; memory is often selective and subject to change over time.

- Because the survey was conducted online, the results are biased by the digital divide; they are limited because they are heavily skewed towards women with Internet access

- On the other side of the coin, the study had several unique strengths:

- The anonymous nature of an online survey and the promise of confidentiality encouraged candor and openness among respondents.

- The open-ended questions, which were answered online, encouraged rich and lengthy responses that permitted a woman to tell her story and express her feelings in some detail, at a time and place convenient for her.
- The survey tapped women from around the world and from many different walks of life.

RECOMMENDATIONS FOR FURTHER READING

∽

"To read a book for the first time is to make an acquaintance with a new friend; to read it for a second time is to meet an old one."

—CHINESE SAYING

"Good friends, good books and a sleepy conscience: this is the ideal life."   —MARK TWAIN

Here are some of my favorite books on friendship.

NONFICTION

Apter, Terri and Ruthellen Josselson. *Best Friends: The Pleasures and Perils of Girls' and Women's Friendships*. New York: Three Rivers Press, 1998.

Barash, Susan Shapiro. *Tripping the Prom Queen: The Truth About Women and Rivalry*. New York: St. Martin's Griffin, 2006.

Carol, Joy. *The Fabric of Friendship: Celebrating the Joy, Mending the Tears in Women's Relationships*. Notre Dame: Sorin Books, 2006.

DePaulo, Bella. *Singled Out: How Singles Are Stereotyped, Stigmatized, and Ignored, and Still Live Happily Ever After*. New York: St. Martin's Griffin, 2007.

Goodman, Ellen and Patricia O'Brien. *I Know Just What You Mean: The Power of Friendship in Women's Lives*. New York: Simon & Schuster, 2000.

Grief, Geoffrey L. *The Buddy System: Understanding Male Friendships*. New York: Oxford University Press, 2009.

Hartley-Brewer, Elizabeth. *Making Friends: A Guide to Understanding and Nurturing Your Child's Friendships*. Cambridge: DaCapo Press, 2009.

Horchow, Roger and Sally Horchow. *The Art of Friendship: 70 Simple Rules for Making Meaningful Connections*. New York: St. Martin's Press, 2005.

Isaacs, Florence. *Toxic Friends, True Friends: How Your Friends Can Make or Break Your Health, Happiness, Family, and Career*. New York: William Morrow, 1999.

James, Sara and Ginger Mauney. *The Best of Friends: Two Women, Two Continents, and One Enduring Friendship*. New York: William Morrow, 2007.

Lavinthal, Andrea and Jessica Rozler. *Friend or Frenemy? A Guide to the Friends You Need and the Ones You Don't*. New York: Harper Collins, 2008.

Mooney, Nan. *I Can't Believe She Said That! Why Women Betray Other Women at Work*. New York: St. Martin's Griffin, 2005.

Paul, Marla. *The Friendship Crisis: Finding, Making and Keeping Friends When You're Not a Kid Anymore*. New York: St. Martin's Press, 2004.

Offill, Jenny and Elissa Schappell (Eds.). *The Friend Who Got Away: Twenty Women's True-Life Tales of Friendships That Blew Up, Burned Out or Faded Away*. New York: Doubleday, 2005.

Pryor, Liz. *What Did I Do Wrong? When Women Don't Tell Each Other the Friendship Is Over*. New York: Free Press, 2006.

Rawlins, William. *Friendship Matters: Communication, Dialectics, and the Life Course*. New York: Aldine De Gruyter, 1992.

Rubin, Lillian B. *Just Friends: The Role of Friendships in Our Lives*. New York: Harper & Row, 1985.

Sheehy, Sandy. *Connecting: The Enduring Power of Female Friendships*. New York: William Morrow, 2000.

Spencer, Liz and Ray Pahl. *Rethinking Friendship: Hidden Solidarities Today*. Princeton: Princeton University Press, 2006.

Yager, Jan. *When Friendship Hurts: How to Deal with Friends Who Betray, Abandon or Wound You*. New York: Fireside, 2002.

Zaslow, Jeffrey. *The Girls from Ames: A Story of Women and a Forty-Year Friendship*. New York: Gotham Books, 2009.

CONTEMPORARY FICTION

Clayton, Meg Waite. *The Wednesday Sisters: A Novel*. New York: Ballantine Books, 2008.

Green, Jane. *Second Chance*. New York: Plume, 2008.

Recommendations for Further Reading

Jacobs, Kate. *Friday Night Knitting Club*. New York: Berkley Trade, 2008.

Packer, Ann. *Songs Without Words*. New York: Alfred A. Knopf, 2007.

Rendell, Joanne. *The Professors' Wives' Club*. New York: Penguin Group, 2008.

Scotch, Allison Winn. *Time of My Life: A Novel*. New York: Shaye Areheart Books, 2008.

Trollope, Joanna. *Friday Nights*. New York: Bloomsbury, 2008.

Volk, Patricia. *To My Dearest Friends*. New York: Alfred A. Knopf, 2007.

Weiner, Jennifer. *Best Friends Forever: A Novel*. New York: Atria Books, 2009.

ACKNOWLEDGMENTS

Thanking an editor is usually a gratuitous afterthought. For this book, it deserves to come first. Few authors are fortunate enough to be approached by a warm and wonderful editor with an idea for a book that is perfectly suited to their background and interests. I am extremely appreciative of Juliet Grames of The Overlook Press, who commissioned this book and shepherded it through publication. With more than 800 Facebook friends—and still counting—Juliet's stories and insights about friendship have been invaluable in shaping my thinking about this complex topic. I'm also grateful for the wisdom, guidance, and support that my agent, Joelle Delbourgo, brought to this project.

While I conducted research for this book, it was a particular privilege to draw upon the collective wisdom of other authors and academics who had tackled the subject of female friendship before I did. Although friendship is a subject of universal and perennial interest, I hope this book offers a fresh perspective that dispels the myths that still remain pervasive.

I am indebted to more than 1500 women who responded enthusiastically and in record speed to the online Fractured Friendship Survey and who emailed me or posted messages on my blog (www.fracturedfriendships.com). They shared their stories of bonding, betrayal, and loss with great candor. Many said that just thinking about their friendships and writing about them on paper was an empowering exercise. It was the same for me. I hope this book sheds some light on the fragility of these relationships and their need for nurturance.

Throughout the years, I've always been blessed to find new friends—usually because we were in the same place at the same time (whether it was at Bayside High School, Queens College, or St. John's University; in my neighborhoods in Bayside, Rockville, or Chappaqua; or at brick-and-mortar or virtual workplaces). Irrespective of the circumstances that brought us together, these friendships have helped shape the person I am. My girlfriends have mentored me on how to be a better wife, mother, daughter, teacher, psychologist, writer, and friend. Thank you Judy Buckner, Donna Dellaero, Vikki DeMeo, Rita Dunn, Pam Foti, Risa Fox, Echo Garrett, Gale Germain, Margie Goldstein, Mickey Goodman, Loretta Haggard, Leslie Knowlton, Judy Kirkwood, Judy Kramer, Linda Ligenza, Dawn Jahn Moses, Hilary Nagel, Linda Rosenberg, Diana Silberman, Elissa Steiner, and Diana Zuckerman.

I'm also very lucky to have two wonderful men in my life: my husband, Jerry, and my son, Andrew. Both have been ongoing sources of strength, joy, and pride, and this book would not have been possible without their support. They are my most critical editors as well as my biggest cheerleaders in boxer shorts. When I ask one or both of them to read what I've written, however boring the topic might be, they rarely turn me down, whatever the hour. Java, my loyal Himalayan, has also been by my side, making an inherently lonely process more bearable.

As I put away all the books and papers related to this project and come up for air, I am selfishly committed to set aside more time for the friends and family who sustain me.

ABOUT THE AUTHOR

Irene S. Levine, Ph.D., is a psychologist and award-winning freelance journalist and author. As the Friendship Doctor, she is a regular contributor to the *The Huffington Post*. She also has a popular blog about female friendships (www.thefriendshipblog.com) and pens an online bi-monthly career column for the American Association for the Advancement of Science. She has written on a range of topics, including health, mental health, relationships, and lifestyles, for leading publications including *Ladies' Home Journal*, *Reader's Digest*, *Self*, *AARP*, *Better Homes & Gardens*, *Health*, *Prevention*, *The New York Times*, *The Los Angeles Times*, *Chicago Tribune*, and *The Dallas Morning News*. Dr. Levine spent the major portion of her career in senior policy roles at the National Institute of Mental Health (NIMH) and the Center for Mental Health Services (CMHS), where she was one of the chief architects of the NIMH Community Support Program and created the NIMH Program on Homelessness and Mental Illness. She was appointed the first Deputy Director of CMHS, part of the Substance Abuse and Mental Health Services Administration. Since 1994, she has worked part-time as Director of Communications at the Nathan S. Kline Institute for Psychiatric Research and has held a faculty appointment as a professor of psychiatry at the New York University School of Medicine. She has lectured locally, nationally, and internationally, and co-authored *Schizophrenia for Dummies* (Wiley, 2008) with her psychiatrist-husband, Jerome Levine, M.D. She is a member of the American Society of Journalists and Authors, the Association for Health Care Journalists, the American Medical Writers Association, the Authors Guild, the National Association of Science Writers, and the American Psychological Association. She resides in Chappaqua, New York with her husband and son.

NOTES

∽∞

Introduction

14   *Make new friends*   Helen Exley, *Friendship Quotations (Quotation Books)* (Chicago: Helen Exley Giftbooks, 1992).

Chapter 1

27   *Each friend represents*   Anais Nin, "The Friendship Page: Friendship Quotes: General," Global Friendship, http://www.friendship.com.au /quotes/quofri.html (accessed June 2, 2009).

28   *complexity, depth, and intimacy*   Liz Spencer and Ray Pahl, *Rethinking Friendship: Hidden Solidarities Today* (New York: Princeton University Press, 2006), 76.

30   *no official friendship counts*   Spencer & Pahl, 23.

30   *10,000 Brits*   Microsoft Press Centre, "Time Pressured Brits Make 396 Friends In Their Life . . . But Lose 363 Of Them," Press Release, November 28, 2003, http://www.microsoft.com/uk/press/content/presscentre /releases/2003/11/pr03170.mspx (accessed June 2, 2009).

31   *seven year expiration date*   "Half of your friends lost in 7 years," Press Release, May 27, 2009, http://www.alphagalileo.org/ViewItem.aspx ?ItemId=58115&CultureCode=en

31   *How many best friends*   http://www.fracturedfriendships.com/blog /friendship-factoids-facebook (accessed on 9/1/07; no longer extant).

32   *five close friends*   Lewis Smith, "Online networkers who click with 1,000 'friends,'" *The Times*, September 11, 2007, http://www .timeson-line.co.uk/tol/news/uk/science/article2426229.ece?Submitted=true (accessed June 2, 2009).

32   *150 people*   Lewis Smith, "Online networkers who click with 1,000 'friends,'" *The Times*, September 11, 2007, http://www.timesonline

.co.uk/tol/news/uk/science/article2426229.ece?Submitted=true (accessed June 2, 2009).

32   *fewer friends than their friends have*   Scott L. Feld, "Why Your Friends Have More Friends than You Do," *The American Journal of Sociology* 96 (1991): 1464-1477.

33   *face-to-face*   Liz Spencer and Ray Pahl, *Rethinking Friendship: Hidden Solidarities Today* (New York: Princeton University Press, 2006), 39.

33   *differences are evolutionary*   Anna Kuchment, "The More Social Sex," *Newsweek*, May 10, 2004, http://www.msnbc.msn.com/id /4879366 /site/newsweek (accessed June 2, 2009).

33   *"tend and befriend"*   Shelly E. Taylor, *The Tending Instinct: Women, Men, and the Biology of Relationships* (New York: Holt Paperbacks, 2003), 15.

33   *more in tune with other people's feelings*   Terri Apter and Ruthellen Josselson, *Best Friends: The Pleasures and Perils of Girls' and Women's Friendships*, (New York: Three Rivers Press, 1999), 21.

34   *Gender Differences in Online Friendships*   Amanda Lenhart and Mary Madden, Pew Internet and American Life Project Report, Social Networking Websites and Tenes, January 7, 2007, www.pewinternet .org/PPF/r/198/report_display.asp (accessed June 4, 2009).

34   *Friendships are discovered*   Herb Galewitz, *Friendship: A Book of Quotations* (Mineola, NY: Dover Publications, 1999), 21.

34   women who are extroverts   Meliksah Demir and Lesley A. Weitkamp, Journal of Happiness Studies (2007), 8:181-211, 187.

35   *share certain qualities that bond*   William K. Rawlins, *The Compass of Friendship: Narratives, Identities, and Dialogues* (New York: Aldine De Gruyter, 1992), 12.

36   *Friendship is a non-event*   Lillian B. Rubin, *Just Friends: The Role of Friendships in Our Lives* (New York: Harper & Row, 1985), 5.

37   *Best friends allow us to try on new roles*   Terri Apter and Ruthellen Josselson, *Best Friends: The Pleasures and Perils of Girls' and Women's Friendships*, (New York: Three Rivers Press, 1999), xii.

37   *Irrespective of a woman's personality*   Meliksah Demir and Lesley A. Weitkamp, Journal of Happiness Studies (2007), 8:181-211, 187.

Notes

CHAPTER 2

39   *A bosom friend*   Helen Exley, *Friendship Quotations (Quotation Books)* (Chicago: Helen Exley Giftbooks, 1992).

43   *un'amica stretta*   Elizabeth Gilbert, *Eat, Pray, Love: One Woman's Search for Everything Across Italy, India and Indonesia.* (New York: Penguin Books, 2006, 57.

43   *incorporate only positive attributes*   Lillian B. Rubin, *Just Friends: The Role of Friendship in Our Lives* (New York: Harper Perennial, 1986), 7.

44   *this usually isn't the case*   Liz Spencer and Ray Pahl, *Rethinking Friendship: Hidden Solidarities Today* (New York: Princeton University Press, 2006), 31.

49   *a positive developmental force*   Apter & Josselson, 63.

49   *two types of readers*   Personal Interview with Jeffrey Zaslow, 4/29/09.

49   *drop out of cliques*   William Damon, Richard M. Lerner, Nancy Eisenberg, *The Handbook of Child Psychology: Social, Emotional, and Personality Development,* ed. Nancy Eisenberg, (New York: John Wiley and Sons, 2006) 1022

49   *friendships may enhance your prospects for happiness*   Published 4 December 2008, doi:10.1136/bmj.a2338, BMJ 2008;337:a2338, Dynamic spread of happiness in a large social network: longitudinal analysis over 20 years in the Framingham Heart Study, http://www .bmj.com/cgi /content/full/337/dec04_2/a2338 (accessed June 2, 2009).

49   *as young women mature*   Lillian Rubin, 113.

49   *Amish Quilting Circles*   America's quilting history, http://www .womenfolk.com/quilting_history/amish.htm, (accessed June 6, 2009).

CHAPTER 3

51   *One who looks for a friend without faults*   Helen Exley, *Friendship Quotations (Quotation Books)* (Chicago: Helen Exley Giftbooks, 1992).

59   *Sometimes you put out your hand*   Personal email interview with Anne Roiphe, 9/18/08.

72   *problem of co-rumination*   Rose AJ, Carlson W and Waller EM, Prospective Associations of Co-Rumination with Friendship and Emotional Adjustment: Considering the Socioemotional Trade-Offs of

Co-Rumination, *Developmental Psychology*, 2007, Vol. 43, No. 4, 1019-1031.

Also, University of Missouri Press Release, July 16, 2007, Girls who complain about their problems at greater risk of developing anxiety and depression, says MU researcher

84 *The Sopranos* "Mergers and Acquisitions," *The Sopranos*, Episode 47, Dan Attias, HBO. Aired November 3, 2002.

CHAPTER 4

87 *Men kick friendship* Anne Morrow Lindbergh, *Locked rooms and open doors*, Harcourt Brace Jovanovich, 1974, *Original from the University of Michigan*

digitized Mar 10, 2008, 7.

107 *forgiveness is good for your health* "Learning to Forgive May Improve Well-Being," *Mayo Clinic Women's Healthsource*, January 2, 2008, http://www.mayoclinic.org/news2008-mchi/4405.html (accessed June 2, 2009).

CHAPTER 5

109 *What do we live for* Helen Exley, *Friendship Quotations (Quotation Books)* (Chicago: Helen Exley Giftbooks, 1992).

110 *the term "toxic friend"* Florence Isaacs, *Toxic Friendships*, (New York: William Morrow and Company, 1999) 16.

130 *friendship killers* personal email interview with Florence Isaacs, August 26, 2007.

CHAPTER 6

139 *"Old friends…* The Country of the Pointed Fir (Boston: Houghton and Mifflin, 1896, 97)

144 *shrunk markedly* J. Miller McPherson, Lynn Smith-Lovin, and Matthew E. Brashears, "Social Isolation in America: Changes in Core Discussion Networks over Two Decades," *American Sociological Review* 71 (2006): 353-375.

144 *no close confidants*   McPherson, J. Miller, Lynn Smith-Lovin, and Matthew E. Brashears, 366.

146 *friendship patterns*   Andrew M. Ledbetter, Em Griffin, and Glenn G. Sparks, "Forecasting 'friends forever': A longitudinal investigation of sustained closeness between best friends," *Personal Relationships* 14 (2007): 343-350.

146 *cautionary note*   "Study Shows What Makes College Buddies Lifelong Friends," Ascribe, August 7, 2007, http://newswire.ascribe.org/cgi-bin /behold.pl?ascribeid=20070807.114545&time=12%2042%20PDT&year =2007&public=0 (accessed June 2, 2009).

146 *2002 survey*   Marla Paul, *The Friendship Crisis: Finding, Making and Keeping Friends When You're Not a Kid Anymore* (New York: St. Martin's Press, 2004), 14.

147 *harder to maintain friends*   Jan Yager, *When Friendship Hurts: How to Deal with Friends Who Betray, Abandon or Wound You* (New York: Fireside, 2002), 13.

148 *sage advice*   email interview with Erin Torneo, co-author with Erin Torneo of *The Bridal Wave: A Survival Guide to the Everyone-I-Know-Is-Getting-Married Years* (New York: Villard, 2007), June 6, 2007.

149 *"I'm part of a club . . ."*   Gail Konop Baker, *Cancer is a Bitch: Or, I'd Rather Be Having a Midlife Crisis* (New York: Da Capo, 2008).

149 *"It's like we share a secret language..."*   Email interview with Gail Konop Baker, January 11, 2009.

150 *a strong network of families and friends*   Press Release from the American College of Surgeons, Patients with Larger Social Networks May Fare Better After an Operation, February 12, 2008, http://www .facs.org/news/jacs/socialconnect0208.html

150 *"friends in low places"*   Helen Russell, "Friends in Low Places: Gender, Unemployment and Sociability," *Work, Employment and Society* (1999), 13:205-224 Cambridge University Press, http://journals.cambridg.org /action/displayAbstract?fromPage=online&aid=39015 (accessed June 2, 2009).

CHAPTER 7

163 *"positives in your life"*   Personal email interview with Florence Isaacs, August 26, 2007.

163 *blood pressure* Julianne Holt-Lunstad et al., "On the importance of relationship quality: The impact of ambivalence in friendships on cardiovascular functioning," *Annals of Behavioral Medicine* 33 (2007): 278-290.

165 *"suppression and accommodation"* personal email interview with Debbie Mandel, May 25, 2007.

170 *school of correction* Terri Apter and Ruthellen Josselson, *Best Friends: The Pleasures and Perils of Girls' and Women's Friendships*, (New York: Three Rivers Press, 1999), 60.

CHAPTER 8

181 *"lost friends, some by death"* Virginia Woolf and Deborah Parsons Wordsworth Editions, 2000, 105.

181 *unable to forgive* "When Good Friends Go Bad," Tyra Banks Show Archives, posted starting from June 22, 2007 http://telepicturesblog.warnerbros.com/tyrashow/2007/06/when_good_friends_go_bad.html (accessed June 2, 2009).

195 EBF Amy Sohn. The Björn Identity, New York Magazine, November 12, 2006.

CHAPTER 9

199 *4 A.M. that matter* Marlene Dietrich, Helen Exley, *Friendship Quotations (Quotation Books)* (Chicago: Helen Exley Giftbooks, 1992).

209 *digital technology* Marketing Charts, "Youth and Digital Tech – Viacom, Microsoft Global Study Challenges Assumptions," Press Release, July 25, 2007, http://www.marketingcharts.com/television /youth-and-digital-tech-viacom-microsoft-global-study-challenges-assumptions-1076/ (accessed June 2, 2009).

CHAPTER 10

211 *"family of friends"* Quote by Gloria Steinem on wowowow, 4/16/2009, http://www.wowowow.com/politics/gloria-steinem-75-feminists-pro-choice-268505FLor (accessed June 10, 2009).

212 right kind of friends Marla Paul, *The Friendship Crisis: Finding, Making and Keeping Friends When You're Not a Kid Anymore* (New York: St. Martin's Press, 2004), 5.

Notes

212 *buffer against stress*   Liz Spencer and Ray Pahl, *Rethinking Friendship: Hidden Solidarities Today* (New York: Princeton University Press, 2006), 28.

212 *psychosomatic illness*   Nicole Knickmeyer, Kim Seton, and Nancy Nishimura, "The Impact of Same-Sex Friendships on the Well-Being of Women," *Women & Therapy* 25 (2002): 37-59.

213 *biological impact of social isolation* UCLA, "UCLA researchers identify the molecular signature of loneliness," David Geffen School of Medicine at UCLA, http://dgsom.healthsciences.ucla.edu/news/detail ?rad_id=8214 (accessed June 2, 2009).

213 *risk of death*   http://boomers.msn.com/articleLHJ.aspx?cp -documentid=376471 (accessed June 4, 2008).

217 *social media*   Johanna Pearce, "Facebook eases freshman fears, fosters friendship," CNNU, http://www.cnn.com/2007/TECH/ptech/09/07 /cnnu.facebook/index.html?eref=rss_tech (accessed June 2, 2009).

224 article in Charlotte Observer by Joe DePriest http://www.charlotteobserver.com/catawba/story/180657.html, (accessed July 6, 2007).

218 *achieving happiness* Nattavudh Powdthavee, "Putting a Price Tag on Friends, Relatives, and Neighbours: Using Surveys of Life-Satisfaction to Value Social Relationships," *Journal of Socio-Economics* 37 (2007): 1459-1480.

222 *Mommy & Me* "About Mommy and Me Products and Services," Mommy and Me, Inc, http://www.mommyandme.com/about-us.html (accessed June 2, 2009).

222 *Mothers & More*   "Mothers and More – About Us: What We Do," Mothers & More, http://www.mothersandmore.org/AboutUs/about _us.shtml (accessed June 2, 2009).

225 *nostalgia* University of Southampton, "Nostalgic thoughts of happier times can help overcome loneliness," Press Release, November 18, 2008, http://www.southampton.ac.uk/mediacentre/news/2008/nov/08 _212.shtml (accessed June 2, 2009).

234 *every fifteen days*   Cesar A. Hidalgo and Carlos Rodriguez-Sickert, "The dynamics of a mobile phone network," *Physica A* 387 (2008): 3017-3024.

BIBLIOGRAPHY

Apter, Terri, and Ruthellen Josselson. *Best Friends: The Pleasures and Perils of Girls' and Women's Friendships*. New York: Three Rivers Press, 1998.

Exley, Helen. *Friendship Quotations (Quotation Books)*. Chicago: Helen Exley Giftbooks, 1992.

Feld, Scott L. "Why Your Friends Have More Friends than You Do." *The American Journal of Sociology* 96 (1991): 1464-1477.

Galewitz, Herb. *Friendship: A Book of Quotations*. Mineola, NY: Dover Publications, 1999.

Gladwell, Malcolm. *The Tipping Point: How Little Things Can Make a Big Difference*. New York: Backbay Books, 2002.

Hidalgo, Cesar A., and Carlos Rodriguez-Sickert. "The dynamics of a mobile phone network." *Physica A* 387 (2008): 3017-3024.

Holt-Lunstad, Julianne, Uchino, Bert N., Smith, Timothy W., and Angela Hicks. "On the importance of relationship quality: The impact of ambivalence in friendships on cardiovascular functioning." *Annals of Behavioral Medicine* 33 (2007): 278-290

Horchow, Roger, and Sally Horchow. *The Art of Friendship*. New York: St, Martin's Press, 2006.

Knickmeyer, Nicole, Seton, Kim, and Nancy Nishimura. "The Impact of Same-Sex Friendships on the Well-Being of Women." *Women & Therapy* 25 (2002): 37-59.

Kuchment, Anna. "The More Social Sex." *Newsweek*, May 10, 2004. http://www.msnbc.msn.com/id/4879366/site/newsweek (accessed June 2, 2009).

Ledbetter, Andrew M., Griffin, Em, and Glenn G. Sparks. "Forecasting 'friends forever': A longitudinal investigation of sustained closeness between best friends." *Personal Relationships* 14 (2007): 343-350.

Marketing Charts. "Youth and Digital Tech – Viacom, Microsoft Global Study Challenges Assumptions." Press Release, July 25, 2007. http://www.marketingcharts.com/television/youth-and-digital-tech-viacom-microsoft-global-study-challenges-assumptions-1076/ (accessed June 2, 2009).

McPherson, J. Miller, Smith-Lovin, Lynn, and Matthew E. Brashears. "Social Isolation in America: Changes in Core Discussion Networks over Two Decades." *American Sociological Review* 71 (2006): 353-375.

Microsoft Press Centre. "Time Pressured Brits Make 396 Friends In Their Life . . . But Lose 363 Of Them." Press Release, November 28, 2003. http://www.microsoft.com/uk/press/content/presscentre /releases/2003/11/pr03170.mspx (accessed June 2, 2009).

Nin, Anais. "The Friendship Page: Friendship Quotes: General." Global Friendship. http://www.friendship.com.au/quotes/quofri.html (accessed June 2, 2009).

Paul, Marla. *The Friendship Crisis: Finding, Making and Keeping Friends When You're Not a Kid Anymore.* New York: St. Martin's Press, 2004.

Pearce, Johanna. "Facebook eases freshman fears, fosters friendship." CNNU. http://www.cnn.com/2007/TECH/ptech/09/07/cnnu.face-book/index.html?eref=rss_tech (accessed June 2, 2009).

Powdthavee, Nattavudh. "Putting a Price Tag on Friends, Relatives, and Neighbours: Using Surveys of Life-Satisfaction to Value Social Relationships." *Journal of Socio-Economics* 37 (2007): 1459-1480.

Rawlins, William. *Friendship Matters: Communication, Dialectics, and the Life Course.* New York: Aldine De Gruyter, 1992.

Rubin, Lillian B. *Just Friends: The Role of Friendships in Our Lives.* New York: Harper & Row, 1985.

Smith, Lewis. "Online networkers who click with 1,000 'friends.'" *The Times*, September 11, 2007. http://www.timesonline.co.uk/tol/news /uk /science/article2426229.ece?Submitted=true (accessed June 2, 2009).

Spencer, Liz, and Ray Pahl. *Rethinking Friendship: Hidden Solidarities Today.* Princeton: Princeton University Press, 2006.

Taylor, Shelley E. *The Tending Instinct: Women, Men, and the Biology of Relationships.* New York: Holt Paperbacks, 2003.

Torneo, Erin, and Valerie Krause. *The Bridal Wave: A Survival Guide to the Everyone-I-Know-Is-Getting-Married Years.* New York: Villard, 2007.

UCLA. "UCLA researchers identify the molecular signature of loneliness." David Geffen School of Medicine at UCLA. http://dgsom .healthsciences.ucla.edu/news/detail?rad_id=8214 (accessed June 2, 2009).

University of Southampton. "Nostalgic thoughts of happier times can help overcome loneliness." Press Release, November 18, 2008. http://www.southampton.ac.uk/mediacentre/news/2008/nov/08_212.s html (accessed June 2, 2009).

Zaslow, Jeffrey. *The Girls from Ames: A Story of Women & a Forty-Year Friendship.* New York: Gotham Books (Penguin Group), 2009.

"About Mommy and Me Products and Services," Mommy and Me, Inc, http://www.mommyandme.com/about-us.html (accessed June 2, 2009).

Bibliography

"Mothers and More – About Us: What We Do," Mothers & More, http://www.mothersandmore.org/AboutUs/about_us.shtml (accessed June 2, 2009).

"When Good Friends Go Bad," Tyra Banks Show Archives, http://telepic-turesblog.warnerbros.com/tyrashow/2007/06/when_good_friends_go _bad.html (accessed June 2, 2009).

INDEX

BEST FRIENDS FOREVER

35

Gilbert, Elizabeth, 43
Girls from Ames: A Story of Women and a Forty-Year Friendship, The, 155
Gladwell, Malcolm, 32, 228
Golden rule, 14

Helping a Friend Who is Depressed (box), 135
How to Forgive a Friend (box), 166
How to Make Yourself a Keeper (box), 235

Identifying the Signs of a Toxic Friendship (box), 119
Isaacs, Florence, 163

Life Transitions that Affect Friendships (box), 143

Jealousy vs. Envy (box), 132
Josselson, Ruthellen, 170
Just Married: Keeping the Friendship Alive (box), 148

Mandel, Debbie, 165
Milgram, Stanley, 228
Minimizing Family Feuds (box), 65
Mommy & Me, 222
Moms & Tots, 221
More than Shy: Could It Be Social Anxiety? (box), 217
Mothers & More, 222
Myth of Best Friends forever, see Best Friends Forever myth

New York, 195, 230
Nostalgia as an Antidote to Loneliness (box), 225

Parents Without Partners, 221
Phone Friends (box), 234
Physical Toll of Love-Hate Relationships, The (box), 163
Playgrounds for Young Moms (box), 222
Powdthavee, Dr. Nattavudh, 218

Queen bee, 128, 129
Recent Novels about Female Friendship (box), 227
Recognizing the Symptoms of a Mental Disorder in a Friend (box), 153
Rosenfeld, Lucinda, 230
Rubin, Dr. Lillian, 36, 43
Rx for Better Health: Friendship, 213

Self-esteem, 34, 76, 132, 186, 212
Setting Healthy Boundaries with a Needy Friend (box), 117
Signs of a Suffocating Relationship (box), 128
Sohn, Amy, 195
Sopranos, The, 84
Speaking Out: When Candor is Called For (box), 69
Steps to Save a Dying Friendship (box), 169

Best Friends Forever

Surviving a Breakup with Your Best Friend

By Irene S. Levine, Ph.D.

Female friendships have their ups and downs—most of them don't last forever—but we are very fortunate when best friends are a constant in our lives.

ABOUT THIS GUIDE

The questions that follow are offered as possible topics for discussion. We hope they will enhance your reading of Irene S. Levine's *Best Friends Forever* and provoke reflection and lively discussion.

ABOUT THE BOOK

Men, jobs, children, personal crises, and irreconcilable social gaps—these are just a few of the strange and confusing reasons that may cause a female friendship to end. No matter the cause, the breakup leaves a woman devastated and asking herself difficult questions. Was someone to blame? Is the friendship worth fighting for? How can I prevent this from ever happening again?

Even more upsetting is that women suffering from broken friendships often have no one to confide in—while the loss of a romantic partner garners sympathy among peers, discussing the loss of a platonic friend is often impossible without making other friends jealous or uncomfortable.

Best Friends Forever is the first self-help guide tackling the complex topic of female friendships, including:

- Why Friendships Fall Apart
- How to Get Over Getting Dumped
- Spotting a Toxic Friendship
- How to End a Friendship That Can't Be Fixed
- Moving Forward with New Friends

Drawing from the literature, her own research, and the personal testimonials of more than 1500 women, Dr. Levine explores the myths of the romanticized notion of "best friends forever," and contends that most friendships, even the best or close ones, are more fragile than permanent.

QUESTIONS FOR DISCUSSION

- What are some of the qualities that make for a "best friend"? Can a woman have more than one? What types of boundaries should there be between best friends?

- How are women's friendships different than men's?

- Thinking back, when were the easiest and most difficult times in your life to make new friends?

- Who is the friend that you have known for the longest time and still consider a close friend? When and how did you meet? What has made the friendship "stick"?

- What are your expectations of your friends on your birthday? Do you communicate your expectations or wait and see if they remember you? How did your family handle birthdays when you were growing up?

- Do you feel like you have to juggle friendship with the rest of your life (family, career, school, etc.)? How do you set priorities?

- Should a woman expect her best friend to provide unconditional support, whatever the circumstances?

Reading Group Guide

- One study from the UK suggests that we keep only one out of 12 friends we make over the course of a lifetime. Thus, everyone has sóme fractured friendships. Why do so many friendships end?

- Have you ever been betrayed by a female friend? Disappointed? Have you ever been replaced by a "new" best friend? Have you ever had a relationship with a friend that felt suffocating? How can women handle such situations? Can they be avoided?

- Think back about a meaningful friendship that suddenly ended. How did you explain it to the people around you? Were they sympathetic? Were you embarrassed? Why?

- What was the loneliest period of your life when you felt like you had a "friendship deficit"?

- What are the signs of a toxic friendship, one that you know isn't good for you?

- Are you comfortable having arguments or disagreements with friends? Do conflicts take a toll on a friendship? If so, under what circumstances? What are best ways to apologize to a friend when you did something you know was wrong?

- Is there any good way to end a friendship? Have you ever ending a friendship successfully? Have you ever tried to end a friendship and then later were sorry for the way you handled it? Is it okay to tell a "white lie" to end a friendship gracefully?

- If you were ever the friend who was dumped, what are some strategies you used to get over the loss? How can a dumpee achieve closure?

- What is your favorite book about female friends (besides this one)?

- What TV shows have you enjoyed that portrayed female friendships? Were they true to life?

- What are some of the potential complications of extended your female friendships to boyfriends, husbands, other girlfriends, your kids?

- Do friendship and work mix? What are the advantages and pitfalls of having a close friend at work?

- Do you favor being part of a group of friends or having one-on-one relationships with other women? How does your personality factor into that equation?

- Are you the type that stays in touch with friends? What are the best ways to achieve continuity in friendships when your lives go in different directions?

- What are some of the myths associated with female friendships? Are they changing for our daughters?

- How have new technologies, like cell phones, e-mail, and social media affected your friendships? Do they strengthen existing friendships? Weaken them? Are online friends real friends?

- Have you ever found a long-lost friend on the internet and revitalized that friendship? How did it happen?

- What are the best ways for grown women to make new friends?